ISBN 9781869409319

9 781869 409319

Out Here

Edited by
Chris Tse and
Emma Barnes

Out Here

An anthology of
Takatāpui and LGBTQIA+
writers from Aotearoa

AUCKLAND
UNIVERSITY
PRESS

First published 2021

Auckland University Press
University of Auckland
Private Bag 92019
Auckland 1142
New Zealand
www.aucklanduniversitypress.co.nz

ISBN 978 1 86940 931 9

Published with the assistance of Creative New Zealand

creative nz
ARTS COUNCIL OF NEW ZEALAND TOI AOTEAROA

A catalogue record for this book is available from the National Library of New Zealand

Design by Kalee Jackson

Cover image: Jack Trolove, detail from
The Thick Skin of a Pronoun, 2019,
photographed by Marlaina Key,
courtesy Whitespace Contemporary Art.

Printed in Singapore by C.O.S. Printers Pte Ltd

Contents

On Naming

Throughout the process of producing this anthology – from soliciting submissions to writing this introduction – we discussed at length which terms we would use for its title. Although many other recent publications and articles have used 'queer' in their titles, we ultimately opted for 'Takatāpui' and 'LGBTQIA+' to reflect Aotearoa's rainbow community as broadly as possible. However, in our introduction we're going to use the word 'queer' for expediency and in keeping with its use in academic and critical texts (although we're not claiming to be academic writers!).

Despite its historical use as a slur, the word 'queer' has since been reclaimed by individuals and groups as an umbrella term for all members of the rainbow community in an effort to acknowledge both gender and sexual diversity. It allows fluidity and ambiguity in a world that would like to pin us like butterflies, through the thorax, with specific details of who we are and who we fuck. 'Queer' gives shelter and room to develop without needing to know the whole story all at once. We acknowledge that this term is not without controversy in the communities it aims to shelter, especially in recent years, and that some still find pain attached to its pejorative connotations. As we discovered through our research and reading submissions, there is no neat term that fully encompasses all lived experiences and preferences. There are arguments for and against all possible terms. Please know that, for the purposes of our introduction, we are giving room to all labels and identities by using 'queer'.

Introduction

As teenagers, the two of us would look for queer texts in public and in private. Regardless of the setting, we did this as secretly as possible, whether it was looking up keywords in the library card catalogue or waiting until our family had gone to bed so we could use our home computer to read about queer TV shows and films we'd heard about but couldn't watch in New Zealand. Deleting browsing histories with a single click was easy, but letting go of the shame that lingered with these furtive quests was a much longer process.

In what is now an oft-quoted essay for *The Pantograph Punch*, genderqueer writer and editor Jackson Nieuwland writes of the historical erasure of queer identities in New Zealand literature as a symptom of our reluctance (and apathy) as a country in engaging with anything that steps outside a cis / heterosexual / Eurocentric perspective. Nieuwland writes: 'I was introduced to queer writers much earlier than I realised. I just wasn't introduced to them as queer writers.'[1]

Queer books and writing were out there if we knew where to look, but a lack of visibility and access meant it was a lonely task trying to find stories where we could see parts of ourselves, if not our entire selves, represented. We became teenagers in the nineties when New Zealand felt a lot less cool about queerness, and gender felt much more rigid. We knew instinctively that hiding was the safest strategy. But how to find your community if you're hidden? How to find the stories you need to read when you're full of shame?

Over time, this erasure has had a profound effect on access to, and the visibility of, writing by queer New Zealand authors. This has meant that writers such as Katherine Mansfield and Frank Sargeson were never discussed in terms of their queerness when they were writing. Decades later the dots have been connected, but even post-homosexual-law-reform queer writing seemed to be a quiet thread in New Zealand literature – easy to miss, easy to overlook.

Queer New Zealand authors have also had to work in the shadow of oppressive legislation and societal attitudes that viewed queer lifestyles as criminal or unsavoury. In 1971, Ngahuia te Awekotuku was famously denied a visa to the United States of America because she was a self-described 'sapphic woman'. Queer characters in books, films and television shows were often reduced to tropes, the punchline of jokes that reinforced damaging stereotypes. When queer creatives took control of queer representation in an effort to provide positive or realistic depictions of queer lives, this often

1 Jackson Nieuwland, 'Working Against a System That is Working Against Them: Contemporary LGBTQIA+ Writers in Aotearoa', *The Pantograph Punch*, 10 August 2018.

resulted in public outcry and controversy. Critics and queer audiences praised the 1980 New Zealand feature film *Squeeze*, which centres on a bisexual man's relationship with a young male lover, for its sympathetic and groundbreaking depiction of Auckland's early LGBT scene. However, there were also vocal detractors who spoke out against its 'objectionable' content. A vigorous campaign from the Society for the Promotion of Community Standards resulted in MPs debating the film in Parliament.

This, of course, was not the only time queer lives and issues were discussed in Parliament. Activists had pushed for homosexual law reform since the 1960s, but it wasn't until the 1980s, as the HIV/AIDS crisis took hold, that the campaign for such reforms began to gain momentum and was debated by both our politicians and the general public. As Chris Brickell notes in *Mates and Lovers*: 'The Homosexual Law Reform Bill gave rise to the keenest public debate since the Springboks' rugby tour of 1981, and those with a strong opinion lobbied furiously.'[2] Although the passing of the Act represented both a legal and moral victory, the public conversation about what rights queer people would be permitted to have has continued through to the present day, from civil unions and same-sex marriage to anti-discrimination measures and trans rights, including the right to self-identify gender. Public discourse around these topics has a tendency to shine a light on the bigotry and hypocrisy that simmers below the surface of New Zealand's carefree veneer.

However, as Nieuwland notes in their essay, queer erasure remains a contemporary issue: reviews of newer writers such as Hera Lindsay Bird, Gina Cole, Kerry Donovan Brown and Courtney Sina Meredith often disregard or fail to mention the queer context or content of their works in favour of something more familiar – that is, something more heterosexual.

For some queer New Zealanders, the lack of visibility of and access to queer New Zealand writers has meant looking beyond our shores for writing that reflected their experiences of sexuality. Perhaps there's a bit of that national cultural cringe at play too – we're often too quick to dismiss our own experiences or question the value of the art this country produces.

Which is not to say there haven't been queer New Zealand writers pushing in from the fringes and gaining critical and commercial success. Peter Wells, Heather McPherson, Hinemoana Baker, Renée, Witi Ihimaera, Ngahuia te Awekotuku, Paula Boock and others had success throughout the 1970s to 2000s. But again, as Nieuwland notes, their work wasn't always viewed through a queer lens, even when writing on queer subjects.

There have been early attempts in Aotearoa to anthologise the writing of gay and lesbian writers *as gay and lesbian writers*, though often separately and often with that binary division of identity. In 1999, Publishing Giant Press produced a pair of queer poetry anthologies, the lesbian *Eat These Sweet Words* and the gay *When Two Men Embrace*. In a review for *New Zealand*

2 Chris Brickell, *Mates and Lovers*, Godwit, Auckland, 2008, p. 349.

Books, Laurence Jenkins noted the difference in the relative sizes of the two anthologies, in particular pointing out the 'poetic poverty' of the latter, and pondered whether the editors 'might have encouraged some of New Zealand's excellent gay prose writers to come out as poets.'[3] Those gay prose writers are comprehensively represented in *Best Mates: Gay Writing in Aotearoa New Zealand* (1997), edited by Peter Wells and Rex Pilgrim. It was the first collection of New Zealand work by gay men and featured mostly prose selections. We've seen other small collections, hidden away and hard to find.

In the decades since the publication of those books, thinking and discourse around sexuality and gender has developed to include more sensitivity, to cover a wider range of experience and to create a broader language. This shift in thinking is evident in the wider history of zines and other self-published works that bring together experiences by trans, queer, Takatāpui and genderqueer writers. One recent example is *this gender is a million things that we are more than* (2019), edited by essa may ranapiri, which gathers emerging non-binary and genderqueer writers. Every single publication is important; essa's zine was well received and even reviewed on RNZ National. Since its initial New Zealand release, it has been published and distributed by independent Scottish publisher Easter Road Press. There is an appetite for this sort of work and an audience ready to read all of us, both in Aotearoa and internationally.

At the same time as we were finalising our selections for this anthology in October 2020, New Zealand made headlines around the world for voting in 'the queerest Parliament in the world', with eleven MPs in the fifty-third Parliament identifying as queer. In the creative world, this shift in diversity and representation has also occurred in our many arts and literary festivals, with dedicated programmes and events designed to showcase our growing pool of queer talent. The first Same Same But Different festival was held in Auckland in 2016 and is Aotearoa's sole rainbow-focused literary festival. In the programme booklet for that first festival, founder Peter Wells wrote that he hoped it would 'introduce a heightened awareness of the timbre and reach of our voice but also celebrate the richness inherent in difference.'[4] That timbre and reach has been evident in subsequent iterations of the festival, which has hosted dozens of our established and emerging creatives and writers from all fields of the arts, including comics, theatre, music and activism.

At this time of growing representation and awareness, a diversity of queer stories and writers is needed more than ever. Public debates about trans rights and gender nonconformity, and about the inclusion of uniformed police in pride parades, show that there is still work to be done for queer communities to have our voices, stories and opinions heard with respect and empathy and to receive the rights we are due as humans. We wanted to collate

3 Laurence Jenkins, 'Smoke Gets in Their Poems', *New Zealand Books* 1, 3 (August 1999), p. 18.

4 Peter Wells, Same Same But Different festival programme, 2016, p. 2.

an anthology that celebrated the depth and especially the breadth of queer experiences in Aotearoa.

We initially assumed that the pool of writers to consider would be considerable, but modest. We had identified about 110 writers, but we also knew a call for submissions would allow people to suggest more writers to read. This would be particularly important for writers whose sexuality was 'invisible' or not public knowledge.

The response to our open call was overwhelming, and reinforced the need for such an anthology. We received submissions from more than 200 writers, of whom only about 30 per cent were already on our radar. There were so many who were completely and delightfully unknown to us. In some cases, they were established writers whose sexual and gender identities were not common knowledge for a number of reasons. Queerness is often talked about in terms of coming out, and for many of us coming out is a regular action due to the way assumed heterosexuality leaves little space for difference. As described in Jackson Nieuwland's essay, it can be hard enough to find ourselves, let alone connect with others like us, and in literature there are many examples where queer context is ignored:

> Hinemoana Baker's first collection *Matuhi: Needle* was covered in a 2005 *Listener* round-up of new New Zealand poetry. While Baker is often labelled a queer poet, this book doesn't contain a lot of explicitly queer content. So I find it hilarious that the reviewer chose the most sexual lines in the book – 'fat strawberries . . . at night // we pick them by touch / listen to the flesh / release the stem' – as the only extract to quote, and then used them as an example of 'pregnant' imagery, rather than queer innuendo.[5]

As we read through the submissions, the focus of our anthology shifted considerably. We'd originally set out to provide a view of queer writing in New Zealand published from 1985 onwards, but the end result is something that is much more representative of the growth and increased visibility of queer writers being published over the last ten to fifteen years. There are many young and emerging writers in our anthology – for some, this anthology was their first time having their work accepted for publication. We have included as many established writers from the last thirty-five years as we were able to, though we acknowledge that there will be some absences, as is often the case with anthologies.

Our goal from the start was to curate a wide-ranging anthology that brings together writers of as many gender and sexual identities as possible, all working across different genres. We specifically asked for submissions to not only focus on queer life events like coming out or first love. We wanted smaller things, bigger things, different things, to see narratives that aren't

5 Jackson Nieuwland, 'Working Against a System That is Working Against Them'.

always shown for people like us. We imagined this anthology as a riot of brightness, life and feelings. We're exceptionally familiar with tropes of queer unhappiness and we wanted to widen the frame and draw more things into the picture to shift the tragic queer life over to the side of the frame instead of the centre.

We chose works that delighted us, surprised us, confronted us and engaged us. We chose political pieces and pieces that dreamed futures as yet only imagined. We chose coming out stories and stories of home. We followed our noses. What our reading revealed to us is that our queer writers are writing beyond the expectations of what queer writing can be, and doing it in a way that often pushes against the trends of mainstream literature.

If there's a common theme to be found throughout the anthology, it's the role that place plays in the works of queer writers. The queer experience is often one of searching for belonging, which is explored in many of the pieces in this anthology. They are stories of finding a place for oneself, whether that's within a family unit or a relationship, or as part of a community, city or country that allows the speaker to flourish. These pieces take place in strip clubs and art galleries, in motel rooms and courtrooms, and move the reader beyond the shores of Aotearoa to Australia, the United States of America and Sri Lanka.

Our original intention was to order the anthology chronologically, or possibly by subject or even by identity. However, as we worked through the submissions and began making selections we realised that all of those groupings would either be difficult or would be making arbitrary calls and separating people in ways that didn't make sense. In the end, we went with alphabetical order by our writers' first names, which is how we had ordered the many spreadsheets we used to manage our submissions and selections. When we stepped back and looked at it as a whole, we loved the way the pieces by the first and last writers spoke to each other in tone and outlook. We also loved the way that some of the works jangled against each other and were mixed up into each other. It's not traditional to use first names to alphabetise an anthology but we're confident in our ordering and it wouldn't be a queer anthology if it wasn't doing something differently.

It's not our intention to present a canon or a tidy history or to make a definitive statement of what contemporary queer New Zealand writing is right now. We wanted to collect as many of us together as we could, but we know there are absences, some due to the physical limitations of publishing a book and some due to our own personal tastes as editors and readers. Since finalising our selection, a number of writers and books have been published that weren't caught in our original net of submissions and reading. Ultimately, we hope that this anthology is a step forward in the visibility of queer identities in Aotearoa's literary history. We want it to serve as a starting point for anyone else who wishes to take on a similar exercise in the future.

This is why we've named our anthology *Out Here* – to acknowledge not only the writers who are speaking up and sharing their stories and lives with readers, but also those who continue to step forward and put in the mahi to ensure that future generations of queers are afforded the space to tell their stories and be themselves without fear of retribution or harm.

We'd like to thank all the writers who submitted their work for consideration, and those who suggested writers and books for us to read. It's been a privilege and a huge responsibility to bring these incredible writers together in this anthology. If you are a queer writer reading this and not seeing your name included, please include yourself. We had to say no to many more writers than we said yes to. By its nature, editing is about choosing what to leave out, and often in queer lives the queerness is left out, papered over or ignored. We know you're there and we believe in a future where we'll all get to be seen and heard as ourselves.

— Chris Tse and Emma Barnes

A. J. Fitzwater

Offset

Preet's wrister beeped: UV levels and temperature rising. She needed to get under cover soon.

She urged the electric scooter another tick faster as she suckled the water-spout in the collar of her cool-coat. Cathedral Square – and the protest – wasn't too far away. A swing along the river promenade, past the rebuilt Kate Sheppard Memorial, and down the Papatūānuku tunnel, the bio-artwork an ever-moving revolution of colour.

A hab wooshed by, leaving behind the faint tang of ozone. Preet craned her neck to see if Keeks was aboard. Nope. Selwyn commuters from beyond the fringe. Keeks was rounding up a group of protesters, friends, from the eastern suburbs.

She'd thought about it, so now she could smell it. The Ōtautahi brine. Preet wrinkled her nose. Even though they'd lived out east for a good twenty years, moving closer to the city as each street was redzoned to the encroaching swamp, Preet had never got used to the smell. Decades on, the council was still dealing with the consequences of the ruptures at the abandoned Bromley wastewater site. She'd taken a job straight out of uni on a clean-up crew. The resulting chronic skin allergy had almost not been worth the offset load, which zeroed out her student loan.

Another smell intruded as she trundled out of the Papatūānuku tunnel: burning iron, choking oily smoke, churned landfill.

Fossils.

Preet parked the scooter on the rank next to beat-up twofers and bicycles, and her wrister gave a cheerful chirrup as she tagged it available. Her carbon credits ticked down more than she'd usually spend for a weekend ride; she'd come all the way in from house-sitting at Nanna's in Avonhead.

A few moments later, Keeks dashed out of the transport exchange tunnel, silver-blue hair flying.

'Had enough CC for a seated scooter, eh love?' Keeks smooshed their face into Preet's hair. Preet breathed deep; Keeks' real-fake leather and mineral scent were her armour.

'Weekend CC highs are depressing.' Preet knuckled her back. 'I'll be walking a couple days next week.'

'Back still hurting, eh?' Keeks crooned, adding their long fingers to the gentle massage. 'You need to tell those nongs at the co-op to stop taking up all the sitting desks. Come on, chai is my shout.'

Keeks was flush with offsets, having saved up CC for weeks just in case they needed to make bail.

The two didn't get far into the upper gallery of the underground market. It was packed with weekend shoppers picking over the best of local produce. Preet's wrister beeped with location-tagged advertising that finally wriggled past her algorithms.

Would she be interested in a display of character vintage Cutes? A Mini, Micra, 500, Beetle, and ElVee, all in a row, pretty metallics gleaming their caustic grins.

Ugh. Bots. The council must be desperate for the big dump of CC into the coffers.

But it was what they were here for anyway.

'Just as well Nanna is on her tank holiday,' Preet said, sliding under the awning of a familiar chai cart. 'Her blood pressure couldn't take another round of yelling at a council meeting.'

'Where she gone this weekend?' asked the barista, Anaru, one of Nanna's friends from the Avonhead co-op. He was a long way from home.

'Mumbai, to visit her cousins. Says it's partly because she misses the white noise.'

'Never the same in full sensory immersion,' Anaru said, liberally spicing the top of their drinks. 'None of the texture.'

'Nah. Your body just knows, you know?'

'Better than never being able to afford the offsets for the real thing, eh?'

'Preet 'n me will always have tank Disneyland,' Keeks grinned, toasting Anaru with their cup.

Another comforting conversation. It helped cool the pressure in Preet's head that had nothing to do with the outside temperature.

Preet glanced around for bee drones as they descended the ramp to the lower floor. 'How many you reckon will turn up?'

'Fifty at least at the last meeting,' Keeks replied. 'Another couple dozen through the secret anarchist group. Add in their friends and on-site randoms. I'd say close to a hundred.'

'I had to quick smart shut down an open check-in group late last night masquerading as—' Preet made quote-fingers '—Friends Gathering To Find Fossils.'

'Shit. Dumbarses.'

A hundred people protesting without permit or prerequisite polite check-in with the council. Even forty years on from the pre-Resolution riots, when the world had struggled to ensure a fair carbon footprint for everyone, governments were very careful about free-speech gatherings. This wasn't sand in the tanks and black-market fuel. The best they could do now was turn up, witness, hold space, negotiate.

And often, that was enough.

But this? Vintage cars, *pollutants*, around a mass of people, food, and in a regulated air space? What was the council *thinking*?

Despite her anger, curiosity poked at Preet. She'd never seen a fossil vehicle in-the-metal before. She pushed through the kaleidoscope of scents and skin. Usually she and Keeks stayed local at the Aranui market, or, if feeling especially cozy, only ventured down to the Japanese bakery in the food court under their apartment building. Preet had forgotten just how many people could pack in here. The See-Oh-Two scrubbers whined hard.

Yup, there they were. Petrol-driven propaganda wrapped up in shiny, rust-free nostalgia. The Cutes were all huggable voluptuousness, the humble-flaunts of the carbon loaded, the kind of people who kept their unmodded vintage Maseratis, Porsches, and Lamborghinis for viewing only by fellow fossil fiends.

Two security guards, one at each end of the display. The usual single guards on the far-apart exits. A couple of plain clothes strolling around.

As if Preet's approach was a signal, people started peeling off. Soon the entrance to the laser-roped viewing corridor was blocked.

'Eh. Where'd the owners go? Too chook to face up?' This too loud from a person with tight braids and a bright, flowing hemp skirt. Preet didn't recognise them, but she was glad they spoke up first. She didn't want to be seen as an instigator.

More protesters took the cue, hooking elbows and shuffling to make space for friends.

A guard wandered over, hand on tool belt. Preet recognised her from other protests she'd attended; tall, broad, efficient. Preet licked her lips and swallowed, glancing between the guard's taser and her face.

'The car owner's around, if you have questions,' the guard said to Preet. '*Proper* questions.' The guard then flicked an up-nod at her partner. They responded in kind, face neutral.

'Look at it,' Braids said. 'Leather seats. Air conditioning. Dripping old fibre electrics. Real rubber tyres. Just a small piece of this could carbon load a family for a month.'

'And the rest,' Preet muttered. She fingered her wrister, expecting notification the police were on their way. Hmm. Nothing yet. She lifted her voice. 'Kia ora, e hoa.'

Keeks started up a karakia and was quickly joined by some elders and stern youngsters looking out for them.

Everyone had a chance to speak. Preet mingled, tapping shoulders as she organised the speaker rotation, offering meaningful glances and quiet words as a reminder to keep it cool. They all spoke with purpose, some with measured, old, cracked voices, others with the simple pride of youthful passion.

They needed people to *remember*.

The stink from diesel vehicles. Noise pollution. Degrading air travel in cattle class. Respiratory illnesses from winter smog. The lost green of the desertified parts of the Canterbury Plains. So much wasted time stuck in traffic. Bad civil design and lack of accessible public transport. Oil spills. Broken promises and pipelines. The endless oil wars, countries broken apart and picked clean. The refugee crisis, still reverberating today. The dead zones of land and ocean. The tiny polar ice caps.

Heckles rose in retaliation. Plants, probably. Some simply annoyed at having their nice day interrupted. They were shushed down with reminders of the Protocols of Public Protest, and that they were on the wrong side of history.

Someone started up a round of 'Fresh Air, Free Land', the popular pre-Resolution resistance song. A guitar appeared; someone always had a guitar. As the song ended, 'kia ora', 'nice', and other heartfelt expressions in many languages peppered through the crowd.

'You call that a protest,' a crowd-baiter sneered. 'Cars will always exist—'

'Post-capitalist rights! Post-capitalist rights!' someone started chanting.

Another interjected: 'You're all just jealous!'

Voices up the back, scoffing. Preet saw Keeks' fibre-optic-laced hair bobbing through the crowd, hands circling in soothing motions.

Preet pretended solidarity with the patient guard, grimacing 'sorry' in her direction.

The guard glanced up at the bee drones.

Then the mumbling began from the crowd about offsets, how the government UBI didn't near enough cover the stepped exchange rate, how gigging secondary tax dug into it. How the carbon rich could still flaunt heavy polluters like this without consequence, even be celebrated for it, I mean, look at it. All that CC just *sitting there.*

'It all feels a bit sideways, eh?' This from a kuia beside Preet, a frown creasing her wrinkles deeper, carcinomas reddening. Her hands clenched and unclenched as if reliving a memory of land finally returned but rendered unsustainable.

The guard glanced at the bee-cams again and touched something on her wrister. Did the drones turn away, or was that just the pattern of the sweep?

The other guard at the entrance nodded.

Preet took a deep breath of the lingering dirty exhaust scent, quick-checking who to cover first. The elder, definitely.

'My grandma used to strip cop cars at protests way back when,' the guard said. 'Black market metals helped pay bail.' She pulled a multi-tool from her belt. 'I know people.'

She knelt and began stripping the first lug nut.

Someone came from a caravan stall with a jack. Anaru appeared with hydraulic jaws. Braids' friends pulled laser-cutters from packs.

Preet watched wide-eyed as everyone over the age of fifty seemed to have some tool on them that could help.

The hecklers were kettled to the back of the crowd, protesters holding up home-made scramblers so the hecklers couldn't stream live and their pictures would glitch. Protesters reminded each other to stop streaming. There would be no way to stop everyone in the market filming, they'd just have to hope whatever security had done to help extended beyond their drones.

In the end, most hecklers gave up, realising there was more profit in joining in. More people kept coming, wanting a piece of what killed the world.

Keeks brushed up beside her, eyes bright, humming the tenor line of 'Fresh Air, Free Land'. Their presence gave Preet back her strength and together they wrenched at a front panel on the Mini. A few tugs and it came away. Nanna had taught them both how to make their hands and muscles useful and quick in these situations.

Forty-five minutes later, the crowd had dispersed as if a wave of righteous glee hadn't descended like ants upon sweetness. Preet and Keeks were shopping in the gallery when a group wearing poverty chic returned to the site of their fossil babies. They watched as the group stood in shock, staring at the stripped frames on blocks.

'Who did this!' the carbon rich demanded of the solicitous security guards.

We apologise, nobody saw anything. How could so many people not notice! Security footage shows nothing. Market management and the police will be right with you.

The market tech team dragged their feet to attend to the bee drones, which still buzzed in a rebooting square pattern.

People went about their business, breathing the fresh air.

Such sweet air.

Maybe there would be consequences, arrests. Maybe there wouldn't. Right now, carbon credits did all the talking.

Preet chose a whole dozen eggs and a pinch packet of oolong for Nanna when she climbed out of the tank. Keeks treated them to black rice for that night's dinner.

As they casually sauntered towards the transport exchange tunnel, Preet fingered the motherboard deep in her pocket and hunched a little against the weight of wiring in her hemp backpack. There was a good couple months of eating there, if they were discreet. Perhaps a few trips to help the regeneration team out at Bottle Lake Forest. Maybe take Nanna on the intercity hab up the coast to visit her sisters in Waiharakeke.

Keeks wrapped their fingers in Preet's. In the space between their cupped palms and curled fingers lay an in-held breath and land of their own making from the ones they were denied.

A. J. Fitzwater is four giraffes stuffed into a racing mini, living between the cracks of Ōtautahi. Their books are the World War II land girls fantasy novella *No Man's Land* from Paper Road Press, and lesbian capybara pirate hijinks *The Voyages of Cinrak the Dapper* from Queen of Swords Press. Their short fiction is available in a variety of speculative venues of repute. They attended the Clarion writers' workshop in 2014, and use their two Sir Julius Vogel Awards as sword hands. They maintain a collection of bow ties.

Alison Glenny

The Propeller Club

Edith Hazzard checked the time on her watch. She was standing outside the Propeller Club in Half Moon Lane, and she had an appointment to meet her cousin, Reggie Anstruthers. Edith wasn't sure she'd recognise Reggie. The last time she'd seen her cousin (in Canterbury, New Zealand), he'd been no more than nine or ten. It was the summer after the end of the War, and Reggie had been a pale, rather delicate boy, with freckles and a bad habit of teasing.

The Propeller Club was located above a shop that sold furnishings. As she waited on the street for Reggie to arrive, Edith amused herself by admiring a pair of table lamps that were prominently displayed in the bay window. The lamps were in the modern style and were in the shape of nymphs, standing on tiptoe with raised arms and holding aloft incandescent globes. To Edith, the slender, golden nymphs seemed like athletes in some Olympic sport not yet invented. She thought about coming back when the shop was open and buying the lamps, but told herself that it was too soon to begin to acquire furniture. Perhaps after she moved out of the hotel and into a flat of her own . . .

Edith glanced again at her wrist-watch. It was a leaving present from her mother, and Edith's initials were engraved on the reverse of the elegant, cartouche-shaped face. Perhaps she had missed Reggie, and he was already inside?

As Edith paused, momentarily irresolute, a man in a long leather coat pushed open the door and began to climb the flight of stairs that lay behind it. Edith hesitated for only a moment before following him up the stairs and into the club.

Edith had never been in a gentlemen's club before, and she gazed at her surroundings with frank curiosity. The Propeller Club resembled a slightly shabbier version of one of the lounges on board the SS *Surrey*. It was furnished with low tables and a scattering of comfortable chairs, and there was a bar at one end. When Reggie had arranged to meet her, he'd explained that the club was frequented mainly by instructors at Handley Aerodrome. There were also a few flying students, and some pilots like himself who were employed by the new aircraft companies that had sprung up to cater for the public's new fascination with what the newspapers called 'airmindedness'.

Edith observed about half a dozen men seated around the tables or standing at the bar. They were all in their thirties or forties, and none of them appeared to be Reggie.

She removed her new gloves (they were made of cream-coloured kid and fit her perfectly – firm without being tight) as a man came from behind the bar to greet her.

'I've an appointment to meet Reggie Anstruthers,' she told him.

'Mr Anstruthers is not here at the moment,' the waiter said. 'Can I bring you a drink? Tea perhaps?'

'Do you serve cocktails? If so, I'll have a martini.'

Edith had been introduced to the martini aboard the SS *Surrey* as it steamed out of Auckland harbour. During the long voyage from New Zealand she'd had ample opportunity to deepen her acquaintance with this elegant yet formidable drink. She seated herself in one of the rather battered club chairs, and the waiter brought her drink over on a silver tray. Edith thought it all terribly British – refined in an old-fashioned way but a little bit worn, as if the contents of one's great-aunt's attic had been dug out and put back into use. It was one of the things she loved about England – how old everything was. But Edith wasn't simple. She saw that beneath the tradition that clung to everything like old varnish, Britain was an industrial nation, intent on being new and up-to-date. A discreetly modern spirit was busily at work, transforming everything from automobiles to clothing. Edith smoothed the soft jersey of the skirt she'd purchased that week at Harrods. It came with a long, belted cardigan that was both elegant and practical. Edith crossed her legs, admiring the gleam of her pearl grey stockings.

London was as rich in *things* as it was crowded with people – hundreds of thousands of people, all going about their own business. For the first time in her life, surrounded by people whom she didn't know and who didn't know her, Edith was experiencing the heady freedom of anonymity, and she had begun to glimpse the endless possibilities it offered for transformation and discovery.

Edith had thought she was the only woman in the club, but as she sipped her drink she realised that she was mistaken. At one of the tables on the opposite side of the room from Edith a tall, rather casually dressed woman was talking to a man with thinning hair. The woman's own hair was blonde, and cropped so that when she bent forward it barely grazed the back of her neck. Edith, who had always been slightly vain about her long, auburn hair, felt a sudden urge to have it cut off. She almost shivered. It was as if this unknown woman, with her vaguely masculine clothing and unselfconscious assurance, had brought a current of sharper air into the room: the pure, cold air of the upper regions of the atmosphere, ruled by winds and cloud. How marvellous, Edith thought, to be able to enter that region at will, like a horseman galloping through the sky!

With that thought, Edith's own vague sense of restlessness and desire suddenly became focused and resolute. She felt a sense of purpose take root and unfurl inside her, as if it too were struggling to ascend into that purer and more exalted realm.

'Edith? Good heavens, is it really you?'

Edith looked up and saw a man who must be her cousin Reggie. She searched for signs of the thin boy with freckles, but grown-up Reggie bore few traces of his younger self. Her cousin was tall, well-built, and handsome in a rugged kind of way. He seemed to be taking in the changes in her own appearance with equal astonishment.

Reggie saw the martini she was sipping and raised his eyebrow. 'I see you've made yourself at home,' he observed. He settled himself in the chair opposite hers. 'How are Uncle Frank and Aunt Dora?'

'Pretty well, actually,' Edith replied. 'Dad says that wool is holding its own.'

'Aunt Dora wrote to tell us about Madeleine's wedding.'

'Oh – yes! She and George are awfully happy.'

Madeleine was Edith's older sister. Edith recalled that at the time of that early visit Reggie had seemed rather keen on Maddy.

Reggie said, 'When my mother heard that you were coming over, she thought you might like me to show you around a bit.'

Edith gave her cousin a considering look. Carefully, she put down her drink and said, 'What I really want is to learn to fly.'

'Gosh, do you really—'

'I know it's dangerous, but I don't care. Actually, I thrive on risk.'

'Oh golly, do you now?' Her cousin seemed bemused.

'Will you take me up with you?'

Reggie rubbed his chin, as if testing it for stubble. 'As it happens, you're in luck. I'm delivering a plane to a client in Rome later in the week. If you like, you can come along for the ride.'

'Fly to Rome?'

'Yes, if you don't have any objections.'

'Heavens, no!'

Three days later, Edith came to be shivering at Handley Aerodrome in the pre-dawn chill. She was grateful for Reggie's instructions on what clothing to wear. She'd spent an entire day shopping for the woollen trousers and men's lace-up boots, the turtleneck jumper, scarf, gloves, and bulky fur-lined gauntlets. Reggie was loaning her the leather flying jacket, helmet, and goggles. On her own initiative she'd also brought along a picnic hamper containing a flask of coffee and some sandwiches.

Edith had known that clothes could alter the way you felt about yourself. But it wasn't until she was standing in front of the mirror in the gentleman's outfitter in the Strand, and the shop assistant was bringing over men's boots for her to try, that she appreciated how they could make you feel almost like a different person. Gazing into the mirror, it felt as if a long-lost twin brother – Eddie rather than Edith perhaps – were gazing back at her, with a slightly mocking expression.

Her confidence sagged a notch or two when she saw the aircraft that would take them to Rome. The plane, a grey, low-winged Avro Avian, was already on the runway and the mechanic was giving it a final once-over.

'Is that our plane?' Edith said doubtfully. 'It looks awfully small.'

Reggie looked at her with a slightly taunting expression. 'Having second thoughts?' he asked, and for a moment she was reminded of the teasing she'd once endured from him.

'Not in the slightest!' she retorted, and began to fasten the buckle of the borrowed flying helmet.

Reggie helped her to climb into the passenger seat, which was immediately behind his own. There was very little room for her legs, and she realised that she would be severely uncomfortable by the time they arrived in Rome. He showed her how to adjust the webbing straps, and to insert cotton wads in her ears. 'For the engine noise,' he explained.

'But how will I talk to you?' she asked him.

'If you have to,' he said, 'write on a piece of paper. If you need to get my attention, tap my shoulder.'

He'd already gone over the route with her. Their first stop would be at Lympne airfield in Kent to clear customs and take on extra fuel before crossing the Channel to Belgium. From Belgium they'd fly to Cologne, where they would refuel and stay the night. The next day, if all went well and the weather held, they would fly to Italy via Switzerland.

Reggie climbed into the seat in front of Edith and strapped himself into the open cockpit. The mechanic swung the propeller repeatedly until the engine roared into life, and the little plane shuddered like a horse at a starting gate. Even through the wadded cotton the engine noise was deafening. The smell of oil made the inside of Edith's nostrils pucker.

Then Reggie pushed the throttle forward and the plane hurtled along the runway. At the last minute, just as they became airborne, Edith experienced a curious sensation. It was almost as if at that moment she'd become two people. There was the Edith Hazzard who was embarking on the unknown, armoured in wool and leather, her face pointed firmly towards the future. And there was the other Edith who was left behind on the runway with her old life, gazing up at the new Edith and raising her arm to her in a gesture that could have been either farewell or greeting.

Alison Glenny is the author of *The Farewell Tourist* (Otago University Press, 2018), which won the Kathleen Grattan Award for poetry in 2017, and *Bird Collector* (Compound Press, 2021). In 2019 she was an Ursula Bethell Writer in Residence at the University of Canterbury. She lives on the Kāpiti Coast.

Annamarie Jagose

from In Translation

Navaz speaks five languages, can write in eight and read two more. Once when she was talking to me about a book she was reading, she asked, 'Do you have any German?' Not can you read German, can you follow it, but *do you have any?* Not having any, and suddenly feeling this as a lack, an impoverishment, I made that open-handed gesture you make when approached on the street to indicate that you have come out without money, that you don't have a light. She had started out as a translator for a government department in the city but soon she was getting enough work as a translator of fiction. These were her own words: *getting enough work*. It was Lillian who showed me the shelves of books that Navaz had translated. *Against the Season*, an award-winning volume of poetry from French Canada; *Cage*, the prison notebooks of South America's most celebrated political prisoner, 'now available in English for the first time'; *The Green Fuse*, a sonnet sequence whose translation was praised by *The Times Literary Supplement* as 'maintaining the easy control, the unlabored phrasing and breadth of allusion, which marked the Russian original'.

Translation seemed to me a secretive business. I never saw Navaz actually translating anything although she spent hours at her work. She had a study at the front of the house and worked at a long desk that overlooked the garden and, beyond that, the street. Whenever I came in to see her – *to catch her at it,* was the phrase I used to myself – she would be looking out the window, a pencil tucked over one ear, dragging slowly on one of the cigarettes that were kept burning at her elbow, narrowing her eyes against the smoke. And the books themselves, their titles and authors' names running along the spine, never looked like translations. I would run my hand along their backs, take one down, open it randomly at any chapter, any page, and read the first sentences that claimed my attention. *This morning I traded my soap for a piece of paper. I have since prepared a hundred sentences in my head but none is beautiful enough to risk that smooth white perfection.* There is no sign that these words belong to someone other than that dissident whose name is displayed so prominently under the title on the front cover, that the author may not even understand the language he claims to have written. There is nothing to suggest that these lines are less real than those unseen and unintelligible ones, choked up with unpronouncable consonant clusters, from which they derive. It is only on the title pages, in the smallest typeface, that Navaz's name appears, *translated by Navaz Nicholson,* or sometimes, more specifically, *translated from the German by Navaz R. Nicholson.*

'Do you translate the titles as well?'

A small smile tightened the corners of her mouth so I knew it was the wrong question, one that would be repeated to Lillian after I had gone home for the night.

Lillian shows me a series of photographs she has taken of Navaz. When she offers to show it to me she says, 'Let me show you one of my pieces.' It is not really a series of photographs but one photograph mounted many times in the same frame. It is stacked in the back room along with Lillian's *other pieces*. In the photograph Navaz is at her desk. You can't see the desk but I recognise the blurred blocks of colour behind her as the books in her study. She is smoking, of course, a yellow pencil resting over her ear, a thick curl of smoke obscuring one eye. Perhaps Lillian has taken this shot through the glass of the front window for Navaz looks straight ahead, her single eye resting easily on the camera's. The picture is titled *Portrait of the Translator*. There is a small piece of card taped to the back of the frame with these words typed on it and underneath it states *Private Collection*. Below each picture of Navaz is a handwritten caption, a careless scrawl of dark ink that I recognise from the invitation in my aunt's letterbox, and now know to be 'artistic'. *Navaz as Milan Kundera*, says one. *Navaz as Nicole Rocquefort, Navaz as Shio Nishimura*. I am giddy with the realisation that I am standing in a *private collection*, one of Lillian's *pieces* in my hands as casually as a breakfast tray, and that I understand completely. It is the first time it has occurred to me that there might be something to understand in a picture, a way of reading that is more than just looking. I can't imagine how I might indicate this to Lillian. I stare dully at the faces of Navaz, feeling as wooden as the frame still held between my hands, Lillian watching the side of my face so intently she might be taking a light reading.

Lillian is always showing me things. It is she who shows me the dust jacket of Navaz's translation of Nishimura's third novel, *Skin Behind Bone*. Nishimura himself has written the back cover blurb: 'I always knew Navaz Nicholson to be a fine translator but her work on my latest novel far exceeds that of translation. Nicholson does not return my work to me, she rewrites it entirely. *Skin Behind Bone* is a new novel and I will say an altogether better novel than anything I have ever written. This does not debilitate me, it revitalises me. From now on, the first appearance of my work will be in Nicholson's translation.' I go to see Navaz in her study. Smoke rising, she is looking out the window. I put the copy of *Skin Behind Bone* on her desk.

'What will happen to the original of Nishimura's next novel?'

'It will come out a couple of years later as a translation.'

'But what is it a translation of?'

'Of the English text.' The corners of Navaz's mouth are tightening in that small smile. I try another line of questioning.

'What did you think when you first heard of Nishimura's intentions? What did you do when you first read this?'

'Translated it,' says Navaz.

These are the scenes I rerun for myself now, the sound of the fans turning above my head like the clacking of film from a projection box, scenes that doubtless continue, diminished, without me. Then the view from my window, the woman on the porch opposite picking over tonight's rice, the children chasing a water truck from the yard, is more remote than these grainy images from that distant country, these jerky takes of Lillian and Navaz. My memories have the hand-held quality of home movies. The camera pans across our faces, Navaz's, Lillian's, mine, swinging too close and pulling back for focus. Our lips move in silence, our unsynchronised voices trail across the next scene: *Do you translate the titles as well? Let me show you one of my pieces.* Here I am, in my aunt's white shirt, hesitating in the gap in the hedge; here we are, the three of us, lunching on the afternoon lawn, sprawled carelessly in the sun like an advertisement for sanitary protection; our faces are overexposed, bleached flat, our mouths unfathomed holes, our movements are spastic, continuity the one thing the camera cannot preserve.

Thinking now of all that is lost to me but to which in my mind I continually return, I remember a dream I had last night. I am at Raroa Road again, in the kitchen with Lillian. She has a pile of flour on the kitchen table and is breaking eggs, one by one, into a well in its centre. I am walking down the corridor to Navaz's study. For once she is bent over her desk, her pencil working furiously. She has another desk immediately behind her and when she finishes writing at the desk in front of the window, she turns on her revolving chair and begins working on something at the second desk. There is no pencil behind her ear, cigarettes burn on both desks. She looks up as if she has been expecting me. She says that she is trying something new, that she is translating Nishimura's novel into English, then back into Japanese, to English again. It never comes out the same. She makes the gesture of pouring water back and forth between two containers. Each time, the plot lines, the characters' interactions and outcomes, are recognisable yet recognisably different from the time before. Nishimura is pleased with her work. His publishing house is bringing it out next season as a trilogy.

This is all I ever wanted, to be moving between Lillian, breaking eggs in the kitchen, and Navaz, turning and turning in a smoky room. It is as if, too late, I realised that Lillian's photographs were the real thing, not the simulation they pretended. I live more fully in the flickering half light of recollection and dream work than I do in this room, in this country whose fiercely bland light allows no deception. Like some old sports hero who watches himself again and again breasting the tape, I understand that my worth is reckoned in terms of what I was once, of what used to be and, unlike that old man, I fool myself into thinking that that place waits for me still, is not lost to me with the passing of time. I wake in my narrow bed in a strange country, cast up, adrift, exiled. Below my bedroom window I see a small dot of light, glowing red, first on one side then the other, as the watchmen downstairs pass a bidi between them in the dark.

Annamarie Jagose

A first-generation New Zealander, **Annamarie Jagose** is an academic and an award-winning writer of three novels: *In Translation* (1991), *Lulu: A Romance* (1998) and *Slow Water* (2003), all published by Victoria University Press. She is currently Executive Dean, Faculty of Arts and Social Sciences, and Pro-Vice-Chancellor (University Schools) at the University of Sydney.

Aorewa McLeod

from Who Was That Woman, Anyway?

The Quickcat, the high-speed ferry to the island, leapt over each huge swell and slammed down in a chaos of spray. I loved the excitement of the catamaran in heavy seas, when they probably should have cancelled the sailing. Kathy cowered in her seat pretending to read the island newspaper. Natalie, our visitor from the States, was as thrilled as I was. That was a relief. I'd hoped for a Pacific calm with sparkling seas and sunny golden beaches and instead we'd got this wild weather. I was doing all I could to make Natalie like Auckland, so that when she was offered the professorship in Women's Studies she'd want to come.

I'd had a party at my house with a bunch of the city dykes and now I was taking her to the island to meet the Waiheke dykes. After all, this was Natalie Burns, author of *The Resistant Virgin*, probably the most famous openly lesbian theorist there was. And she was applying for a position with us! Massachusetts-pale, bespectacled, sturdy, fleeing as far as she could (we later found out) from a collapsed long-term relationship. I'd fitted her out with a weatherproof parka and gumboots.

Our resident Waiheke poet met us on the wharf amidst sleeting rain and we drove to the Waiheke house, where the car, turning on the lawn, got bogged down. Kathy, the rather small resident poet, and Natalie Burns, famous lesbian theorist, all got out and pushed. I got towels from the house and put them under the back tyres. It was our island car, so the tyres were indubitably worn. Those were the days when there was no resident policeman and the grapevine would spread the news when one was coming to conduct Warrant of Fitness tests, at which point many cars would vanish from the roads for the duration. Natalie got sprayed with mud and lumps of lawn as we sludged the car out.

She loved it and we loved her. So famous and so much at home with us! After the water heated up and she'd had a shower, we sat around the open fireplace and talked feminism and lesbianism. She discussed the way heterosexuality is taken to be normative.

'The word "virgin" didn't originally mean a woman who was untouched by . . .' she paused, and looked around at us '. . . by a penis.'

There was a chorus of, 'Yes, of course, no penis.'

'Never again,' shouted Kathy. 'I've had enough penises to last me a lifetime.'

'Where did that come from?'

'Ngaio here was my first woman. I had so many men before that. So many penises.'

'Any ten-star dykes here?' asked Natalie.

Silence fell as everyone looked at everyone else, waiting.

'So we've all been touched by a penis. Virgin originally meant a free woman, one not betrothed, not married, not possessed by a man.'

'Absolutely,' said the poet, bouncing up and down.

'It meant a woman who is sexually and socially her own person. A virgin is an independent feminist who refuses to kowtow to patriarchal norms of femininity, attractiveness or sexuality.'

'Gosh,' said Kathy, 'that sounds so impressive.'

'I can quote anything from my book by heart,' said Natalie smugly.

'Could we lesbians call ourselves virgins?'

'Nope,' said Natalie. 'We might try.'

'How about Monique Wittig's statement "a lesbian is not a woman"?' I asked. Was this a way out? As lesbians we did not conform to these patriarchal norms the way that hetero women did. But as I said it I knew it was not true. Plenty of lesbians conformed to common concepts of femininity and attractiveness. Even those of us who once had bravely but briefly let any facial hair grow now stood in front of the mirror, plucking. As we grew older I noticed how many of us dyed our hair interesting heteropatriarchal colours, mainly shades of blonde. Perhaps it was especially because we were lesbian that we wanted to look likeable by society's standards. It was impossible to free ourselves totally from heteropatriarchal society and its norms.

But it was great to sit around with the famous lesbian theorist, poking the blazing embers, safe from the rain outside, and talking as if we could. Natalie was relaxed and friendly. Claudia, the island's DJ, was snuggling up to her and Natalie had draped her striped arm over Claudia's shoulder. We'd brought an assortment of nibbles that we'd thought would appeal to a feminist theorist who might or might not be a vegetarian – olives, hummus, pretzels, salmon, mussels, pickled mushrooms, stuffed peppers, chunks of exotic cheeses, nuts and chocolate. There was a renegade store in Oneroa, the main settlement on Waiheke, which had a huge assortment of delicatessen goodies sold cheap because they were past their use-by date. So we ate flamboyantly well on the island. I noted that Natalie liked the chocolates. And she liked New Zealand chardonnay.

As we nibbled and drank our discussion morphed from being about lesbian feminism to being about heterosexuality. Natalie was in great form. 'I'd like heterosexual women to be as curious about how and when and why they became heterosexual as I have been about how and when and why I became lesbian.'

'Yes,' I said, 'yes. There's so much pressure to be heterosexual. It's so predominant, so ubiquitous that we can't see it. And you get rewarded for being good at it. I did.'

'Right,' said Claudia. 'Hetero women in my feminist group say, "Women just don't turn me on." And that's that.'

I told Natalie what had happened to Tahuri when she was ruled out of consideration for the professorship Natalie was now being considered for. Tahuri, a Māori lesbian radical feminist activist, had been one of the first candidates for the chair, two years earlier. I'd been on the interview panel then, and to my delight the majority of us agreed on Tahuri. After a lengthy discussion we'd walked back through a clear black night to the hotel where the overseas committee member was staying, laughing and excited. This, I had said, would make our new Women's Studies Department world famous – an indigenous radical feminist head.

The next morning we were told that a group of senior academic women had gone to the Vice-Chancellor and said they would refuse to work with Tahuri, that her credentials were shaky, her academic record immature, and that she would ghettoise the projected department. So the decision of the selection committee was overridden.

'And it wasn't even the men, it was the senior academic women – all white, all heterosexual, all claiming to be feminist.'

'Of course,' said Natalie. 'The connection between lesbianism and feminism has made many women nervous. There's a real fear of approving of lesbians, fear of being identified with lesbians, fear of being suspected of being lesbian – and that's a frightening, even a disgusting thought for them.'

'Or fear of actually *being* lesbian,' added Claudia.

'And it means that since they aren't lesbians and would never in the world become lesbians and since they believe lesbians are the real extreme trouble-making feminists, they have an excuse for not thinking or acting radically feminist. These senior academic women of yours aren't feminists, whatever they claim.'

A quiver of doubt entered my mind. It was these same women who would be on Natalie's appointment committee. And Natalie's work was not only radically and overtly lesbian, but she looked like the stereotypical soft-butch lesbian. No make-up, flat shoes, trouser suit, low voice and attractive to lesbian eyes. Oh dear. I slanted the discussion.

'I loved your article about lesbian sex. The one arguing against those statistics that seemed to prove that heterosexual married couples have sex more than lesbian long-term couples.'

Natalie giggled and ate an olive. 'Uh huh. What the heterosexual couples call sex takes on average about eight minutes. What a lesbian couple does can take thirty minutes, an hour, an afternoon.' Kathy and I grinned at each other. Natalie caught the grin, and laughed with us.

That evening we had a party. Rosine and Adah, Hannah and Ser, the poet, the clinical psychologist, Claudia who DJed at the women's dance, all came. Natalie was exactly my age so she liked the music of my youth, and of course, lesbian music: Dusty Springfield, Marianne Faithfull, k.d. lang,

Dory Previn, Diana Ross. She danced with everyone. She danced the way I imagined the character Mo from Alison Bechdel's lesbian-famous cartoon series *Dykes to Watch Out For* would have danced: enthusiastically and clumsily, jumping to and fro, shooting her arms up in the air to the beat. She even wore the same long-sleeved stripy T-shirt that Mo did. When Kathy and I conferred in our bedroom, after putting Natalie in the spare room with a pile of New Zealand novels, we reckoned that we'd done all we could to ensure that she'd want to accept the professorship here.

'Did you notice, she was definitely flirting with Claudia. A romantic interest! That's good.'

We left the island early in fine weather. We ate muffins and drank coffee among the suited commuters. This was the day of the interview for the chair in Women's Studies. I was not on the new selection committee; none of those who had voted for Tahuri, except for the overseas member, were reappointed to it. But I was almost confident they would have to choose someone as distinguished as Natalie.

I was always an innocent in the ways of university politics. The decision to reject Natalie should not have surprised me, but it did. My one friend and ally on the appointments committee, the professor from Australia, told me that the committee had declared Natalie was 'old and tired' and that they, mere associate professors, had published more than she had.

Back in her hotel room Natalie told us, 'Walking into that den of vipers that was the Women's Studies committee was eye-opening. They were downright rude to me from the beginning. I was astonished they had got the university to pay the enormous amount to bring me out when they were just playing a game to get whatsername into the job.'

Kathy and I, together with Claudia and the poet, waved Natalie goodbye at the train as she headed south following a trail of lesbian connections to meet up with friends of ours in Hamilton and Tauranga and Napier and finally Wellington. Two weeks later, we welcomed her back when she returned with an extremely bad cold, and put her on the plane for the States.

The final appointee, 'whatsername', was white, heterosexual and not politically active. After ten years, the Women's Studies Department collapsed due to inadequate student numbers. They didn't want to study opaque male theorists like Lacan, Derrida, Baudrillard, Barthes.

Aorewa McLeod was born in 1940 in Auckland. She studied at Auckland, Victoria and Oxford Universities, and taught at the University of Auckland's English Department for thirty-seven years, specialising in women writers and feminist theory. She had her first lesbian relationship when she was twenty, and after a lesbian-focused life has lived with her current partner, Fran, for thirty-five years.

Ash Davida Jane

Good People

O soy milk carton   I just want to recycle you   I just want
you to go on and fulfil your life dreams
of being pulped
            and reused to make new cartons
and hold other consumable liquids   like orange juice   or almond milk
except we can't call almond milk
                        almond milk anymore
because it's too misleading   and causes innocent shoppers to
imagine almonds with tiny almond teats being milked by
almond farmers who get up at 4am every day
            Nobody wants to think about that while they do
their grocery shopping

            You can't be a good person even if you recycle
If only everyone didn't already have their own piles of used plastic
            maybe we could find someone to buy all of our piles of used plastic
Synthetic clothes release
            particles into the ocean every time you wash them
and I have dreams of drowning in a sea of bubble wrap and single-use
            plastic bags
while around me people lounge on cruise ships drinking
piña coladas and saying   But I Use Them For Bin Liners

I have dreams of me and all my friends buying
organic compostable biodegradable faux-plastic wrap
made from buckwheat and coconut fibres
while billionaires build single-use bouncy castles the size of islands
and we panic like housewives in the '80s doing bad jazzercise
choreography in front of the television while the house
burns down around us   Pump those arms girls
            Can you feel the burn yet

water levels

we're in the bath together but not in a sexy way   the lights are off
because the fan makes too much noise   so it's dark
except for a few blooms from cheap tea candles on the vanity
and the windowsill   I close my eyes and you rub shampoo into my hair
        like parents do when you're a kid   I cup my hands and raise them
filled with water   a tiny bath for a tinier person   who is washing
the hair of their beloved   and carefully wiping the soap bubbles
from their forehead   I hold them with a calm determination so as
not to spill their bathwater   you sit back and the water sloshes up
the ceramic wall and spills over the edge   because I filled it up too much
        or because the giant person holding this moment has small hands
it's a new kind of intimacy to know whose fingers wrinkle into old prunes first
        and to discuss the benefits of conditioner   I lay back and
put my head under and you're talking but the sound is muffled   my heart
pulses a very emphatic beat   on a tiny underwater drum
        you tell me our fingers and toes wrinkle
so we can hold on better in the water   which is good to know for when
the sea levels rise   the bathwater is starting to go cold   and when
I take out the plug I imagine the giant parting their giant hands very slightly
        to let the water pour out the gap in between   and it recedes
like the tide while I sit very still   reluctant to upset the balance

in my memory it is always daytime

in my memory it is always daytime, midsummer, and you and i are lying on the bed in that trapped room, the sun drawing stripes across our skin through the blinds. they were moments of sweetness in the worst summer of our lives. we don't get to choose what we remember. i'm scared of the things i will forget. one of my earliest memories is of the time i answered the phone and spent 20 minutes telling a stranger she was my mum when it was just some other woman with the same name. do you picture the world. how it changes an ear to have it filled with birds' chirping all day. i'm scared of turning bitter. i always want the possibility of running through a field and into somebody's arms. we can see in our memories a species laid bare, the nakedness of our wants. i think i'm in control but this has already been decided. to see the future all you have to do is look around. every raindrop is prophetic, a crystal ball to look into. they cascade down and shatter on the concrete. if you listen closely you might hear the breaking. solid walls amplify it, brick and glass. it sounds softer in the bush, soaking into the undergrowth. a distant memory of the groundwater, splintered.

Ash Davida Jane is the author of *Every Dark Waning* (Platypus Press, 2016) and *How to Live With Mammals* (Victoria University Press, 2021). Her poems have appeared in *The Spinoff, Sweet Mammalian, Starling, Landfall, Sport* and more. She lives in Wellington.

Cadence Chung

Girls just wanna have fun

Girls just wanna have fun   girls just wanna
be fatal   eyeliner like slits in their skin
lipstick like bloodstains   nails like claws

Girls just wanna escape   but there is no escape
when the past rattles   from all directions in time
so they find escape   in their own bodies

until they no longer sit   in their own skin
but watch themselves laugh   (until laughter
sounds like a language)   high above

on a streetlamp. They escape   into each
other, clawing like animals   to be let in
because they know how a girl can close

herself off, shut herself up.   No time
no need for pretext   just straight to the
clawing   the wanting   the finding.

Girls just wanna poison for 24,000 years
flay every foolish being   who walks into
the fallout zone   want their bodies

to vibrate beneath the earth   create
earthquakes   make teacups fall
from their shelves   make violets grow

make something happen   when their hands
can't reach the big buttons   that change things
that gloved hands in business suits   are always,

always pressing. Girls just want whispers and for
whispers to turn into shouts   and shouts turn into
law. Girls just want an anodyne   a quick fix

for their pain assigned at birth   that they
are forced into   that aches like no other pain
that has no cure   except witchcraft

The spells that are chanted   at pride parades
and protests – *what do we want? what do we want?* –
or whispered in the secrecy of night to each other –

I want, I want, I want. Girls just wanna cut
with their glowing bodies   bright with bottled
time, from being told time and time again

that they should not fall   into bed
into whispers   with each other
should stay as white and pure as

they were painted, were carved from
Adam's rib. Girls then turn their heads
inwards   gather their arsenal

of calligraphy brushes   create scripts
and books   and languages   only they
can speak   because they created them.

They use these languages   to say
what they've always wanted to say   without
anyone knowing – *I want, I want, I want, I want*

I want, I want, I want.

女 (Woman)

See what she's sacrificed
slipping   in   and out   of skins
a thousand unlived lives wait in her mind –
she could have been anyone; she chose to be no one for you
In the blue-lit nights, effervescent with thunder
she bared her skin under the ever-watchful stars
as they rode fiery chariots of eternal vigilance
she went gently into the stranger's arms: she did this for you
The stranger from the movie cinema
she never even got a glimpse of him before she was his
she rode the cold waves of love that couldn't be chosen
she loved someone she didn't, so that she could love someone she did
Look   what   she's   done
the prettiest girl in *Bak Shek*; she could have run away
with any man she chose, she could have kissed him
and they could have escaped from the thunder and light and noise
They could have lived together; free spirits
roaming the fields, searching together for forgotten snippets
of thoughts and feelings and love and this way, she never would have
become an empty ghost, doing laundry forever
You. She carried you inside of her
knitted her sinew and marrow into a whole new being
just like her mother and her grandmother and everyone before her
all living ghosts, pouring their spirit into vessels that would never return it.

The End

The ocean rears her head down in
Ōwhiro Bay – it is like a scene of rapture
frothy and green and suitably dark;
suitably stormy for when the end is nigh

even though, knowing this world
it will probably end on a calm, sunny
Saturday when we feel everything
is settling. Just to keep us on our toes.

Social media is bursting at the seams and
the Twitter bird swoops about like a bad
omen, foretelling ruin, fights with itself about
the economy until its sharpened claws rip

blue feathers to shreds. I read poems instead,
poems about the end of the world
and I wonder why they all talk about love. Not
soft love, sweet love, not the love that Victorian

poets smeared onto pages with ink-stained sleeves
but raw love. Stinking love. Love thick with seaweed
and swarming with flies, bloodied hands pressing
together and mingling stale blood – was it

yours or mine, I don't remember, doesn't matter. I
picture a wasteland but can only see the flowers
that will grow in the soil, fertile with charcoal
from the fire, and of course, free of us.

Everything we have built has always
been temporary; colosseums crumble, temples
sift into dust, stone tablets grind into a few
unrecognisable runes. We have tried to impose

this decay onto nature, but she'll always return
with a new leaf to grow in the cracks where our hands
once foolishly lingered. I've never been to Pompeii
but sometimes I wonder what the two lovers

were thinking, before the ash hit them. Did they
know? They must have – so I suppose they just didn't
care; too caught up in the raw, dirty thick of each other
that it didn't matter. This is how the end will be –

we'll be so entrenched that we won't even notice
that the earth has stolen the singed crown from our heads
and the ground has begun to shake with indignance. Those men
made love right as the heat scorched them, and

I'll be too busy staring at my crush's icon when
they broadcast the Great Flood (and subsequent rapture)
over a Zoom meeting. Everything we've built
is teetering; it is hovering over our heads

and bound to crush us if someone doesn't move
quickly enough; but we pull out the phones for a
quick kiss and a selfie, for old time's sake. Our
intertwined arms will be too coiled to untangle in time

so we won't try and run. We'll hold hands as the
waves come, and drown with our eyes open, staring
at each other. The historians will laugh and wonder
why we were so stupid, but will do it themselves

someday. The end of the world hides in the foundations
of everything we've built, and you can find it
if you tilt your head just the right way. When threatened
an animal will revert to its most natural instincts

and when you walk into a Greek ruin, you can smell
the people all turning to each other and pressing
bodies against bodies – love may make us fools
but we still come back to it, time and time again.

Cadence Chung is a student at Wellington High School. She has been published in *Stasis*, *The Spinoff*, *Awa Wahine*, *Starling* and *Milly Magazine*, among others. She identifies as a sapphic person of colour.

Carolyn DeCarlo

Winter Swimmers

We are not
swimming pools,

our faces
never submerged in water
long enough to breathe,

never dipped
below the surface,
eyes absorbing the
chlorine and urea
flushing milky pink.

We do not
share the sunblock,

our fingers
wet and greasy
against each other's backs,

never slipping
out of hands
and towels and lycra
to perform our skin
against the density
of 1,000.00 kg/m^3.

We do not
scrape the balls of our feet
against the concrete

playing spider
in the corners,

nor do our toes
gather grains of sand
to be sucked out later
in the bathroom
by hungry lifeguards.

We are in pieces,
not limited by bodies
of water and skin,

we turn ourselves
inside, we float up
like plastic bags
on the sea,
rising to form clouds.

The Year I Let My Heart Go Asunder

Scraping into the basin with both hands
I let the waves lap against them,
pushing my giant hands to and fro.
The waves are gentle and they make my hands bob
like moths do when they're not being harassed by lights.

I am crouched down on the bank of Wellington Harbour
and I am huge as the hills.
I am squatting with my bottom on Khandallah,
my feet in the harbour and the water barely splashing my ankles.

When I stand, I am wondrous.

Get back! I want to cry out
at the men in their cars and their ships and their helicopters
slowly circling.
Get away, don't look.

I push them, but not with my hands
just with my mind,
not hurting them but just bending –
bending them with my mind until they go.

Equilibrium of a Rigid Body

Think about the things you like,
like an old brooch or a handful of gemstones,
fresh cut grass between your fingers or
the smell of a flower you picked
in the gardens in Hamilton last summer,
the one you can never remember the name for.

You'll need them all next winter
when your legs grow numb
and you sit at work thinking about degeneration
until you feel like you're rising up out of your body.

Get a glass of water,
close your eyes, and breathe deeply.
Take the time to do this even when others are watching.
Remember the times this has happened to you before,
walking across campus two years prior
or for the first time, at the end of a run,
back when you were a student yourself.

This will help you keep perspective.
You are not dying.
You are not going to be captured
and put in a wheelchair
like when you were at the airport
and the woman in the United Airlines uniform
told you it was the only way you'd make it to your flight.

Don't have flashbacks to this
or to when you sat cross-legged on Venice Beach for so long
that when you tried to stand your legs had gone numb
from the waist down and you had to crawl on your hands and knees
in the sand thinking, this is what it feels like to be paralysed.

These are normal things,
they happen to everyone,
so don't worry.
Everyone around you is just as uncomfortable as you are.

Breathe and keep breathing.
Drink water and keep drinking.
Don't go to work when you're in pain.
Working in an office isn't good for your body
and it is important to maintain your health
when your soul feels so light
it might float away one morning
without you even realising it.

Carolyn DeCarlo writes from Aro Valley, where she lives with a full house of animals and humans. She works in a bookshop she started in Newtown with her partner Jackson Nieuwland, called Food Court Books. She loves it.

Courtney Sina Meredith

Jam Sandwich on the Lawn

I miss being back at Law
only because
you used to kiss me in the toilets at Rakinos
and say I aimed sky-high sitting on roots in Albert
park
eating triangle sushi, kissing the wasabi away on
your sleeve
   Too hot! Too green! Now my
   dad is in town again and horny for Goat Curry,
   a few months in Indonesia spent pining
the Rialto, don't know what happened
we used to watch
explosions and missionary sex, no one dies in festival
films they
            haunt,
stay contracted and kind of French.
I
appreciate the garlic steaks in Khartoum Square,
drink beer through a smile,
and who's special now
we want to say but can't,
that you don't turn the hand drier on with your ass
anymore, borrow my books and hide them,
imagine yourself listless (you fucking romantic).
And Dad's thinking the same thing as my boss, how
expensive it is to produce
          such tall children.
When you put your hand up
(remember) how the board would unhinge
            and some poor educator in tweeds
                        saying *quiet*
                        quiet would run after it, trying to
reinvent the moment
analogising his pen for a wand!

I don't know what happened, and why I want
        my crimes tried in a Marae, for someone's
Koro to rush me with an umbrella
Auē moko auē!
            Auē moko auē!

The Coconut King

The coconut king sends me a text
/ he wants to meet up and give me some coconut oil
/ it isn't cold pressed
/ his mother made it the traditional way in the sun
/ he's from a different island where the women are in charge
/ their men wait on them at home like wives in the west
/ Helena says it's fine to have a holiday fling
/ even if it's with the blackest guy on the island
/ my aunty says to keep away from him
/ he's a heart breaker
/ she should know
/ always getting caught on rusty men like rusty nails
/ smartening up in a blue floral dress
/ she puts on dangly earrings and does a twirl
/ pretty as a picture
/ I watch her leave the house smiling
/ promise not to see the black animal
/ lying through my teeth.

Helena's scooter works again
/ hear it turn into my aunty's drive
/ look down at myself in a pink mood singlet
/ blushing into red at the end
/ wipe passionfruit pulp off my shorts
/ stop in the mirror
/ turn my neck both ways
/ clean and slender
/ hair smelling like honey
/ skin soft like butter
/ take some deep breaths
/ watch the black ants march across the bench
/ Helena yells out over the spitting engine of the bike
/ hurry up and lock the house.

We get to the markets while it's still light
/ the coconut king is sitting in a circle with his boys
/ they fish and hunt together
/ bark at tourists in hotels
/ wearing next to nothing
/ stamp and wail about the gods
/ pull white women up from the audience to dance and dance

/ warriors for hire
/ call it round the world but it's just round the room
/ round and round the same island playing the same songs every Tuesday and Thursday
/ he looks up
/ sees my face
/ jumps to his feet
/ tells the boys to shut up
/ does his best impression of a gentleman
/ pats down the black curls of his chest
/ creeping out from under his singlet
/ wades towards me
/ used to living underwater
/ wades through an ocean of women staring
/ saying dirty things behind his back
/ looks at me like I'm the only girl at the market
/ gives me a kiss on the cheek and two containers of white cake
/ Helena's eyes go wide
/ she grabs them out of my hands
/ stalks off to a table with shade
/ takes out her phone to text her papa'a boyfriend
/ snaps a picture of the cake
/ then a picture of her bust
/ gleaming behind a sunburst knot.

I walk around the food stalls with the coconut king
/ watch his leather skin glistening in the heat
/ beads of sweat push their way through his temples
/ I let him rest his fingers on my elbow
/ let him hold my hand for a second before my steak roll is ready
/ we walk to the back of the markets and cuddle by the toilets
/ he melts in my arms.

The church took my grandmother's stove
/ she signed the house over in her will
/ I go to the flat land where she used to live and feel all the hairs on the back of my neck stand up
/ she was a quiet woman
/ always by the window lathering coconut oil into her hair
/ combing until the white teeth turned red
/ pleased when her scalp was raw
/ my aunty says not to think about it
/ the missionaries gave her something to believe in
/ we drive to a garden on the other side of the island to pick frangipani for guests arriving from America

/ more old white men to line the pockets of the island
/ my aunty asks why I keep smiling
/ tell her the truth
/ I'm still drunk from the night before
/ when we get to the house there's only babies rolling around on the deck and two dogs in chains
/ the mum and dad aren't home
/ we fill up a plastic bag with flowers and take off.

The darkest moments of the island unfurl in daylight
/ geckos cluck
/ fat with spirits
/ in the car we talk about moves
/ I want to inhabit his body
/ how to move inside the coconut king like water moves inside the land
/ Helena talks me through her wardrobe
/ I can borrow whatever
/ I'm going home in three days anyway
/ her papa'a boyfriend thinks I can do better
/ someone with a brain
/ we smile at each other while my aunty drives
/ his blonde eyelashes shine
/ Helena's riding shotgun and making a long list
/ a shopping list
/ a beautification list
/ not that the coconut king will notice
/ my aunty's given up
/ I'm old enough
/ girls my age make up their own minds
/ their own beds
/ their own faces with clouds of powder.

Studying the coconut king one night drinking cheap vodka
/ dark and wide like a massive shadow with paws
/ after the vodka he kisses my hand and leads me down the beach far away from Helena and her papa'a boyfriend
/ closer to the edge of trees and rocks
/ as clouds cover the moon
/ the coconut king takes off his shirt
/ lays it across the wet sand
/ he takes off his pants
/ kneels down on his crumpled clothes with both hands reaching out to me
/ come and dance he says
/ the waves are playing our song.

Sheets on the line hold their breath
/ show off sharp ribs
/ hold hands breathe out
/ everything is moving on the island
/ old faces reappear
/ asking the same old questions
/ why did they send you away
/ were you a bad girl
/ is that why your tongue is a dead fish
/ did you kill your own tongue
/ spitting city trash
/ sitting unconscious in your own skin
/ far away from your people
/ sitting on the surface
/ is it like being covered in plastic
/ they ask over and over again
/ flicking their dusty tongues between English and gibberish.

Helena lies in the sun
/ waits for her glass to be filled
/ I pour pinot noir
/ her papa'a boyfriend has turned to gold
/ he sits down on the grass beside us
/ rolls a joint
/ they've got a cat who likes to fight
/ maybe they'll get married and stay on the rock
/ teach the cat to love the heat
/ Helena wants to study long distance
/ do it on the internet in town once a week
/ they've both gotten used to seeing the dead
/ things go on here
/ the elders are healing people by ending their lives
/ moving their souls into animals
/ that explains red-eyed roosters and goats looking for privacy
/ why the wild pigs cry like boys
/ they say that's what happened to my grandmother
/ the church swapped her for a dog
/ took all of her land
/ sold all of her jewels
/ Helena's papa'a boyfriend jokes about me and the coconut king
/ does he seem like a normal man
/ how can I not feel what he is
/ sleeping with a mountain ghost.

The coconut king turns up on his motorbike
/ I kiss Helena on the forehead
/ wave goodbye to her papa'a boyfriend
/ think about staying away for a while
/ send my aunty a text that I won't be home tonight
/ she replies with a smiley face.

We curve our way around the land
/ climbing high above the sea
/ pull up in front of a small house
/ he says it belongs to him
/ inside there's no electronics only coconut shells and soft fabrics
/ a single bed neatly made
/ boxes of beer and posters of wrestlers on the walls
/ I hitch up my long skirt
/ fan my face with a car magazine beside the bed.

The coconut king sits on the floor in front of me
/ rests his hands in his lap
/ goes soft around the mouth
/ everyone wants me to stay
/ goes soft around the eyes
/ tells me to cancel my flights
/ it's easy he knows the number
/ his brother will answer
/ my aunty will get a refund
/ I can stay with him on the mountain
/ my tongue won't be a dead fish
/ he knows where they've taken my grandmother's stove
/ we'll make them pay.

He says all of these things with the back of his head bleeding handfuls and handfuls of blood
/ the room fills with small red waves
/ staining the heavy flowers of my long skirt.

Courtney Sina Meredith is an Auckland poet, fiction writer and musician. Her award-winning work includes her play *Rushing Dolls*, poetry collections *Brown Girls in Bright Red Lipstick* and *Burst Kisses on the Actual Wind* (Beatnik), short story collection *Tail of the Taniwha* (Beatnik) and her children's book *The Adventures of Tupaia* (Allen & Unwin). Courtney has held various international residencies, including at the International Writing Program at the University of Iowa, where she is an Honorary Fellow in Writing. She is the director of Tautai, Aotearoa's leading contemporary Pacific arts organisation.

Eliana Gray

Sometimes I wonder if my salt water mouth should be allowed to speak at all

Sometimes I wonder if my poems should have been tweets:

GOODBYE TO EVERYONE BUT THE SUNSHINE
        AND JEFF GOLDBLUM'S ASS

The best thing about living in Dunedin is the crushing sense of loneliness

I'm crying at the wall for no reason! More info soon

Give us all this trash in a pile and we'll take it home
figure out how to make it say what we want

Here's the pile of things we unwished
Here's the one we set on fire
Here's the links you saved to forget

Sometimes I set my ears alight on purpose
Lean my eyes outwards towards the heat
Boil the sides of my brain, flake the skin

It's only falling ash, darling
Like the giant fires in Nelson
that ate up all the pine and
a house full of belongings

Left behind a nursery
A cushy bed of destruction
A metaphor about the power of rebirth like:

REALLY FEELING MYSELF TONIGHT MIGHT DELETE LATER

Summer's hot and so is everybody else

I've never tried less to do anything wrong
Wrapped up in the mohair feeling of yesterday
And tomorrow
Or anytime that doesn't currently exist because

The present is bleeding and my first-aid certificate has lapsed

You can't kiss a moment on the knee
Plaster a big bird band aid over the puckered flesh
You can't kiss a moment and you can't kiss anyone

Because the present is bleeding and no one has a compatible blood type

But believe me we've tried
Hooked ourselves up to the emotional drip
Fed the hungry like a horror movie about a vampiric slave
Lapping up droplets from a fresh cut arm

There's way too many poems about blood and kissing
You'd think there'd be nothing to say by now

But everyone is shouting in salvation square and
Everyone is confused and dehydrated
Shaking alms cups in their own faces
Dropping coins on the ground and picking them up

No one's looking at each other
You can't look at people in summer because everyone turns
Into their bodies

And we've been through this
People don't like it when you make each other feel
Good without letting them know

We've become so used to receiving information in advance
To be a spectator feels like leaving
Like being left out in the sun too long
Waiting for the hand of god

To tell you summer's over
It's time to take stock of our retina
Find out where we've been burned

Dirt.

It expands
this idea of hurt

This overgrown
garden I tend
with blooms like

11 – one time
14, 16 – 18, 24, 25

I turned away
learned how to hide my head
keep seeds under my tongue

After ten years
I have only just begun
to notice the weeds and hedges

How good they have been to hide behind
How I've clipped the wilds in my sleep

Eliana Gray is a poet from Ōtepoti. They like queer subtext, astrology memes, and absolutely nothing else. They have had words in *Sport*, *Landfall*, *Poetry New Zealand*, *Mayhem* and others. Their debut collection, *Eager to Break*, was published by Girls On Key Press in 2019, and in 2020 they were writer in residence at Villa Sarkia, Finland, and artist in residence at St Hilda's Collegiate, Ōtepoti.

Emer Lyons

poppers

in the future we'll black bag
that shit
badges bracelets so much inappropriate
the old man sells through a hole in the wall
in the centre city mall
if he lets you through the small side door
you've struck gold
the kind of gold we leak into lucozade bottles
and take on buses to underage discos
the gold my cousin tells me is for gay men
the gold that widens our assholes
and reddens our faces
if only for a few seconds
we pressure each other to sniff it up our noses
and feel all the older for it
mature with our drug taking
but nothing tastes as good as vodka
the best stuff is always regrettable
see-through
and lethal

Baptism

she was taught the ways by the same woman who taught a man how to
conquer   to capture her
                                                        is that romance   it is

in the same breath she slides a
                        sword into her boot and a babe to her breast

                                        two things i'll never do

this is a history poem   i said
this is a history poem

                        some people know their people as far back as eve   i don't
                        know where my mother's mother's family are from   i only
                            know the ones that named me

she
                                who needed death
to prove love
            she who had an only jealousy

  i heard our dream in Adelaide   threaded through
a violin

                                                                on the face of love
                                                flies land
the body indecently dying   she
                                mourns alongside her rivals

                                                        grief bleeds from her hands

my body learns
the cold
of holy waters

                                our lines run into
unconsecrated ground

dune

'ever seen a blind man cross the road trying to make the other side'
'Handbags and Gladrags', The Stereophonics

i.
everything opens out
except our ears
filled with sand
the brown dull noise
as if inside
a conch shell
i can live like this but
if i lose sight
send me out to sea
on a pyre maybe
something low-key
i couldn't live a day
with the thought
that your face
might fade
from my memory
i follow your pointing
finger towards the tide
sweeping in and out
the stones getting wetter
the horizon promising
i turn and nod
even though you aren't
looking
you pull back your hand
get up and leave

ii.
plenty stones to see from
step must be minded
the odd swamp disguised
no signage for miles
all the fields have views to kill
you   an oasis in the distance
i call out through cupped hands
your sights set on the sea
not a sense left for hearing me
i think how the sky compliments you
as if you were here first
i'm convinced you're here to torment me
i've developed a new tone especially
i'm better and i'm worse than i ever was
sitting in this bog land
wishing i was the water
you are captivated with
wanting to shore up at your feet
foaming teeth washing your skin
i'll go home with you
in your hair   on your clothes
on your clothes   in your hair
i'll go home with you
and i swear
you won't
even know

Emer Lyons is a lesbian writer from West Cork living in Dunedin, New Zealand. In 2017 she was the recipient of the inaugural University of Otago City of Literature PhD scholarship. She has been shortlisted for the Fish and Bridport poetry prizes, her play *The Green* was nominated for Best Narrative in the 2018 Dunedin Theatre Awards, in 2019 she was the Otago Regional Slam Poetry Champion and in 2020 she was nominated for a Pushcart prize for fiction.

essa may ranapiri

knot-boy ii

an open space where?
not here   not here   knotboy!   that's me   sat behind the
turbine of   brain
exposed to water
ungalvanised

it turns   how i turn in a dress
sat behind a counter with   gabble
asking questions like   these questions
what kinds of   jokes
spin   in focus behind their mouths
it's telling
they're telling me it's not
alright   to b

wood clap on wood   if they see me alone   i   am

gay man   or transvestite   or drag queen

if they see me with u   i   am

straight man   or nothing else   or lying to myself

---*---

– just smash me to pieces brave boys! just fucking have at it!
and at it and at it and at it   till i am meltdown   complexity
is a devil   horned   and writhing

my body is something i would like to see in writing that   flat
and perfect and dead

---*---

the beetle pushes shit along the ground

on parts of itself it makes to move

if the dress is short

it knows this to be true because it
feels the object
it tells itself it smells nothing

i get an ironic version of the
attention cis women get

u r so hot
what do we have here
those legs
u need to shave

scribble furious shapes onto
swollen board

the pen will be knife before long
before my body turns into

the letters will turn into splinters
a song

---*---

i can not be my self without verbal communication but my
mouth is turned inside out
doughnut meated inadequacy walk down aisle at
countdown
hold up mixed veges under the light
what nutrients are left in frost

people passing
from the rotting avocadoes black and soft
to the fresh-baked bread held in sheaves of cardboard
demarcating price and contents labels if you're able
push a week's worth of survival around in a cage with

a look that shakes my spine a look
on so many different faces but still
the same fucking stare a snare

that hooks the lip
or a smirk that
highlines the forehead

---*---

wet saws battling themselves out chains clacking to the ground when will we realise the door is unlocked and a corpse is holding it closed when they realise they're utterly outnumbered way too late // severed ideas floating back into a vacuum where nothing is written and nothing lives the sun screams with no air to carry its screams i speak with nothing to carry my—

---*---

the stars are all out   of their comfort zones here
sweaters cover   a wetness   of intent
a specific cast   lasered into the stone
we wear around broken bones   and broke-ass wallets
key chains hanging from flayed minds

a clatter   a   tear   in the eye   drop
in the ravenous   gloom
in the titan   of dust
smote in the memory of burying itself alive to feed

the earth a story

gut me for chances   gut me for clever designs   gut me or cut me
smudged
on the wood that he grew
from his spine
a whole fucking tree   how could you miss it???

---*---

trick question   is a tired   coda

or a code to crack before the chemical   hit

it takes to the sky on the polish   of promise

leading a bull on a leash made of tissue paper
to the very centre of the circle where there /
any place could be

essa may ranapiri (Ngāti Wehi Wehi, Waikato-Tainui, Takatāpui, Na Guinnich, Highgate) is a poet from Kirikiriroa. Their first book of poetry *ransack* (Victoria University Press) was longlisted for the Ockham New Zealand Book Awards in 2020. They are the featured writer in *Poetry New Zealand Yearbook 2020* with their work 'HAUNT | HUNT'. They will write until they're dead.

Gem Wilder

Te Awakairangi

My first memories of Te Awakairangi smell like rubbish. It'll be a weekend, any weekend. Dad's home and there are jobs to do. The lawns are mowed, the catcher on the mower emptied over and over onto an old stained drop cloth. Two-stroke and grass clippings stain his hands and invade our nostrils. The seats are folded up in the van and it is filled with the clippings and other garden waste, rubbish, broken toys, punctured tennis balls, furniture that is beyond repair, magazines, newspapers. We climb on top of the pile for the ride to the tip, and then explore the mountains of other people's rubbish when we get there, tiny treasure hunters. Dad empties the van, and we pile back in with whatever we've salvaged, after he gives it the okay. And we drive down the hill, heading for the river. We fling all the doors and windows open, pile out again, making a beeline for the water. Water and children are magnetic forces. While Dad sweeps out the van and gives it a good airing, we paddle in the shallows, throwing stones, sometimes going in ourselves if the sun is out. Dad is one of those 'If a job is worth doing it's worth doing right' kinda guys, and this is how you finish a trip to the tip – with a well-swept and aired car, leaving no sign of the load that it's just carried. We never go to the tip without going to the river afterwards. The two places are indelibly linked in my memory.

I am six, and my cousins are visiting from Brisbane. The afternoon they arrive, our dads take us to the river to kill time before dinner. They stand on the shore, catching up, while we giggle in the dappled shade of the willow trees, ignoring our skinny ankles turning numb in the icy water. Zara, who is ten days older than me and therefore my extra special cousin, sings a new song that hasn't made it to New Zealand yet, 'I can call you Betty! And you can caaaallll meeee Al . . .' My uncle joins in. 'Don't you know that song?' they ask, incredulous. Weeks later it will be all over the radio, but not yet. We have to wait, anticipating its arrival like an expectant mother, knowing it will arrive eventually, but not able to pinpoint exactly when.

Zara and I need to wee. 'Go in the river,' my uncle tells us. More giggling. Zara doesn't hesitate, but I'm shy, unsure. Do they really mean do wees right here, in front of everybody? But I do really have to go. And so that is how I learn about Paul Simon: ankle deep in freezing water, the tiny pink hand-me-down hot pants with maroon piping pulled down around my grazed knees, bare bum sat on a cold rock, pissing into the currents of Te Awakairangi.

One weekend when my mother is at work, Dad drives us up to the Silverstream rail bridge. It's us four youngest kids. My oldest sisters are teens, and do their own thing on weekends, which is avoiding being round the house where they could be called on to babysit. Dad produces a large black inner tube and the four of us eagerly clamber aboard. He pushes us out into the current, calling out that he'll meet us downriver. It is exhilarating, this adventure. Where did Dad even get an inner tube from? How is it that we find ourselves so carefree and wild? Does Mum even know this is happening? I don't know how long we are on the river for that day, but it feels like an age. We are pioneers in untravelled territory, boldly navigating rapids. My entire body is buzzing with excitement and adrenaline. There are shallow sections where we have to get out and lug the massive tube back to deeper water. There are deep stretches too, and inevitably we capsize. I find myself underwater, paddling urgently to the surface, expecting my head to clear the water only to come up against the underside of the inner tube. I can't reach fresh air and I'm starting to panic when a skinny arm reaches under and drags me up, up, until I'm once again perched atop the black rubber vessel. My brothers have got this. They are in charge, and take their responsibility seriously.

Years later when we talk of the great inner tube outing, my sister says she was the one who fell in and got trapped, that she was the one who had to be saved. I wonder if I stole her story. But I remember gasping under the cold, the feel of my head hitting the rubber as I search for the surface, the resigned panic, the rescue. Perhaps we were both under there. Two little sisters struggling, two big brothers keeping us safe. And at the end of it all, Dad, downriver, waiting to collect us.

At my primary school, someone's mum comes in to teach us te reo Māori. She writes our school song to be performed at pōwhiri and assemblies, to the tune of Rod Stewart's 'Sailing'. 'Tēnā koutou, tēnā koutou, tēnā koutou . . . katoa . . .' The first verse welcomes guests to our school, the second verse tells where we're all from, the third verse names our marae, Hato Mikaere, the church. And then 'Ko te awa,' we lower our arms. 'Te Awakairangi,' and we move them back and forth, mimicking the movements of the water, the current.

We know this river. If we have bikes, we ride them here after school. Those who don't have bikes still gravitate here on foot. Sunny weekends see half the community at Taita Rock, the local swimming hole. On the far side of the river is the titular rock that you can jump off, and kids spend their summers here, perfecting their bombs. This is the landmark of our neighbourhood, more so than the alien monolith of the Avalon TV studios, a little further downriver.

We walk to the river one lunchtime before school camp, to practise making fires, which we cook our lunch on. Sausages, mostly, and Lisa brings pineapple rings because she's decided she's a vegetarian. We stack up river stones and find willow branches to build our fires. We eat our cheese sizzlers, then fan out over the stones, exploring. We've brought our togs, but the spring water is too cold for us. Not for Iritana though. Iritana is in form two, a year older than me, but the gap between us feels cavernous. She is tall, smart, good at everything in a quiet way. She's not shy. She's already comfortable with herself at thirteen years old. Humble, but not ignorant of her skills. Iritana takes to the water, swims confidently over to Taita Rock, and sits, bathed in sunlight. She tilts her head back to the warmth, eyes closed, and laps it up, as if she is completely unaware there is an entire class standing knee deep on the far shore, each one wishing they were as brave as her. Even the way she sits is grown up – no crossed legs, just knees together, feet tucked to one side. The Pania of Taita Rock.

Gem Wilder is a Hutt Valley-born, Wellington-based writer. They have published and performed their work in *Sport*, *Turbine | Kapohau*, *The Spinoff*, *The Sapling*, LitCrawl, Kava Club Chop Suey Hui, Enjoy Gallery and The Dowse.

Gina Cole

Melt

Rena looked from the back seat of the factory truck towards Rangitoto Island glittering on the horizon. The giant volcanic cone sat hovering on a mirage layer of quivering blue as though skimming along the surface of the ocean. It looked like an alien spacecraft about to take off. Vivienne sat beside her, but Rena dared not say anything to her or even look in her direction. They both stared out of the windows as Manu Koula steered the truck across the northbound wing of the Newmarket overbridge towards SkyCity. His brother, Tommy Koula, rode shotgun. Their huge Afros filled the front cabin.

Rena heard the radio announcer say that Auckland had not recorded a temperature this high since 1872: it was a sweltering thirty-two degrees. Such high temperatures are normal in Rabi, Rena's first home. Her home was now in Howick, but her first home would always remain Rabi, and Marenanuka Tonganibeia would always remain Rabian. Kiwis struggled with the correct pronunciation of Rabi. Rena tried to explain the invisible M in front of the B: you said it 'Rambi'. But they didn't get it. One time for a laugh she had written 'Rabid' on a form that required her to state her ethnic origin. Although why ethnic origin held any importance for a Las Vegas ice sculpture competition remained a mystery to her. On your birth certificate or a census form, she could understand, but an ice sculpture competition in a desert city founded by gangsters? The Las Vegans had rejected her entry on the basis that she had entered a non-existent ethnicity. She had tried to point out to the organisers that Rabi was an actual country, a Pacific island.

'Those ignorant Las Vegans think I'm joking or something,' she said to Vivienne.

Vivienne had intervened on her behalf and explained to the organisers that in fact Rena was a New Zealander. After much to and fro the Las Vegans relented and let her into the competition. So began her famous partnership in ice sculpture with Vivienne. They carved intricate and complex pieces, and had won a gold medal at the Las Vegas competition with a rambling undersea fantasy, complete with Venus rising from the sea in a fluted scallop surrounded by the winged Erotes twins Himeros and Pothos and gigantic pearls inside enormous oysters, mermaids, whales, taniwha and the entire city of Atlantis.

Their partnership in life had begun much earlier, as children in the Polar Bear crèche in Auckland.

After the incident with the Las Vegans, Rena grappled for a while with giving herself an appropriate autonym; she had discussed it with Vivienne on many of their delivery runs.

'After all, would you call people from the Gobi Desert Gobid or Gobian?' said Rena.

'What about Gobits?' said Vivienne.

'No, then I would be a Rabit and Gobi children would be teased at school and called Hobbits. And Malian children would be called Malits,' said Rena.

'What if the Malits hit the Hobbits on the head?'

'Haha, so funny.'

'What about Raboid, or Rabo?'

'Nah, then I'd be called Rambo or Rainbow.'

'And Rabo is a Dutch bank,' said Vivienne.

'What about Raboi? Yes, we have it. I'm a Rainbow Raboi.'

'Rainbow Raboi it is. You can't call your people Rabis either. Such a name would be problematic for the vets and the Jews.'

Rena shared this joke with her Jewish doctor, Rachel Firestone, although Dr Firestone understood the dilemma and said, 'Meh. In Hebrew "he" means "she", "dog" means "fish", "rock" means "soft", "cuckoo" means "ponytail" and "mafia" means "bakery".'

To which Rena retorted, 'Well I've been to the mafia city, and it did strike me as half baked.'

In the end she settled for Rabian. Most people could not make out her racial or gender identity, and would construct it for her according to their own reality. One day a white woman having trouble being understood by a Saudi Arabian shopkeeper turned around to her and said, 'Young man, can you speak English?' Another time a tourist on the bus spoke to her in Spanish. Another time a small child at the beach ran up to her yelling 'Japanese man! Japanese man!' She would stare at these people in disbelief.

Those who knew the troubled history of Rena's home would debate whether she was truly Rabian at all. In fact Rena was of Banaban descent; her people came from the raised coral island of Banaba within the Gilbert Island chain, more accurately known as the Republic of Kiribati. The British had displaced the Banaban people to Rabi to suit their purposes, and in turn displaced the Indigenous Fijian people who had been living on Rabi to the nearby garden island of Taveuni. In unguarded moments, so the Banaban story goes, the English were heard to whisper among themselves that they had used phosphate royalties from Banaba to purchase Rabi in order to resettle (that is to say, get rid of) the inconvenient Banabans so they could strip-mine Banaba of its remaining precious phosphate, in a carelessly circular process. Today this is well-known history, and still a topic of angry debate for Banabans and I-Kiribati and Fijians when they gather around the kava bowl. Of course, nobody in England remembers or even cares one jot about any of it, as you would expect. This is way too complicated to explain to a woman seated opposite you when you're speed dating and you only have three minutes to talk.

Rena had tried speed dating once with her ice queen, Vivienne. Vivienne wanted to go for a laugh. Rena went along, as she always did with Vivienne, because she had loved Vivienne from the first, since their childhood together running around in the Polar Bear crèche. They would often tiptoe past the ice room and Vivienne would squeeze Rena's brown face and hug her and then run away laughing and puffing white steam from her mouth, her shiny orange hair folding over and over as she looked back at Rena. She had no need to explain anything to Vivienne, and so when the circle changed and Vivienne sat across from her at speed dating, Rena said, 'I love you' straight off. Vivienne looked at Rena and said, 'I love you too.' And then she laughed, and they'd sat there for the next two minutes and fifty-eight seconds laughing and talking about ice, as they always did. Ice, the first love of Vivienne's life and the second love of Rena's life.

When Rena was very young, her parents had continued the displacement tradition and travelled to New Zealand looking for opportunity, settling in Howick. Her father had found work as a labourer at the Polar Bear Ice Factory, delivering party ice to supermarkets and petrol stations. The owner of the factory, Mr Watson, had started with block ice and then diversified into party ice. Out of a sense of loyalty to some of his customers (old-timers in historic Fencible cottages who hadn't made the change to refrigerators) he had continued delivering block ice to them for their ancient ice boxes. Rena's father would saw the ice blocks into slabs and carry them on his shoulders into refrigerated trucks. Other labourers at the factory also hailed from the tropics (Mr Tugia from Samoa, Mr Koula from Tonga and Mr Singh from Fiji), and they each had children, lots of children. Mr Watson, a staunch Catholic, had six young and boisterous daughters who ranged around the factory during the holidays like a flock of lambs. Rena joined the Watson flock, as did Fagaloa Tugia, Manu and Tommy Koula and Priya Singh. Having eleven children running around at holiday times meant the warehouse was more like a childcare centre than a centre of business. Mrs Watson came up with the idea of converting the unused storage room at the back of the warehouse into a holiday holding pen for the children, and the Polar Bear crèche came into being. The dusty room was cold and echoed. But Mr Watson swept and mopped the floors and the walls. He painted the room white and dragged in old signs saying 'Polar Bear Ice Factory' in elaborate lettering, and old cardboard figures of polar bears and snowmen, and fluffy toys with the stuffing coming out.

Rena and Vivienne would escape from the rest of the flock to watch their fathers in the ice room, cutting massive steaming ice blocks into cuboid lumps that they would slide into cardboard boxes and stack in the freezer. Sometimes Rena's father would stage a show for them, heating a fat nickel ball bearing with a blowtorch until it glowed red-hot. Using a mammoth wrench to pick up the glowing ball, he would place it on top of a cut-away block of ice. Rena and Vivienne would clap and laugh as the red-hot ball sizzled and melted its way right through the cracking hunk, water gurgling up behind it, overflowing from the top and spurting out of fractures it left behind as it tunnelled its way to the gravelled floor. They would play with the left-over ice blocks wearing their fathers' old ice gloves, pushing the blocks about and smoothing them into shapes on the rough concrete. Even as young children they saw shapes in the blocks, and would compete with each other to see who could make them into the best dice, face, cat, igloo.

Inevitably, Rena and Vivienne melded into the Polar Bear work force. Many of the flock joined the business. The Koula brothers worked in the ice room and drove delivery trucks. One of them had his own courier company. Fagaloa Tugia burrowed his way into the Watson fold to become floor manager. Diane Watson went to university and became the accounts manager. Caroline Watson became the dispatch manager. As for Vivienne and Rena, Mr Watson made a strategic decision to capitalise on their talents, and diversified one arm of the business into ice sculpture: ice bars, ice glasses, party pieces, ice wedding cakes. Vivienne and Rena could sculpt whatever the customers ordered.

SkyCity became their main customer, making continuous large orders of ice sculptures for medical conventions and trade fairs and fancy dinners for government dignitaries. The most recent order was for a large curved ice bar with corner features of ice dolphins and winged horses for the Nightclub and Alcohol Trade Fair, where it was rumoured there would be many Las Vegans in attendance.

Rena and Vivienne needed six days to make the sculptures. On the first day Rena half-filled the curved bins with water and left them in the freezer to solidify.

The next day, as Vivienne placed bottles onto the frozen slabs, she said to Rena, 'Fagaloa asked me to marry him.'

'What a fool!' said Rena, and she laughed.

Vivienne put down the bottle she was holding. 'Rena . . . I said yes.'

'You're joking, right?'

'No, I'm not.'

'Well, you're an idiot. That's stupid. He should just fuck off.'

Rena ran from the freezer and didn't come back until the fourth day, when she returned through the loading bay. Fagaloa was standing on the dock, directing the load-up of a truck, officious with a clipboard. She ignored him and went straight to the ice room. The curved bins lay open in a line. Each one stood half full with frozen water. She could not see Vivienne anywhere, but it was clear that she had been working in the room. As planned, she had placed bottles of green and red top-shelf spirits in ordered rows on the flat layer of ice inside each curved bin. Rena straightened one or two bottles, her hand lingering on their smooth surfaces, before filling the bins to the top with water so as to submerge them. She left the cold ice room to do its freezing work, to grip the colourful bottles in icy suspension. Fagaloa had left the loading bay, and so had the truck.

The next day Rena returned to the ice room to start carving the corner-piece dolphins and winged horses. She hesitated at the thick plastic vertical blinds hanging across the entrance to the cold room. Vivienne's figure moved in ghosted profile behind them. Rena put on her waxed ice coat and gloves and drew the hood up over her head. Shuffling into the ice room sideways like a crab, in bulky boots, with a toolbox in one hand, she looked over at Vivienne, who was wearing red gloves, busy carving outlines onto new slabs of ice. They didn't talk, merely worked. Rena blocked out the shapes around Vivienne's grooved outlines with a small orange chainsaw, the noise loud enough to drown out any hope of talk. They carved for hours, until the dolphins leapt higher than usual and the winged horses reared up in anger rather than trotting in orderly ranks. But by the time it came to polishing and finessing the sculptures, the ice animals appeared calmer. Rena and Vivienne melted the dolphin noses into shape with tiny blowtorches and smoothed them to a clear shiny finish with heated spatulas. They chiselled the horse wings into light feathers.

Fagaloa poked his head through the plastic blinds as Rena sat putting her tools away. He hovered there as if decapitated and held in place on a pike staff, until the rest of his body slithered vertically into the room. He looked at Rena for a second and looked away. She ignored him. Vivienne hunched over her work, smoothing the curves of a dolphin's icy tail. He squatted next to her and whispered something. She stood up angrily and left the room. Fagaloa shook his head and looked at Rena, who lifted her chin and stared at him as he stood and followed Vivienne. Rena finished packing away her tools and went into the moulding room to talk to the Koula brothers. They wore white overalls and white gumboots with full-length white ice coats, and hoods drawn up over their massive black Afros. She felt calm in their presence: they were like her brothers. They had an uncomplicated view of life. From the ice mould machine they had produced one thousand hexagonal ice glasses and packed them into cardboard boxes.

'How's the bar looking?' said Manu.

'Finished. We need to winch it out of the bins. How are the glasses?' said Rena.

'All done. We'll get the bar into the truck in the morning. You will be here, won't you?'

'Of course I'll be here. How's she going to install it without me?' said Rena.

Manu stared at her for a moment. He had always been there for her, since childhood. He looked at her with a strange tilt of his head.

'What?' she said.

'I know how you feel,' he said, his eyes soft.

'How could you possibly know?' she said, and walked out of the room towards the loading bay.

Her ice coat swung as she walked, shedding ice particles onto the ground behind her. Vivienne and Fagaloa gesticulated at the end of the dock in heated conversation. Rena ignored them. The hot loading bay oppressed her, and she walked quickly to get away from their sordid carry-on. She returned late the next morning to help load up the ice sculptures. Fagaloa and the Koula brothers had winched the bar blocks onto pallets and were leaning into them trying to slide them into the refrigerated delivery truck. Vivienne stood watching and fanning herself in the heat of the loading bay. She had piled her hair in orange layers on top of her head. Her shirt was open at the neck, and she held a melting piece of ice to her clavicle. Her eyes looked fluorescent pink, as if she had been crying. She saw Rena and came over.

'Rena . . . I . . .'

The heat on the loading dock felt unbearable. Rena pointed with her eyes at the pallet loaded onto the truck. The edges of the cardboard boxes had begun to crinkle as melt water seeped through.

The traffic had come to a complete standstill half an hour ago. Rena cast her eyes over the cursed incline of Mount Hobson, with its tennis courts of heated pitch surfaces. Nothing moved except the shimmering heat waves coming off the roofs of the air-conditioned homes below. Vivienne turned to look out the window, red and green light from the dashboard reflecting onto the curve of her cheeks. Rena wanted to apologise, but not here in the truck. Tommy and Manu Koula sat in the front of the cabin with their round Afros filling the roof and their muscled brown arms resting on the door frames. Manu tied a bright red bandana around his head, pulling his hair into a tall tube. The RT radio chirruped and beeped as Tommy spoke into the mouthpiece.

'We're stuck on the overpass,' he said.

Caroline Watson's voice echoed through the tinny RT box and into the corners of the truck cabin.

'Truck and trailer jackknife at the Khyber Pass off-ramp. How's the diesel?'

'Should be okay,' said Tommy.

Rena sat quiet, listening to the idling engine, the hum of the air conditioning fan pushing cool air around her face. She could hear the rhythmic beat of the motor, and thought about the ice in the back. She turned to Vivienne.

'You're pregnant, aren't you?' she said.

Tommy looked at her in the rear vision mirror, his eyebrows raised. Vivienne's eyes brimmed with tears.

'We might as well turn the engine off. It'll run out if we leave it going, and then we'll be stuck here,' said Rena.

'We can't turn off the engine; the ice will melt,' said Vivienne.

'What the hell do you care?' said Rena, and she opened the passenger door and jumped onto the sticky asphalt bridge.

As she exited the truck a blast of hot air enveloped her, and she gasped at the shock of heat. Traffic packed the bridge, bumper to bumper. People climbed out of their cars and strained their necks above their rooftops to see what had happened ahead of them on the bridge. A Sikh taxi driver leaned against his car in the next lane, a white dastar, white beard and handlebar moustache lending him an air of nobility. He nodded at Rena.

'This isn't going anywhere,' he said.

Rena looked at him and was about to say something when Manu appeared at her side.

'Wow, she's hot out here. What a pile-up,' he said.

Rena sighed.

'We don't have enough fuel to run the truck for hours.'

'Well, the bar will be a goner then, and the glasses,' said Manu. He looked down at his feet in their white gumboots. 'Look, I think it's a stupid idea for them to get married. But you know what the boss is like.'

'What? Catholic?' said Rena.

'I know it's crazy. But she's stuck.'

'No she's not. It's fucked and Vivienne knows it. So does Fagaloa, the drip.'

Manu shook his head and laughed. They leaned against the blue logo on the side of the truck, a polar bear on an iceberg bobbing in an azure sea of melting ice cubes. A baby cried in an old Peugeot behind the truck. Steam hissed from under the hood of the car. The driver, a Nigerian man, had turned off the engine and stood looking at the mist-shrouded bonnet with concern while talking in rapid Igbo to a woman in the front seat of the car holding the baby.

'I'd be careful opening that hood. The radiator could blow,' said Rena.

'Oh, this is not good,' said the man.

Four children in the back of the Peugeot peered out of the window at Rena. She smiled at them and waved. Their mother looked worried as she sat in the front seat holding the crying baby. Manu ambled over to the man, who greeted him in Igbo. Rena walked around the truck into the shade, and there was Vivienne leaning on the bridge railing. They stared at each other.

'It was just once. I was curious,' said Vivienne.

'Why do you have to marry him?' said Rena.

'Because he asked me.'

'Because he asked you! If he asked you to jump off this bridge would you do that too?'

'We're not kids any more, Rena. Don't try to mould me.'

'You told me you loved me.'

They stood silent, listening to the baby whimpering. Rena climbed onto the ladder and unlocked the back door of the truck. Vivienne didn't try to stop her. The truck doors swung open over the bonnet of the Peugeot and a cloud of ice fog poured out of the truck door onto the overheated car. Rena climbed into the back of the truck.

'What are you doing?' said Vivienne.

Rena disappeared into the wispy darkness and came back with a box of hexagonal ice glasses. She opened the box and handed it to Vivienne.

'We should hand these out,' she said, pointing to the Nigerian family.

Vivienne looked at her for a moment, her hands trembling. Rena jumped onto the road and carried the box of ice glasses to the Nigerian woman in the front seat of the Peugeot. She handed her one of the icy receptacles. The woman took the freezing glass from Rena and held the cold ice to her cheek, thanking her and jiggling the baby. Rena touched the baby's hand, and his little fingers closed around her forefinger. The baby laughed and Rena drew back in surprise, and then laughed along with him and his mother. She handed ice glasses to the children in the back seat, who squealed in surprise when they took hold of the cold objects. They talked in animated Igbo and laughed and drank from the ice glasses already melted full of water.

Rena turned to see a trail of meltwater leading to Vivienne as she walked along the line of traffic handing ice glasses to frazzled people in their heated cars. She looked to Rangitoto, floating suspended upside down above the horizon in Fata Morgana mirage as if a ship could pass underneath. She walked back to the truck and opened another box of ice glasses. She looked back along the line of cars and saw Vivienne shining in distant heat waves at the limit of the vaulted highway, turning and weaving her way back to her.

Ko Te Moana-nui-a-Kiwa te moana. I te taha o tō **Gina Cole** māmā, nō Whītī ōna tīpuna, arā, nō ngā moutere o Serua me Ono-i-lau. I te taha o tōna pāpā, nō Kōtirana me Wēra ōna tīpuna. Ko ia te kaituhi o *Black Ice Matter* (Huia), i toa i te Hubert Church Best First Book Award for Fiction ki te 2017 Ockham New Zealand Book Awards. Ko āna kōrero pakiwaitara e kitea ana i roto i *Black Marks on the White Page* (Vintage), me *Home: New Writing* (Massey University Press). Kua whakawhiwhia ia ki te Tāhū Paerua o te tuhinga totoko e te Whare Wānanga o Tāmaki Makaurau me te Tohu Kairangi e te Pūtahi a Toi.

Gus Goldsack

It's a body

The last time I had blood taken
He told me it was too thick
Said, did you drink last night sir (I did) or
Is there something you ran quickly from tonight sir
(there was)
and
For how long *have* you been a corpse, sir?

You tell me, I said
When did my body end, I said, and

He said,
Wet is a characteristic of bodies until the
Conditions are no longer met, and I said
What are those conditions
And he said he did not know, because by
Nature this transaction relies on the
Knowledge that he won't one day, too, dry out.

33/34th Year

For my birthday I want: six blind kittens lapping loudly at their bowls, the 5th through 15th seconds after two spritzes of eucalyptus oil hit a column of steam, for the 31st state I visit to be anything but Ohio. My landlord to fix the lock.

To finally become a citizen of a country that perpetually feels alien to me, to swallow the load of a man in a suit and tie with his pants pulled down *just* enough, a business class flight class to Auckland, a business class flight to anywhere. A flight in any class. A flight in any class to anywhere.

I want to have a tasteful cake made with a lesser-known citrus fruit, to be left alone with a knife. I want tiny waves sloshing rapidly against an inner-city beach on a calm morning. To be left alone there too.

I would like to explain to my pets what it means to go to the vet for anything other than euthanasia. I would like to be supported by a more sensibly shaped spine. I would like expensive skincare products with long, scientific names. For my birthday I want to swallow every (loraze / temaze / diaze / clonaze)pam in my medicine cabinet, to experience *my* year of rest and relaxation. I want to ride a bike between two vineyards on the North Fork, to bang Justin on East 8th St without coming so quick this time, to find a preventative measure for what I believe to be early onset macular degeneration.

For my birthday I want to not look like this, to not feel like this, to not live like this, I want to burst into screams on the C train at rush hour but without bothering anyone else. I want to shiver beneath a blanket on Karekare Beach, to look at a waterfall, to run to a car as the rain pours

Searches related to state

I'm in a state
i'm in a state of disarray   i'm in the state of new jersey I'm in a state of
disrepair, I've stated one too many
times that I shouldn't be here

I'm a state-owned enterprise operating as a for-profit business on the taxpayer
dime, I'm for statehood for the District of Columbia I'm stateless in that I'm
overwhelmed by an overwhelming sense of feeling neither here nor there
i've stated some of my intentions with your son   I'm the status (denied) of
a claim I made with State Insurance in 2003 because technically, *technically*, it
was stated that an act of God (god) would overrule the rules that were stated
('set out henceforth') that would usually apply, I'm stating on the record that
The status quo regarding the conservation of Māui dolphins is nothing less
than state-sanctioned animal cruelty   i'm the state of it
The state of things, the state of it all   I know some of my statuses
(separated, negative as at January 20, Online Now)
Today I must take an original bank statement produced within the past 119
days to any office of the
Department of Motor Vehicles in the State of New York so
they can state
empirically (ha) that this is all above board, even though on some things I
stayed silent
for 14 months just because I was afraid of what would happen if I walked out
the door and allowed my ex to tell a division of the United States Department
of Homeland Security that no we weren't actually very happy in our state
of cohabitation.

The closest thing I have to growth rings re Wellington (other than hospital
records, a scar beneath my left eye and a stack of Tommy Benefield EPs) is
a paper-thin memory that from my gay uncle's window over a period of days
I watched a sheet metal Bank of New Zealand chevron peeled inch by inch
from the city's second tallest building and replaced with a rather utilitarian-
looking wordmark

I don't know what his view is like now because we don't really talk any more.

Gus Goldsack is a poet, cat dad and black-sand-beach enthusiast. He grew up in Te Whanganui-a-Tara / Wellington and Tāmaki Makaurau / Auckland, and lives in Brooklyn, New York. His work has appeared in *The Spinoff*.

Gwyn Easterbrook-Smith

Stone Femme

There's a line in Leslie Feinberg's *Stone Butch Blues* that I quite like – it talks about camaraderie and a lack of shame between butches and sex workers, because sex work is a 'stone profession'. I sometimes call myself a stone femme, in a way that sounds like a joke but isn't. Some people seem to be able to work for years and turn themselves into shimmering beacons of sex positivity, discussing the importance of eroticism and the possibilities of spiritual connection through pleasures of the flesh. I am not one of these people. If I'm honest, discussions like this make me want to peel off my skin with a combination of mortification and jealousy.

It always feels fraught to discuss any pitfalls of doing sex work, to acknowledge it is something you carry out of the brothel with you. It feels like handing ammunition to people who want to save us by making our work impossibly dangerous, so instead you're left with half a story. I think it is sort of stupid to pretend the sex you've had in the past won't have some bearing on how you approach sex in the future, but I understand what's at stake.

Today I had sex with two men. One of them pried for details of if I was a sexy teenager then asked me to piss on him. I don't think it's uncommon that I was sexualised before I had any desires of my own. That is nothing to do with sex work, by the way, it's just a fact. The other told me he was a Gemini / Cancer cusp, so I thought about how cusps don't exist and how I'd arrange the introduction to this essay while I sucked his dick. He was definitely a Gemini. I suppose both of these things are supposed to be degrading or reflect the traumatic nature of my job, but mostly they're just boring.

Sex work does an excellent job of turning you into a prude. I'm great at talking about sex in a way that's funny or dispassionate, but I would sooner dive into a wood chipper than admit any actual desire myself. When sex is your profession, sex acts as hobby or identity can seem unappealing. I don't think this position is more objectively correct or evolved or anything like that, but I'm also not in a hurry to add 'sex-positive feminist' to my Twitter bio. Sex work can feel like you've been given the ability to peer through the window dressing of sexual cultures and norms to see the armature beneath. It's also difficult to express this without it sounding like disaffected posturing, so I'm conscious I run the risk of sounding like a joyless asshole here.

Trying to explain that sex to me is boring and routine – something I do without any issue with hundreds of strangers every year, but also find intensely private and shameful – might be impossible. I wonder if the whiplash back into shame after my embarrassing baby-hooker phase might be a reaction to dealing with raw desire so often. You see all the soft parts of it, all the ways it makes someone vulnerable, how it can be disgusting in its earnestness – desire feels very abject. I've dated enough straight men to know an aversion to vulnerability isn't unique to long-time hookers though.

I don't think that's the entire shape of it either – there's a bone-deep tiredness of what I'm going to call sexual admin, for want of a better phrase. It's hard to say what is my own desire and what is actually oily jealousy of the ease with which so many men can presume their desires needn't be communicated and should instead be intuitively discerned. The observation that many men are interested in their partner's pleasure because it strokes their own ego isn't an original one, but I assure you it doesn't get less tedious the thousandth time you're reminded of it. People assume that sex workers lie, but if you're clever you don't need to – you just leave blanks people happily fill in themselves.

Ironically, I think I've finally come to appreciate exactly what clients get from seeing us. It's unlikely, though, that I'll ever say 'I want to do what you enjoy', then expect something effortless that feels safe and pleasurable. I'm acutely aware of the multiple vulnerabilities of asking for what I want – risking that I'll end up back in the position shoring up someone's ego; a two-way mirror but not a lie. It feels easier sometimes to absent my own desires from the discussion and turn to stone. I've come to a point where what I actually eroticise is intimacy, but you can't very well write that on a dating app, can you.

Ultimately, this is a long-winded way of saying: please stop asking me to be on your fucking podcast.

Gwyn Easterbrook-Smith (they / them) is an academic and sex worker based in Te Whanganui-a-Tara (Wellington). They completed a PhD in media studies with Victoria University of Wellington in 2018, looking at news media representations of sex work and workers, and are interested in considering questions about how ideas around intimacy, labour and authenticity interact.

Hannah Mettner

Opening night

Miss Burlesque NZ 2012 is flirting with you and winking
at me, one hand on my shoulder while she's trying to fit
on your knee. She has Marilyn curls and a waist that doesn't
show the passage of time the way mine does. The put-on
voice of a little girl. And everyone's doing that forties pin-up
thing these days anyway. She offers to strip for whoever
gets her next drink. You don't know what to make
of each other: both used to charming the room
for yourself. Real talk starts again when she
goes outside to smoke. When she comes back she sits
between us, tells me about her suspension piercings, how
she has to watch her weight so that a few well-placed hooks
can hold her up as someone brings her to a leg-jerking
orgasm in front of a crowd. When I mention
the Mandan tribe she says she likes her scars, polka dots
are so hot right now. And maybe sex is *the* spiritual experience.
That night I dream of coming to the Issues Desk and actually
tearing your clothes off in that way that never happens
really. No clumsy stepping out of socks and shoes and
underwear; your fabled body pushed so hard against the
shelf behind that back issues of *Architectural Digest* are
coming down all around. In the morning you try to wake
me up by giving me head. But I wake up kicking you in the
face instead.

Gender buttons

An object on a shelf; a self with words inside that never came out.
Your finger down my spine; fine singing in my bones. Umbrella avoiding
the rain: the celebrating hat you wear. Tell me a little more about myself.

The food you forgot; what you got for biting at my breasts. The coloured
loss of uneaten toast on the bench and your tongue of loving pepper.
Hunger heavy in my mouth.

This room we bed down in, be wed down in. White roses growing
on the ceiling.
You want in a variety of colours, but a rose is a rose is a rose
and a bunch of them placate the air much better than one.
We couldn't grow anywhere else.

The teasing is tender and trying and thoughtful. Melting without mending
you undo my gender buttons till all of me is myself.

Obscured by clouds

I don't want to start an argument, especially about love
but remember when we watched *La Vallée*

and were so high we thought we were trees
and Viviane was walking between us with a painted face

and the bright whip of a snake at her neck. We were at the start
of the world then – the green as profound as the smut

of last night's sex. Just a smudge of guitar across the valley –
all songs with minor chords make my insides bloom.

Later, you say you saw me with a parrot on my back
its wings beating – the only time you ever witnessed

a bird wanting for hands. And I had my eyes closed
and you thought I was leaving, or dying

but I was just concentrating on feeling something
that wasn't about us.

Hannah Mettner (she / her) is a Wellington writer who still calls Tairāwhiti home. Her first collection of poetry, *Fully Clothed and So Forgetful*, was published by Victoria University Press in 2017, and won the Jessie Mackay Best First Book Award for Poetry at the 2018 Ockham New Zealand Book Awards. She is one of the founding editors of the online journal *Sweet Mammalian*, with Sugar Magnolia Wilson and Morgan Bach.

harold coutts

poems about boys

my first order of business in this poem
is to discuss how i want to stop writing
        poems about boys:
it felt aimless and painful to be entered the last
my asshole is no odeum for a performance
churned forth from loneliness
        dancing among the boys again and
abiding disregard from the masses is
a hurtling of bones; ceremonial over parapets
falling is an art form if you wink on the way down.
        my eyelid is working overtime

i'm going to throw up my arms and say,
'what's the point?' to my reflection for four hours;
        the last time a boy made me feel anything
was when i listened to sophie by goodshirt
a week ago. pressed replay on the footpath
and the wind grabbed my hand
        a more romantic act than forced flowers
can't believe togetherness comes from alcohol
and still learned loneliness. kissing in the moonlight
because we miss the touch. now i want to
        scour my skin of you

my second order of business in this poem
is to actually discuss how i want to stop writing
        poems about boys:
i am immortalising those who wrong me
and those who i have wronged. it holds a sourness
to my lips and parts them like a gate
        sucking dick only does so much for the psyche
but my, have i flown. until i find a love that stains
my skin, stubborn around each arm hair, i will stop.
the moon will hawk a name at my feet
        and then i will write again

my gender

my gender is a prince guitar solo
my gender is the shrill HA joanna newsom makes in *colleen*
my gender is karen o screaming 'stress' over and over again at the end of the yeah yeah yeahs' *mysteries*

i bide my time and bite my thumb and bind my boredom to myself
in the depths i ask questions:
can i sell my gender on trademe
can i use my gender to kill god
can i slow-cook my gender and feed it to my friends
i get no answers

with my gender i have a card house comfort
with my gender i am cavernous
with my gender i learn to curdle in the funhouse mirror

john milton wrote my gender as a poem that i memorised at birth
having been read it every day by a caring parent
and then i attend university to be taught it by fellow poets
eyes burned out at 9AM from behind the podium
while i doodle my freedom on the refill

i bide my thumb and bite my boredom and bind my time to myself
foolishly, i'm asking more questions:
can i leave my gender with a grindr hookup
can i reupholster my gender into a swivel chair
can i enchant my gender to make it more powerful against undead creatures
i know i won't get answers

with my gender i am a beast of flux
with my gender i am a mediocre poet at best
with my gender i am caught in the headlight

i'd much rather read any other poem by john milton
which isn't saying a lot because i quite like *paradise lost* and i fucking loathe my gender
consider me always just slipping out the door
gone for a quiet moment or returning to bed –
whenever you wonder which bathroom i piss in
know the answer is: not a public one

farewell to a gender i never loved

first i from the closet, then it from me
it deserves the grandeur of release as i do the absence
doth it kiss me before we part
or does its rejoice overtake the parting of the ways

the miasma curdles in me before i let it out
sour in the frenzy of my skin
it unfurls like the hand of a lover
that i've been too lazy to break it off with

the tide at wharariki beach tells me i am doing the right thing
my soul burns on the silver sand at my approach
a manicured hand reaches inside and plucks my gender like one does a grape
and i leave it behind in all that beauty

without me it bounds down the dunes
flourishing in the low light of mourning
no shape to hold it rigid allows oneness with the breeze
never so bedazzled in my husk, now it shines

harold coutts (they / them) was born in Whakatū but lives in Pōneke. Their work has featured in *Re-draft, Starling, Several Hundred Fools, Poetry New Zealand Yearbook, Best New Zealand Poems* and *Stasis*. They write poetry and are working on what they hope will be their debut novel.

Heather McPherson

Sniffing the roses

poking my nose in roses

I metamorphosise
into a wasp, a bumblebee,
an aged dyke in a ditch,
a broomstick witch

whose eternity is
to stretch into plaiting
just-dropped petals as linings
for pliant rose-nests exuding
hundreds of dusk-smeared
scents.

Or maybe like Rip Van Winkle
I'll wake hog-eyed, hairy-faced,
and be wildly transfixed in
some garden waving a telegram
from the Queen and assigning
my longevity to frequent
guzzling of hot pink
rose-blood . . .

mixed maybe with bulging
pomegranate juices violent
as honey-gatherers' suns
that blaze through volcanic
dust while visitants
hungrily graze
a bee-stung calyx
and somebody enterprising bottles
rose-breath for when reality
needs a slant or blood
needs mopping up
or desolate lost loves

and family face nightmares
or we become a butterfly
waffling a dottily drunken
sun-dance up a trellis
before a sudden blackbird
swoops low and snaps
no no . . . first we dream
we end up transposed
into a rose

Sometimes after I've seen you

I come away disorientated
You have just the same charm as you ever did
Your eyes sparkle in the same way
and little crackles of electricity so glitter
and busy up the air I never hear
the thunder as a warning

just God rolling his rain barrels around in heaven
and house and city-shift furniture toppling off
van-loads of old planks bricks cans politics
and redressals crumbling in a pile of liberated
kindling while we talk lively family friends

and goddesses we know after fourteen years who's
trustable who's a worry and who'll slither by which
slant on which foreshore and seabed mining whose
grandchildren still face islands and continents
with no guardian laws or the wrong ones and why
a ranting god-mouth turns some women torturers
or suicide bombers not just widows and childless

while risky winds sweep nor' west arcs and refugees
land no passports and exploded homes and might
we have worked but for quirks between ghosts
in flailing pasts and misconceptions and jailors
strutting across border bridges as if in a silent film
somewhere we took part in and fell out of

and somebody else touches you now
and I squat in a doorway facing a hail-storm through
a spiky red-horned tecoma hedge with a bit of meteorite
or what might be a pale fist stuffed in its twigs or a fat
little goddess behind gritty ice pips that bounce off
the steps like sparks in a particle accelerator that slash
the idol into a flat-fish skeleton that glimmers wetly
with a hole for an eye and dark green shoots
poking through do I know you

Things shift

for Fran

But I don't have lots of things in
my work – like Anna does, you said;
ah, I said, but your paint traps

amazing movement in it – it moves,
it moves – whether or not your
subject does – it moves internally

& moving, spills – to tell you fills my
head with your strangely edgy quilt
of many skin-colours – from this

rackety stuffed-to-overflow storage –
this 20th century glorybox behind my
eyes where samples bask in viscera

& rich plates simmer suggestively &
your paint's a palette, a book of fabrics,
a blueprint for – is it walls, floors,

carpet strips, tiles, beds – dense, intense
bold, flickery – a heaving sea-bodied
skin whose gulf-dips & flesh

tinctures ease into a shadowy pinkish
terracotta, its red-flecked browns & blue
green tints that bungy us – surprised –

in outrider curves – & drip-drop rips
& glistening shooting-stars & the startling
starting-place shifts that biff back lids,

flip open shutters & change – & changing
shift – & each shift changes our eyes – & this
& us – & the way I see – you – others – me . . .

Heather McPherson (1942–2017) was a mum, grandma, poet and activist. She was the first out lesbian to have a collection of poetry published in New Zealand. Heather co-founded the Spiral Collective, whose goal was to bring attention to female artists. She has been published in mainstream and lesbian-feminist-specific publications over the course of several decades. Heather continued to support lesbian and feminist writers to achieve recognition right up until her death.

Hera Lindsay Bird

UNTITLED 404

after a Cindy Sherman photograph

Recently someone scolded me for speaking about Cindy Sherman
because Cindy Sherman was an instrument of the patriarchy
Like an evil saxophone, that plays hold music for a bank
Bad financial jazz pouring out of the telephone
O sometimes I get so tired I want to blow the stars out, one by one

Every year people demand to know what art's feminist and what art's
        un-feminist
Sometimes I wonder if it's ethical to be a woman at all
It's a great stupidity to waste your life on right-seeming behaviour
Like putting a coin in a jukebox that only plays whale song

I like this picture because it reminds me of loneliness
And the great, unspecific boredom of life
It's the expression I get whenever someone tries to hold me accountable
The critical theorists advancing, with black leather pompoms

Once there was a time in which I had many ideologies
Many self-pleasing ideologies with which to chastise others
The theme of these ideologies was: however wrong you are,
that's the exact amount I'm right by
I felt them in my blood, like too much money

Once upon a time, I had many ideologies
Many superior ideologies, with which to cheerfully educate my family
        and friends
Forget crying myself to sleep, I wanted to cry everyone else there
Then drive off in my Cadillac, black wig blowing

Once upon a time I had many ideologies
And by ideologies I mean specific ideas about things other people should
        and shouldn't do

But proving yourself right is a bad career
Then you have to prove yourself even righter, in a blue satin pantsuit

Sometimes the world is so backwards all you can do is stare
Stare and stare, from out behind your waterproof mascara
Oh it's a great responsibility to be your own misogynist
There are so many beaded handbags with which to oppress yourself

I don't think the great project of art is ideological messaging time
Like Monet, spelling 'fuck you' in waterlilies
All I want is to pour my eyes into the world
The sunset blazing overhead like too much eyeshadow

People are always on the lookout for new ideologies with which to
    punish themselves
Contemporary ideologies, studded with hashtags
It's like not being able to wear a sexy nurse outfit unless you apply for a
    sexy medical licence
You have to take someone's blood pressure with your skirt hiked up

There are a lot of punishments in this world
And some of these punishments look a lot like life
Some things cannot be transformed, only endured
The moon shining over all of us, with its clean white handrail

The imperative to be correct is the great failure of the left
Sometimes you just want to wash lettuce in despair
It's like buying a second wig, and putting it on over the wig you're
    already wearing
You cry and cry, impressing no one

I AM SO IN LOVE WITH YOU I WANT TO LIE DOWN IN THE MIDDLE OF A MAJOR PUBLIC INTERSECTION AND CRY

is not how you are supposed to start love poems
but I'm too far gone
to work up to it gently

your naked back in the mirror
has cured at least 3–4 major diseases

for you, I would set myself on fire in a smoke detector factory
for you, I would ride through the mall on a Segway knocking juices out of the hands of thirsty real estate agents

your lungs like Christmas stockings waiting for Santa
to climb down the chimney & put cancer in
your face like the face of a dead French revolutionary in an out of print children's textbook
my stupid heart . . . like a snowglobe . . . filled with blood

If you left me, I would be forced to gaze despairingly into the middle distance
If you left me I would be forced to emotionally distance myself from the situation as a self-preservation technique until eventually I healed enough to be able to consider romantic relationships with other people, all the time secretly resenting you for failing to sustain your attraction to me despite the totally involuntary & uncontrollable nature of human desire

your teeth like a graveyard . . . in springtime
your tongue like a mattress . . . in a graveyard . . . in springtime
your tongue on my cunt like a mattress . . . in a graveyard . . . in springtime
my pubic hair like the black carpet on the titanic
my ass . . . like an ass buffet

you put me in a friendly but uncompromising headlock
you bite me all over my neck and shoulders

I do not know how to write a love poem
because love is indescribable
it's this feeling you get
when your mind gets hot
and everything else gets insignificant . . . with diamonds on it
and you have to laugh and laugh at things in your second-hand dress

the slow rising of your eyelid
like a girl's skirt

my eyes like two envelopes stuffed with snow and no return address
my eyes like a pair of pale blue cowboy boots walking slowly down a street
towards you

it's like
you've finally found someone that interests you
and you get more and more interested
like a fascinating disease
it's like
for some reason, you have to think of the wild west all the time
but it doesn't make any sense???
because you don't really care about the wild west!!!!

it's better than tv
to look at someone and feel so much happiness
your smile a single arrow, quivering in a tree trunk

it's like . . . life is not a punishment
and sometimes good things happen for no reason?
I stare and stare at you like you were a distant mountain in a homeopathic
video game
with rare medicinal flowers on it

LOVE COMES BACK

Like your father,
twenty years later with the packet of cigarettes he went out for
Like Monday but this is the nineteenth century
& you're a monied aristocrat with no conception of the working week

Like a haunted board game
pried from the rubble of an archaeological dig site
You roll the dice & bats come flooding out your heart
like molten grappling hooks
your resolve weakening
like the cord of an antique disco ball . . .

Love like the recurring decimal of some huge, indivisible number
or a well-thrown boomerang
coming to rest in the soft curve of your hand

Love comes back . . .
like a murderer returning to the scene of the crime . . .
or not returning . . .
yet still the crime remains . . .
like love . . .
observed or unobserved . . .
written in blood on the walls of some ancient civilisation
in an idiom so old
we have no contemporary vernacular equivalent

Love like Windows 95
The greatest, most user-friendly Windows of them all
Those four little panes of light
Like the stained glass of an ancient church
vibrating in the sunlit rubble
of the twentieth century

Your face comes floating up in my crystal ball . . .

The lights come on at the bottom of the ocean
& here we are alone again . . .

Late November
we ride the black escalator of the mountain
& emerge into the altitude of our last year

The rabbit in the grass gives us something wild to aim for
It twists into spring like a living bell

I have to be here always telling you that
no matter how far I travel beyond you
love will stay tethered
like an evil kite I want to always reel back in
As if we could just turn and wade
back through the ghost of some ancient season
or wake each morning in the heat of a vanished life

Love comes back
from where it's never gone . . . It was here the whole time
like a genetic anomaly waiting to reveal itself
Like spring at the museum, after centuries of silence
the bronze wings of gladiator helmets trembling in their sockets . . .
Grecian urns sprouting new leaves . . .

Love like a hand from the grave
thrust up into the sunlight of the credit sequence
the names of the dead
pouring down the screen
like cool spring rain

Hera Lindsay Bird is a poet and writer. She was a 2017 Arts Foundation New Generation Award recipient and the winner of the 2011 Adam Prize. She currently lives in Auckland where she is not writing any poetry, and hopes to continue not to write any poetry for the foreseeable future. One day she hopes to have enough money to get seriously into miniature railroads like Keith Richards (look it up) but as she works as a children's bookseller, this seems unlikely. She is currently working on a novel for children instead.

Hinemoana Baker

rope

He roped me, he roped me twice, the second time
it caught, fell at the right angle and landed around the bones
of my dress. He roped me from the East like light rising, from the
West like light falling, in the arrangement of his cutlery,
the bubbling land moving on its plates. Without words
or entertainment and without true silence he
roped me in the mud, in the kind of mud people call sucking,
or stinking, it sticks to one's body, one's feathers and folds.
I couldn't bear the thought of soup or vast pastures, he roped me
without heart or dancing, when he called me his *wriggly little girl.*
It was like freezing, when he roped me, I watched a thousand
doors clap shut in the clouds. He roped me and began to pull,
in spite of his own injuries, and I allowed him to be lonely.
With a shovel I buried the turquoise feathers, warm from the sun,
winter in the blood. In my mind I wrote letters to all those I'd
wronged *I want to be buried with a family resemblance.*

* This poem takes its recurring motif, and the first words of the penultimate line, from the novel *Winter in the Blood*, by Blackfoot writer James Welch (Penguin, 2008).

follicle

The follicle is shown on screen as black,
a fullness that looks empty, something like snow
a static interrupting. As the camera
draws near, the image swells towards
us, warps, then curves away

disappears into its own dark. All week
I've been walking into spiderwebs, says the doctor
plucking at his face and hair, at the ghost
of the sticky silver and the spider hunting
on the back of his neck. My pathway,

he says, has become a kind of tunnel
through interlocking glass-green ferns.
I water the plants at high noon forgetting
it'll boil the roots. It's not my strong suit,
he says, gardening. Not my superpower.

born again māori

I board my aunty's knee waving tickets, a guard comes past with syrupy coffee in a large tin can, sugar and Laughing Cow Cheese my airline of choice. Jokes are made about crates of chickens and milk bottles, white pigs. I alight, spend a moment on the sand face down, digesting a fermented delicacy, a sizeable crab climbs onto the bare back of my calf, collects my tickets, legitimate passengers smile me into the carriage.

As we board the canoe the hardcase steward says *Mōrena* to my *Tēnā koe*, his is the most beautiful handkerchief-in-pocket, placards rain from his mouth, he gives us each a tracksuit jacket emblazoned with the name of our team, kōhanga, Te Ataarangi Language school, wānanga, marae, hapū, Family Reunion.

The names on my jacket are the same as everyone else's. The embroidery covers us breast, belly, backbone, on the wing of a collar a sewn cotton Mount Taranaki with a small drifting cloud. I drag around my own set of grinning gates, Thegodofthesea-Longbreathgreatbreath hoists me by the bicep.

Across the aisle my dead Ancestor picks up her *KiaOra* in-flight magazine *the rise and rise of golfer Danny Lee born in Korea and every bit a kiwi*. Grave dirt and rugby trivia, pre-pixellated, fall from her expression into the pagefolds. Her jacket is a real stylie one without sleeves and we are all a little bit jealous, we resolve to put in a complaint, go through the submissions process and bequeath our babies to the honourable members of the Select Committee.

Wairewa meets Ōtākou, we applaud through the ages. Donning life vests and skirting the bold poetic figure in the riverbend we discuss the verdant green of the icing on the two-headed cake. *I am a descendant of Te Uri Taniwha* says the man who is utterly free. *Really?* I respond *I think we've already eaten that part.*

Nylon rope in my fist, I one-and-two-and-three-and-four my way behind the heaving emphysemic into the tiny craft, being able-bodied I am seated at the emergency exit, proud to be the possibility. *Aren't we related* I say to the rope – *it's all about the surnames*. All the passengers answer in unison: *if you have to ask you don't deserve the answer.*

Cartoons pass riding on the backs of moa birds, one shouts *there's no word for 'hectic' in Samoan*. I disembark at Muri, it's summer and the tracks have warped so they're putting on buses. This happens every summer but they never seem to predict it. Like *leaves on the tracks* and the ever-shimmering *body on the tracks* we are carried by our four limbs into different directions by a horse.

The boatman takes our messages from one side of the river to the other. He is dressed in pale pink, standing on the silvering wharf with his eleven pink companions. As we board he says *It's basically just electricity*. Many passengers disagree – *it's the woman who went missing, it is manufactured in the liver, which is the heart, the Darling Seat.*

Someone suggests a theme and we finger the margins, watching the instruments bow as they walk on – harmonium last, trailing the raggedy-sham kōauau and the chatoyant Maitai River pounamu, *they love this* says the boatman, *oh yes, they all love the proper welcomes we put on.*

Speaking to the dinosaur at the bus shelter I say *You haven't been to the doctor in thirty years, think of your blood pressure*. It's about life expectancy, breaking the one-page barrier, holding up mauri next to DNA, cocking the head, favouring instead

steam from the hāngī pit fogging the uncles in blue overalls, the nephews in beanies, the shovel under the forearm of the leaning Satisfaction Wrangler, goat tethered to the stack of wooden crates, snow on the black of the mountain.

last born

I am the last born
I move through the crowd with my shiny red wheels
I bring with me large animals and flaming spikes in cages
I am the last born and I know who I want to vote for
I know the identity of the figure in black
Low prices are written all over my face
I am the last born and I have a long following
Everything and everyone is my elder
I move through the relatives in my green leaves
I eat canoes and drink inlets
I have a beard and a small fat crab inside my shell
I am the last born the pōtiki the tēina
Everything breaks its back over me but there are
Many ways to build from scratch and in spite of the fact
That every fourth corner of the land has been walked
Over I make everything ready, being the last born
I am desired at each event, to lay down the
Cow leather, to direct people to the location of
The demons, the devils in the tarmac
We all bite something for a living
I know not to rave and shout when I reach these places
I bring children with me, just the right number
Of pumpkins and I sing completely out of tune
Buying up all the land around with my lucky sand dollars

He uri a **Hinemoana Baker** nō Ngāti Raukawa, Ngāti Toa Rangatira, Te Āti Awa me Kāi Tahu, ā, he Pākehā hoki, nō Engarangi, Tiamana me Ahitereiria ērā o ōna tūpuna. Nō Ngāi Takatāpui hoki ia, he taera rua. I te reo Pākehā e whakamahitia ana ngā tūkapi 'she / her'. Kei te noho haumaru a ia i Berlin, ā, e whai ana i te tohu tākuta.

Isabelle McNeur

Dancers

It was winter when I went to the strip club, a few months after graduation. After ten minutes – are you here for a job interview? No? I just figured, y'know – I found myself outside with the dancers, smoking their cigarettes, huddling into my jacket and wondering how the hell they were coping in their bras and undies. When it was my turn for the cigarette, I pursed my lips around multiple lipstick marks and inhaled.

It had been Tuesday at 6 p.m. Hardly anyone was in the club then. It was the magical time of night where it was just us girls – walk in and the receptionists were girls. Walk further and the dancers were standing around the bar. The booths were empty except for one guy sitting in the corner, looking lost. I sat down just as the first girl came on.

She was introduced as Helena, 'the best girl in the house', but when I went outside to smoke with the dancers they told me it was a term given out at random. Every girl got their turn. The lights were low. The lights were always low except for the ones turned right up: beams of colour highlighting the stage and more importantly the dancer, circling the pole or sliding down. The dancers moved like they were underwater or maybe they were the water, all liquid. Sitting in that club, pitch dark except for the streams of colour, was like being dropped in a glass of vodka. Everything was clear and hazy all at once.

Two more girls came and went as Helena did a lap around the club. She stopped to talk to the other dancers at the bar before coming up to me, beaming like diamonds. They didn't do polite customer service smiles here.

'You did really great,' I told her.

'Aw, thanks!'

She beamed harder and held out the waistband of her lace undies for me to slot the club's version of money into them. Then she pulled out a chair and sat next to me, asked my name and how my night was going. I told her it was good and kept my eyes on her face. If I looked down I'd see the nipple piercing that was visible through the sheer material of her bra, crafted to look like a set of sharp silver teeth closing around the nipple. I wanted to compliment her on it. It was a nice piercing. Instead I said, 'You're all really talented. You guys must work out a lot to get the kind of muscles you need for the pole.' Her 'aw, thanks!' felt more solid this time. Her shoulders relaxed as she started telling me her workout routine.

When she invited me out for a smoke, I went. There were two other girls standing outside the club, huddled against the cold. One of them had a jacket and it was buttoned over both of them, so they looked like a strange creature with too many limbs, one of them with a cigarette they were holding out to me. I let Helena borrow my scarf and watched their faces as they talked. They were all wearing make-up that glittered when it caught the light, and their skin looked very soft.

They were talking about a movie they saw together last week and one of them that wasn't Helena asked me if I'd seen it. I had. I didn't love it as much as they did, but I didn't want to bring the mood down so I kept that to myself. When the dancer asked me what I did, I told her I recently graduated with a Textiles degree and now did Not Much, what about her? Also university, she said, but not my one.

Her name was Stacy and she studied Commerce. Her friend, who was buttoned into the jacket with her, didn't say her name, but she studied History.

'What are you doing after?' Helena asked. It took me a second to realise she was talking to me.

'After this? Or after I stop doing Not Much?'

'Both.'

'After this, I'm going to sleep. As for anything else – I'm trying not to think about it.'

Helena laughed. 'Same, girl.'

In the lumpy space of jacket between the other two, there was a movement that might've been a nudge from History girl, who said, 'Hey, watch this,' and pursed her lips, blowing small round Os of smoke. Helena laughed, delighted.

'Where'd you guys learn that,' she asked, and begged them to teach her. We spent the rest of their break forming our mouths into circles and blowing shaky Os.

When their break ended, Helena gave my scarf back and she and the other two smoke-ring girls headed into the staff-only door. I went and sat back in my seat. There was a dancer doing her rounds, and I was in the middle of slotting a flimsy three dollars of the club's money into the strap of her underpants, which she held expectantly away from her hip, when Helena came back through the staff-only doors. She pointed at me.

'Hey! Textiles! That means you sew, right? Properly, I mean.'

'Sure.'

'Wanna come backstage and help us out?'

I excused myself from the dancer, then got up and followed Helena through the door.

There was no neon back here. It was dim, but in the way that a secret, misty forest might be dim. Back here the lights were moon-bright, circling around a short line of mirrors like in every rock star movie I'd been jealous over as a kid. The room was narrow and also sparse, except for the vanities under the mirrors, all of which were stacked with all kinds of make-up, glitter, jewelled and sheer underwear. There was also an open textbook that had something to do with statistics.

History girl wasn't there, but Stacy was bending over a vanity. She had what looked like a first-aid kit open next to her, but on second look it was filled with spools of thread and needles and for some reason, a lone crochet hook. She was braced over a bra, which had a strip of lace hanging off the top of the left cup, and she was swearing as she tried to insert thread through a needle.

'Was she still—' Stacy looked up, saw me and sighed.'Great. Textiles, yeah?'

'That's me,' I said. 'Do you want me to—'

'Oh god, yes please.' She held the needle and thread out. 'The lace and everything – it's so fiddly, and the last time I tried this it didn't come out great. Fine from far away, but up close a mess.'

What she said made me think of Monet then – the closer you got, the more the lake or clouds blurred into nonsensical smears. I was still thinking of this as I took the needle and thread – not so much the smears, but the colours and light he managed to put into the paint, whether the landscape was sunset or snow.

At a closer look, I went into the supply kit to get a different type of needle, then pinched the thread and pulled it through its eye. The music was muffled back here. You could sense the beat – rhythmic, hypnotic, something to spin and step to – but not much else. Whatever was on now, it was strong and steady like a heartbeat. It pulsed up my legs, and as I stuck the needle carefully into the bra I glanced down at the dancers' bare, previously high-heeled feet, imagining how the pulse would feel without the barrier of shoes.

Helena sat down at the next desk and leaned towards the mirror. She ran a finger around her eyeliner, clearing the smudges. It came away with glittery specks, purple and gold, and one tiny silver star.

'That must be hard to get off,' I said as I sewed. Helena snorted. She kept wiping her finger.

'You know it. This stuff sticks around like a bad smell. Thank god we can call it an accessory. I swear, glitter's just part of my look now, no matter how far away I am from a stage.'

'It'll still be there when they bury us,' Stacy agreed. 'At least it's pretty.'

'It's very pretty,' I said. There was, I now noticed, glitter everywhere – even in the dim light, the glitter caught the light and reflected it back at us.

I had to concentrate on the bra after that, I'd gotten to a particularly fiddly bit and I had to do a lot of small, precise stitches. I stitched and listened as the dancers sat next to each other and talked – they were going on a trip in the summer, they said. Probably Queenstown, but maybe somewhere more exciting. A few more dancers came in as I sewed, and I ended up standing so they could use the vanities. Helena and Stacy hung around, talking about Queenstown and maybe Greymouth, where they had a knife-making workshop, until I held out the bra and said, 'Ta-da.' Stacy took it and tilted it around. She grinned and said 'Oh, wow! This is so good. You should do this as a job.'

'That was the plan,' I said. Stacy let another dancer walk between us, then orbited forwards and kissed my cheek.

'Thank you thank you thank you. You saved my night, this was the only one that fits properly.'

I hadn't sewed anything outside of class for a long time, and nothing at all since graduation. It was good to do it again. When Stacey tugged gently at the lace, it stayed fixed to the bra. The stitches were small and close together, and white to match the material. If I squinted, it looked like a ribcage. But only if I squinted. Good stitches stay out of sight.

'No worries,' I said.

The one guy had left when I came back out. The bartender wasn't at the bar, so for a moment it really was just us girls. There was a different dancer on the pole now, a smoke-ring girl, the one studying History. She had a hula hoop act but now she was dangling from the pole in a way that made me think of circuses, like for her next trick she'd be halving herself. She'd explained through smoke that she was new, so she was using these quiet hours for practice. There was an art, she'd said, to unclasping a bra, to walking one heel-click in front of the other. As she climbed to the top of the pole and dropped her head back, I thought about Monet again, all that impossible light he got into the paint. History girl extended an arm. It was a long line down to her neck, her bare chest. The lights bathed her in gold until she dripped with it. She slid down the pole, a slow spin, and all of her shimmered.

I didn't stick around for much longer. It was getting to that time where men started to actually show up. After four milled in, I was out of there. Helena stopped me as I passed by, catching me by the shoulder. She'd been standing at the bar, one of the last ones to stay instead of head to the back room or towards customers. I waited, but she didn't say anything as she raised a hand and smudged a thumb down my cheek.

'Lipstick,' she said. She smiled. There was a silver-studded star next to her eye where a dimple would go. She rubbed her thumb on her bare arm until the red vanished into her skin, or maybe it didn't. It was hard to tell in the dark, even when it was punctured by neon pink, which skimmed over her whole body and then back towards the stage.

'Right,' I said. 'Thanks.'

'Anytime,' she said. 'Thanks, Textiles.'

'No worries,' I said. I waved. She waved back, and then I was gone.

Outside, I checked my coat and my pants. Both were a mess of glitter, although I was sure I hadn't come into that much contact with things backstage. My cheek might be dusted with it as well, after getting that lipstick rubbed off. I thought of glitter on my cheek, transferred by her thumb, the whole way home. In my head, the glitter caught the light from every streetlight and refracted it all over. The light grew, gathering from apartment windows and cellphone screens and clubs with dyed bulbs that throbbed like heartbeats, collecting in one big firefly glow until the whole city lit up like a stage in the dark.

Isabelle McNeur has been published in journals such as *Starling, Poetry New Zealand Yearbook, Flash Frontier, Wizards in Space* and *Headland*. She completed a masters in creative writing at the International Institute of Modern Letters, Victoria University of Wellington, in 2020.

Jackson Nieuwland

I am a version of you from the future

Of course you don't recognise me;
you grow into something you cannot yet comprehend—

I am a version of you from the future.
I can prove it.
You used to lie in the bath and masturbate to the idea of Hazel hugging you—

The light tastes different here.
I forgot.   *Then I forgot I forgot.*

I am a version of you from the future.
I'm running late.
Where did you put the keys—

I am a version of you from the future.
You will become close with David
but please don't move to Auckland with him.
He will leave you all alone.
It will become the worst year of your life thus far—

I am a version of you from the future.
I'm just here to warn you
that in a few moments
dozens of future versions
of you will begin appearing—

I am a version of you—
Is it raining?   I love the rain!   I've missed it so much.
Remember when we used to set up the tent in the backyard
and fill it with cushions and blankets and snacks
and read our book while listening to the raindrops on the fabric roof?

The black box in your chest will never fully go away
but it will shrink so small   *for so long*
that you will forget it exists   *for years at a time.*

I am a version of you from the future.
Teach yourself to garden.
Don't give up on drawing.
You're doing so well.
I'm so proud of you—

I am a version of you from the future.
On your first day in the new house
you will take all your pills.
        You know it's not enough to kill you.
        You just need to escape for a while—

                    I need blood.
You are the only viable donor left—

I am a version of you from the future.
Remember how excited you were
the first time you kicked the ball at soccer practice?
Your best basketball memory won't be representing your country,
it will be playing with your friends—

I am a version of you from the future.
Don't let them prescribe fluoxetine.
Tell them to put you straight on citalopram—

I am a version of you from the future.
Make sure none of us find your keys.
You don't want to get where they're trying to go—

I am a version of you from the future.
You will meet someone named Carolyn on the internet.
You will fall in love.
She will move to New Zealand to be with you.
The government will refuse to give her a long-term visa.
This will lead to years of instability, stress, and international travel.
Eventually, expensively, she will gain residence.
Don't let the obstacles deter you.
It's more than worth it—

Our body begins to shake.
At first just the legs
but it spreads through the rest of our frame.
We can tense the muscles in one area
and cause that part to stop
but the vibration just travels to a different section—

I am a version of you from the future.
You get a job as a librarian.
Occasionally you are given the opportunity to test new technology the library has acquired
like virtual reality headsets and 3D printers.
One day, you get the chance to try out a time machine.
You travel back in time to speak to your past self,
not sure what exactly you're trying to achieve by doing this
or what the repercussions might be.
You confess that you have spent your entire adult life trying not to feel,
that you yearn for deep human connection
but have built a protective shell around yourself
which you don't know how to escape from.
You avoid voicing your opinion
because you don't want to disagree with anyone.
You're incapable of handling conflict, confrontation,
or responsibility.
You can't risk the people in your life abandoning you.
You need everyone to love you.
Your past self looks at you with sympathy.
They pull you into a tight hug.
You begin to sob
releasing years of tears
that had been held inside
due to the conditioning you received
from a patriarchal society
and the overload of testosterone
pumping through your body.
As you sink into your own embrace,
the two versions of you merge into one
and you begin again
given a chance to do it all over
but differently this time,
with an open heart
like quadruple bypass surgery.
The risk of death is high
but what other choice do you have?

I am a version of you from the future.
This is just the beginning—

Jackson Nieuwland is a genderqueer writer born and based in Te Whanganui-a-Tara. They are the author of *I am a human being* (Compound Press, 2020), which won the Jessie Mackay Best First Book Award for Poetry in 2021.

Janis Freegard

Exhibition

On the Formica table in the centre of the gallery are
five shoebox-sized boxes. The entrance to each box
is via a fake vulva, the sort you can buy in one of those
shops on K' Road or Vivian Street that are frequented
by middle-aged men who don't meet your eyes. A visitor
to the gallery will insert their hand through the
vulva of each box in turn, uncertain of what they might
encounter.

The first box is lined with fur.
The second box is lined with satin, which feels crimson, but is really an intense blue.
The third box has a fan that blows cool air over the back of the hand so that the hairs will stand to attention.
The fourth box is full of popcorn.
The fifth box holds a snake.

The walls of the gallery sport the traditional line of frames.
This is the plastic shopping bag exhibition. Plastic is made
from oil. This is an exhibition of things made of oil that
don't need to be. The few remaining children of the future
would look at these bags in wonder and shake their heads.
Each bag is from a different shop, a different town, a
different country. Some have slogans. Many are beautiful.

Floral bag circa 1995, from a gift shop in Newcastle-upon-Tyne, England. Once contained earrings shaped like Viking ships.
Yellow bag with a red sailboat on it. Wellington, New Zealand, circa 2011. Slow Boat Records. Once contained a compact disc.
Large grey bag, no markings, provenance unknown. Once contained five fake vulvas.

From each corner of the gallery ceiling, video cameras record the visitors' reactions. Some glance at the fake vulvas and move quickly to the framed plastic bags.

Visitor A. Woman with white hair. Waits until there are fewer people at the table before she tries the first box. Smiles when she feels the fur.
Visitor B. Thin man wearing corduroy jacket. Looks alarmed. Doesn't linger.
Visitor C. Young man with goatee. Tries each box with enthusiasm. Says, 'Man, this is cool.' Tries them all again.
Visitors D & E. Female couple. Slide hands expertly through the openings. Decide they like the popcorn best. Express surprise at the snake.

Trinity

I

Once there was a woman with a big mouth.

She opened it wide in hunger.
She opened it wide in anger.
She opened it wide in laughter.

Her mouth was so wide that when she was hungry,
she could eat you whole.

Her mouth was so wide that when she was angry,
lightning sparked from her throat.

Her mouth was so wide that when she laughed,
the whole earth shook.

One day when she'd had enough of the world,
she opened her big mouth & swallowed it
& kept it quietly inside her.

II

Once there was a woman who grew hair on her face.
She didn't grow it to make people snigger behind their hands
& she didn't grow it to make a point.

When her friends took her aside to talk discreetly about
depilatory creams & electrolysis
she just smiled a smile of serenity & grew her hair a little longer
(soft hair, womanly hair).

She didn't grow it so people would stare at her in the street
& she didn't grow it so they'd turn away from her in lifts.

& when small children tugged at their fathers' hands & said
'Look Daddy, that lady's got a beard!'
she just smiled a little smile inside, all to herself
& grew her hair just that much thicker
(lustrous hair, feminine hair).

So that the hair on her face grew & grew
all soft & curly & growing
until it developed into a dense, tangled thicket
& Pīwakawaka the fantail came to live in it
& sang sweetly in her ear.

III

Once there was a woman who asked the Great Goddess:
What shall become of me?

And the Immense Goddess spoke to her
in her huge roaring voice saying:
You will have many husbands
& several wives
(not all at once, necessarily)
because I have chosen you
you who are a great lump of onyx amongst women
to go forth and, well,
not exactly multiply with all these folk,
but at least have a very jolly time of it.

Lay hold of the Tree of Life, said the Enormous Goddess
(oh yea) and sip at the Endless Well
You go for it, she said.
Go get 'em.

Thus the woman knew she had been sanctified
& that is why she recommends
you just open your heart as wide as it goes
& damn well enjoy yourself.

Janis Freegard

Mikey

Mikey's dead and I found out about it from the ground, literally from the ground because it was written on the ground outside Te Papa because he used to be involved with that light show

Mikey's dead and one summer we flatted together in Maarama Crescent after Griff moved out

Mikey's dead and once he told me that if he liked a woman, she smelled like biscuits

Mikey's dead and for a short time I was sleeping with his friend Symon in the flat in Maarama Crescent except Symon kept coming in really late which woke me up and I wouldn't have minded if he'd wanted to fuck but he'd just go straight to sleep and I'd be awake for hours and had to work the next day and one time after Symon had come in at three in the morning and gone straight to sleep in my bed I got up and mentioned it to Mikey who was in the kitchen and we had a cup of tea and after that Symon stopped sleeping in my bed

Mikey's dead and after the flat broke up, I lent him my guitar for a few months, because he needed it more

Mikey's dead and for a while he and our flatmate, Jane, had a thing going on

Mikey's dead and when I saw him at the Girlies Project in Cuba Street that time, he told me Symon was dead, except Symon was called Patrick by then and it was suicide and I hadn't known and I was sad

Mikey's dead and I remember when he first started calling himself Mikey, and Greg and I were calling each other Greggy and Janny because we thought it was funny

Mikey's dead and I remember him saying that the Turbines would be a good name for this band he was in and I said you might as well call yourselves the Combine Harvesters

Mikey's dead and when I was flatting with him he used up Jane's expensive hair products and she said not to and he said he would have shared his things with her and she said he didn't have any things to share anyway

Mikey's dead and one time I ran into him at a book launch or an art opening, I forget which but that's mostly where I saw him, and he'd got this job taking wildlife photos on some island and he was planning to use a disposable camera and said they were just as good as ordinary cameras and years later, when I was travelling in America, I bought myself a disposable camera on the strength of that

Mikey's dead and he was too young and you're always too young but he was too young

Mikey's dead and he told me once how he had a daughter and how great she was, I never met her but I feel sad for her

Mikey's dead and I don't know how he died, the message on the ground didn't say, but I want to thank the person who wrote it because I wouldn't have known otherwise

Mikey's dead and I didn't know about it in time so I didn't go to the funeral and I wish I'd known because I would have gone, I would definitely have gone

Mikey's dead and the last time I saw him was at Neil's art opening and if I'd known it would be the last time, I would have talked to him longer, I would have said, Mikey, don't die, it's too soon, you're great, Mikey, I thought I'd see you again

Janis Freegard is the author of poetry collections *Kingdom Animalia: The Escapades of Linnaeus* (Auckland University Press), *The Continuing Adventures of Alice Spider* (Anomalous Press), *The Glass Rooster* (Auckland University Press) and *Reading the Signs* (The Cuba Press), as well as a novel, *The Year of Falling* (Mākaro Press). She was the inaugural Ema Saikō Poetry Fellow at New Zealand Pacific Studio and has previously won the Katherine Mansfield Short Story Prize and the Geometry / Open Book Poetry Prize. She grew up in the United Kingdom, South Africa and Australia before her family settled in New Zealand when she was twelve. She lives in Wellington.

Jessica Niurangi Mary Maclean

Kāore e wehi tōku kiri ki te taraongaonga; my skin does not fear the nettle

A dimension of colonisation that has until recently escaped mainstream scrutiny is its impact on Māori gender and sexual identities. We know, through the linguistic evidence, that often no particular emphasis was placed on gender; there are no gendered pronouns in te reo. But this is not to say that gendered roles did not exist in te ao Māori, only that there was not the denigration of 'women's work' we so commonly find today. Ritual gender roles related to, and were governed by, tapu and noa; removing or mitigating tapu was essential for humans to navigate safely in the world. Tapu can be thought of as the presence of a spiritual force and an indication of potential danger, which entailed a series of restrictions and rituals in order to whakanoa, or make noa. Tapu perplexed early settlers and was often erroneously described as sacred, but sacredness is a Christian concept that should not be applied here. Noa is the complementary state of normality, a relaxed state of safety and access. Women, along with karakia, cooked food and water, were powerful whakanoa agents. Crawling between the legs of certain women, in conjunction with the appropriate karakia, was a frequently used act that removed the tapu associated with war, for example. Early ethnographers were quick to assign an inferior status to noa, conflating their own deeply Christian notions of the profane with their contempt for women. Women and noa were collapsed into each other in a profound denial of the tapu and mana of women. This colonial context throws into sharp relief current cultural practices that are determined by gender.

Whaikōrero, the art of formal speech-making during pōwhiri, is sometimes controversial for the exclusion of women from the pae; I affirm the right of iwi, hapū, marae and hapori to determine their own tikanga at the same time I affirm my own right to think and to question. I also want to note that the exclusion of women from the pae, like much else in Māoridom, is not universal. But it would be fair to say that on a majority of marae, it is men who whaikōrero.

There are a couple of responses to be made here. The first is that the original context within which these practices developed no longer pertains; previously, men, being considered somewhat expendable, performed whaikōrero in order to minimise the risk to women, who were considered more valuable because of their role as whare tangata (literally, the house of humanity). Pōwhiri encounters posed certain real dangers that simply do not exist today. This is not to deny their tapu nature, or the spiritual dimension that occurs during a pōwhiri, but many formerly strict practices relating to tapu have been modified or abandoned completely. Therefore my argument is not that we should not preserve tradition, but that we should pay careful attention to what is maintained, what is amended, and what is discarded.

The second response is then that the maintenance of this particular tikanga must be interrogated in light of colonially imposed, and too-often internalised, notions of male supremacy. As Ani Mikaere notes:

> It is obvious that some two centuries of persuading our men that they are superior to Māori women and that patriarchy has always been a central tenet of Māori philosophy has produced the desired result. . . . The Crown does not have to look far to find a small group of Māori men who are prepared to assume the right to speak on behalf of their whānau, hapū and iwi, accepting false flattery and short-term material gains in return for subordination masquerading as power.[1]

Harsh criticism indeed, and although Mikaere is careful to point out that '[t]his does not mean, however, that all Māori men behave this way, or that Māori women have any intention of putting up with it',[2] it is a criticism which must be brought to bear on the respective roles and rights of wāhine and tāne in contemporary Māori society.

Having spoken of whaikōrero, I must speak of karanga. During a pōwhiri, it is women's voices that are first heard, calling visitors onto the marae, weaving the two parties together, describing the take or reason for the pōwhiri, and dealing with the dead and the spirit realm. Karanga and whaikōrero are each essential to the pōwhiri process.[3] In contemporary times though, I believe it is no coincidence that it is karanga, the domain of women, that is so often dispensed with during mihi whakatau, a less formal variation of pōwhiri now popular with public institutions and agencies; perversely, implicit rules seem to remain regarding whaikōrero. If strict gender roles must be retained for pōwhiri proper, surely the institutional mihi whakatau could see a relaxation

1 Ani Mikaere, 'Māori Critic and Conscience in a Colonising Context – Law and Leadership as a Case Study', paper presented at the 27th Annual Conference of the Law and Society Association of Australia and New Zealand, Victoria University of Wellington, 10 December 2010.

2 Ibid.

3 The natural corollary of an argument in favour of women performing whaikōrero is that men should be able to perform karanga, but there does not seem to be the same level of agitation for this development.

of this tikanga, especially given the omission of karanga? After all, a public institution is not (usually) a marae.

Having said all this, I think it's worth bearing in mind the possibilities that my understanding of what constitutes equality is shaped by dominant gender discourses; and that gender equality has its own connotations within te ao Māori. I want to be careful here as I am still feeling my way through this thinking. Gender equality in mainstream New Zealand thinking means *sameness*; it is on the basis of this sameness that equal value and rights are predicated. This is understandable, as difference has been used to justify all manner of atrocities and oppressions. But can things not be different *and* equal? Can the notion of difference be rehabilitated, and in doing so, cast a different perspective on the contemporary interpretation of gendered roles?

This is where gender equality, according to Māori, might look quite different to the equality envisioned by the West. Such a notion of equality, of fundamental sameness, arises in response to the West's own deficiencies, with its predilection for de- or sub-humanising all who do not meet the implicit normative standard of able-bodied whiteness and maleness. But for Māori and other peoples who did not routinely sub-humanise women, equality might celebrate complementary difference, rather than seek to eliminate it as the source of a problem. Although Māori did not use written language, sophisticated concepts were nevertheless expressed in visual terms. A deep and enduring feature of Māori thought is exemplified in the use of positive and negative space in the art of tā moko; that of balance and complementarity. There are clues to be found here that speak to different understandings of equality. What these clues suggest in relation to gender, equality and difference requires further thought.

Mana Wahine thinking has engaged with gender in relation to colonisation for some time, and sexuality and gender-diverse identities are now coming to the fore. Elizabeth Kerekere's 2017 doctoral thesis 'Part of The Whānau: The Emergence of Takatāpui Identity – He Whāriki Takatāpui' and Jessica Hutchings and Clive Aspin's 2007 book *Sexuality and the Stories of Indigenous People* form recent engagements with the topic. Attention has been paid to the term takatāpui, its traditional definition being that of an intimate companion of the same sex. Ngahuia te Awekotuku was one of the first to re-examine and reclaim takatāpui as an inclusive term for Māori who do not neatly fit into colonial sexual and gender identities in her 1991 book *Mana Wāhine Māori: Selected Writings on Māori Women's Art, Culture and Politics*. The same year, the Spiral Collective's *Spiral 7: A Collection of Lesbian Art and Writing from Aotearoa/New Zealand* used the term in the same vein. Since then, takatāpui has been reclaimed by many Māori to describe ourselves, in part because takatāpui is as much a statement of cultural and ethnic identity as it is about gender and/or sexuality.

Given that culture forms part of the identity being expressed via its usage, we must be careful not to reduce takatāpui to Western sexual and gender constructs; as Kerekere notes:

> [T]he definition of takatāpui has generally been reiterated as a sexual identity that is inclusive of transgender people. This study takes pains to point out that 'transgender', or the more inclusive 'trans', is not a sexuality. It is an umbrella term for a range of gender identities and, having transitioned, many whakawāhine, tangata ira tāne and trans people may identify as female or male and as heterosexual. The binary use of 'women and men' here is also problematic in two ways. The first is in relation to intersex people who embody both female and male in remarkable ways but experience unwanted surgeries and discrimination based on their diverse sex characteristics. The second is in relation to people who are gender diverse and do not experience their gender identity as strictly female or male. All are excluded when takatāpui identity is confined to sexual orientation and binary identities.[4]

Diversity is a thing; we find it often in nature, of which we are a part. But, and importantly, the ways in which it is conceptualised, expressed, and restricted are culturally determined. Diversity has always existed and therefore certainly existed i ngā wā o mua, in the olden days. As Ngahuia te Awekotuku before her, Elizabeth Kerekere provides the example of Hinemoa, Tūtānekai and Tiki. In brief, Hinemoa, a woman of high rank, falls in love with Tūtānekai, a man of low rank. Their families conspire to keep them apart but one night, lured by the sound of his flute, Hinemoa heroically swims out to his island, and the rest is history. Already celebrated as a famous love story, Kerekere foregrounds the relationship between Tūtānekai and Tiki, a man usually described when the story is told as Tūtānekai's slave, but who is described by Tūtānekai as his hoa takatāpui. Tūtānekai mourns the loss of this relationship as he prepares to marry Hinemoa, to the extent that he arranges for his sister to marry Tiki. Kerekere concludes, as did te Awekotuku, Aspin and others, that it is clear from the evidence that diversity was sanctioned and accepted within Māori society in pre-Christian times. Going beyond this, Tūtānekai is never described in terms of his sexuality, which suggests that no particular attention was paid to it.

My own experience as takatāpui has been relatively unproblematic, largely due to the consistent love and acceptance I have received. Indeed, I would describe my experiences in this regard as decidedly . . . normal. In Western parlance, I am a biracial, queer, cisgender woman, but identifying as takatāpui feels to me simpler and more appropriate. I have a takatāpui aunty; growing up, it wasn't considered necessary within my whānau to make explicit reference to her sexuality, she was (and is) simply accepted as normal, her sexuality, as mine is, unremarkable in the best of ways. For many takatāpui, though, this is not the case. The unabashedly homophobic and heteronormative rhetoric of Brian Tamaki is an obvious case of deeply internalised colonial thinking, but it is not isolated. We must be wary of this

4 Elizabeth Kerekere, 'Part of the Whānau: The Emergence of Takatāpui Identity – He Whāriki Takatāpui', PhD thesis, Victoria University of Wellington, 2017, p. 24.

colonial influence when considering tikanga around the places takatāpui hold and the roles we should play. Where gendered roles and practices are to be maintained (and I assert here the right of Māori to do so), the place of gender-diverse and trans Māori must be considered. Is it enough to identify as a particular gender in order to perform the associated role/s? Will even surgical gender-affirmation interventions satisfy the criterium of gender?

With regards to karanga and whaikōrero, merely possessing the required physiology did not in any case constitute a *right* to certain roles and practices; at most, perhaps, physiology could be said to confer the right to earn the right. Whakapapa, birth order, training, natural aptitude and circumstance (including sheer necessity) were all factors influencing who *in particular* was allowed or required to perform karanga and whaikōrero. And who performs these roles has changed; previously, only ruahine, or certain post-menopausal women, could perform the karanga due to the extreme tapu involved with calling the dead. These days it is common for much younger women to karanga. This is not a 'good' or 'bad' thing; it is a pragmatic response to the needs of Māori communities. Its importance lies in the fact that it shows that, even within relatively rigid practices, tikanga can change.

Pou Temara suggests that:

> If tikanga doesn't have a philosophy attached to it, then it is tikanga made by man and, therefore, it can be changed. . . . It's a bit harder with tikanga that have an underpinning philosophy. We need to be careful if we want to change them.
> I offer the view that we are always open to new tikanga if we can actually tie those tikanga to a philosophy. And one of the great philosophies that overrides everything is manaakitanga. If you can create a tikanga with a whakapapa that pins it to a philosophy of manaakitanga, then I see that as a good tikanga.[5]

This emphasis on manaakitanga should be embedded in any consideration of evolving tikanga – and it is clear that tikanga do evolve. In relation to women performing whaikōrero, Temara states that:

> Some tikanga belong to another era. For instance, the tikanga in the greater part of Aotearoa doesn't allow women to speak on the paepae. There's a need to re-evaluate that. The current numbers tell us that there are more wāhine Māori than Māori men speaking te reo Māori.[6]

Tā moko provides another avenue for considering gender diversity. Men traditionally receive mataora (full face moko), whereas women usually receive moko kauae (chin and lip moko), and sometimes moko on the side of

5 Dale Husband, 'Pou Temara: A Modern Tohunga', *E-Tangata*, 6 June 2020, https://e-tangata.co.nz/korero/pou-temara-a-modern-tohunga/

6 Ibid.

the nose or the forehead.[7] Given that moko kauae and mataora are, at least implicitly, statements of gender identity, the following questions are raised. Should ira tāne receive mataora? Should ira wāhine receive moko kauae? What facial moko is appropriate for someone who does not identify as either male or female? How strict are the 'rules'?

I will speak to the last point first. Innovation with regard to both technology and design is evident throughout the history of tā moko. Tohunga tā moko were quick to adapt to the introduction of steel for chisels, then needles, which allowed for ever more elaborate designs to be developed. The earliest mentioned moko, such as Mataora's painted version, the double Xs that Niwareka wore on her cheeks and forehead, or the archaic moko kurī, were vastly different from the elaborate styles of the 'Classical' period. A proliferation of different forms has occurred in recent decades. Formerly children were not usually represented in moko (although other relatives might be), whereas this is commonplace now. Tāniko and tukutuku patterns, bright colours and representational figures are often found in contemporary tā moko. Thus moko has always evolved in technique and form.

Moko is usually described as a means of expressing tribal affiliations, with another of its prime purposes to make the wearer more attractive. Broadly, we can think of moko as a statement of identity, and for many now, wearing moko is an act of reclamation and/or celebration of an identity. However, there has crept into some minds the idea that you must earn a moko, particularly facial moko; that you must wait until various criteria have been met (such as fluency in te reo, or a high degree of standing); that you, somehow, are not worthy in and of yourself. I reject this. It's clear that moko were commonplace; if you had the means, you got one, usually beginning after the body had stopped growing, which would have warped the designs. Moko is therefore a birthright via whakapapa. If we accept that one of the primary functions of tā moko is to express identity, and that its form has evolved, and continues to evolve, then it follows (to me, anyway) that you should be able to express your identity with the form of moko that best expresses that identity. This right must be balanced against the right of tohunga tā moko to determine their own tikanga, but I would be surprised if all kai tā refused such work. From the conversations I have had it seems at least some tohunga tā moko would perform such a request where a person was settled in their identity, which, come to think of it, is not so different from any other person receiving moko.

When Māui sought his grandmother Murirangawhenua's aid, she gave Māui te kauae raro, her lower jawbone, a potent symbol of the knowledge of 'things terrestrial'. This knowledge enabled Māui to slow the sun, and fish up Te Ika a Māui, thus bringing a country into being. Te kauae raro pertains

7 There is at least one early written account of a Ngāi Tahu woman with full-face moko, showing again that little was universal in te ao Māori.

to earthly knowledge, and also represents tikanga; the lower jaw chatters and moves, while the upper jaw ('things celestial') remains fixed. Tikanga is (somewhat) mutable, and context dependent. It needed to be flexible in order to accommodate change, which is a natural feature of the world. Tikanga pertaining to gender roles, and sexual and gender identities and expressions, should be revisited from time to time. This is a job for whānau, hapū and communities themselves; but these discussions mustn't happen without takatāpui being central to these processes, and we must uphold manaakitanga at all times. Tukua kia tū takitahi ngā whetū o te rangi; let each star stand out clearly and be seen!

Jessica Niurangi Mary Maclean is a seedling of Ngāti Kahu, Ngāti Hine, Clan MacGill-Eain and Clan Ó Eaghra. Borne along by various winds and tides, she came to rest in Ōtautahi, where she has remained since.

Jiaqiao Liu

as my friends consider children

after Marilyn Chin & Heather Green

follow the bled tongues
the wood's logged

by the fourth marriage: silence
O Wanderer, home spins thin

did it hurt when u fell from the vending machine
cos ur a snack, unsealed like that

bang the microwave shut
before my nightly cry

born green & bald, Big Father cast her out
unseen at last, she scuttles the soles of her feet

we joke about our quarter-life crises over boba
I still dream of a facility of steel

courtly machinations eat your heart out
the emperor can afford new sleeves

missed more than the funeral, so
no time to feel like this, all plural tensed,

a child dreamed of being doctor and woke up poet
& each day she woke up boy she broke something

having walked alone through the valley of my body
of death tucked inside my body for years – suddenly, stars!

the sad boy's friends set him a place at the fire
I'm too fogged out to feel love

deep in a crescent-shaped scar
an unmanned drone considers unhappiness

encrypted your nudes like a good wife
suddenly I smell my own stink

myth: a rabbit dies of loneliness

after Alice Notley & Mitski

. . . she told me her love told her to walk down quiet roads. She said this in the glassless room above the park with the drowned shopping trolleys. I met the shopping trolleys in bed. One of those post-snooze prophecies. They squeaked and quacked like industrial machines. Today we are starting a unit on birds. Batteries clogged with bread. Magnolias clogged with birds. Sparrows, silvereyes, scarabs. Sky's full of them (something in the water). If boy met Rabbit God in a carpark in a shopping trolley rocketing at 8kmph jandals slapping tarmac *ba-dump ba-dump ba-dump* boy joyriding his girl deep-frying, is it still an invitation? is the water still? is the water still starling? They are good mimics. Shot for the moon and landed amongst the ducks. Lower. Deeper. Come duckling season, pūkekos crow, she said I said who said that of course he did.

For example:
she keeps rabbits. she keeps the girl rabbit and the boy rabbit in separate hutches. she keeps the boy husband and the girl husband in separate hearts. if she doesn't, the girl husband won't eat. the boy rabbit's belly is full of wind. Last night I ate an egg whole because there was nothing else within reach, & I can't remember the last time I felt so full or the last time I drank so hard or the last line of:

Come into the water
Do you wanna be my baby?
Are you waiting to touch me?
You look so good, but I keep my hands

He did it. Shot up the moon and landed the ducks. A brace of 'em, good lad. Never mind the fallen never mind the wishes I don't I do my father doesn't either he's an immigrant I don't wish him luck. Haven't the pockets for that, not in these jeans wait 'til I'm feeling boy again, chest full of red, ceiling plaster in my mouth Oh God I still can't wake up. Could you pump my heart for me? I still can't throw up. Home's gone and cracked her knee on the satellite dish. Could you cancel the order for me? The static smoked me up. Spinning never stops, but underwater: the silty green, kids kicking in the mud, in my bubbling belly, polka-clapping on pleurae *I'm liquid smooth come touch me too, I'm* losing something but I'm not sure what, and anyway I keep forgetting too little and forgetting the little things forgot to water the dog feed the car clean the chrysanthemums, forgot to keep clean to say thank you to let the boy rabbit out, keep him clean, keep him centrifugal.

that hand is for holding

after Jupiter

I have
only what I have:
        a tiny snail shell
        a pitted pāua, a spray
        of baby's breath

and the kaleidoscopic cloudburst
I become
when left
        unsupervised in your presence

and anyway I left all that in the car
and all I really have is my body and its changes
and my narrow, unchanging heart
and my handfuls of chamomile
and honey

                I want
        to hold you
        by the eyeballs

Jiaqiao Liu is a Chinese non-binary poet living in Auckland / Tāmaki Makaurau. Their work has been included in *brief*, *Atlanta Review*, *Blackmail Press* and *takahē*.

Josiah Morgan

what i wanna be when i grow up

Not many would be turned on by that
man with the pot
belly smile and the hairy
tongue. Not many would want what he had
to give them, not if it would kill
them to take it from him like a curse.
Not many would stay up at night googling
what to do with a positive test result in a homo-
phobic family. Not many would pray for
the text saying 'Kia ora Josiah, all tests
sent from NZAF were positive, infections
found, please call to arrange another
appointment' but I'm not many I am
one who wants so much inside
me even people and things that will
kill me I want even someone who
hacks violent like a meat grinder at my
ends someone who can show me his pot
belly and his smiley feet someone who can
tell me he loves me for my hurting who can
cover my happiness all up in
routine and disarray who can
stuff my mouth with latex who can
bleed my belly dry who can
give me what I could take from him like a
curse what I can google like it's a positive
test result and imagine I'm in a homo-
phobic family who can help me get past the
text saying 'Kia ora Josiah' like it's
culturally sensitive. Who can be the many to
my not.

BODY

Well you see what I know best is the colour of glass. The result of lots of hours not listening, or ignoring the cutlery. It's two or three panes, all closing in at once, that's what I know well best you see. There are bars, naturally, good-naturedly, promising to the glass that I'll always be there, I'll never leave, it's ok, we know each other better than everyone, I see through you.

Well you see when I left I knew I'd have to go somewhere far away so I went swimming in the cathedral. Knew it was impenetrable, maybe imaginary. It's the reason, all lightning bolt logical, that's why I left I knew you see well. The water's deep, clear, with clarity, someday I'll sink inside it and everyone will wonder what happened to him, was he okay, did he want that, was he happy, well he took swimming lessons as a kid, so there's nobody else to blame, really.

Well I suppose you don't see why I turned my back. That's what happens when your eyes open inward, or else encourage cataracts. My back's the most attractive part of my body, I'd love it if you loved to look at it, that's why I turned my back you see don't I well suppose. My back is uncracked, hunching, unhunched, it needs too much treatment and it's breaking my bank account so if you just look at it please, look at it then I'll know I exist and I can stand up straight once and for all.

Well I suppose you want me back I don't see why. That's after we left and keep leaving, or opened another door. All the other doors are sliding but ours is analogue, I suppose you don't see why I want me back well. Some of the best doors I've ever been through orbit public toilets, slide engaged like a ring over the finger, vacant like the look in my eyes or something like that, maybe in another life I'm an architect or something like that, maybe I'm building something right now.

Well my finger's free if you want it. Cracked skin dropping all over the place, looking like a mirror. It's always rubbed raw and a ring's at least committed, if you want it my finger's well free. But then all of the people I can't stand wear rings, rings that seem to signal status or a house and a family and somewhere to go home to at Christmas instead of the local patisserie or shift job or straight bar or roadwork or roundabout or rest home, so if you lock me up I'll turn into something new and worse.

Hell I've been locked up before the whole world saw. Forced and flaccid, lazy tiger enclosure. Even the stage I stood on recognised it: the audience pointed and laughed and cheered, the whole world saw I've been up before locked hell. The problem is I was assigned my own guard and I let myself run a bit free, they let me run free too, it was all plastic like an erect latex enclosure that I could snip with the scissor, so I was something worse for a while but I left my locks behind too.

Hell I don't know how Goldilocks made it out of the bear trap. Brute force and a twink-like grin. Even in my imagination she's imaginary, Goldilocks I don't know how the bear trap made it out of hell. That's the thing, she's a memory of freedom when child porn and pirating metallica music were just as bad as each other and the companies had free reign over both, Little Red Riding Hood would never make it in this day and age, probably get sidetracked, distracted before the big bad wolf, what a shame, I guess grandma won't be okay in the end.

Hell, my grandma said I'd go to if I carried on like this. Bareback dreams, but they look like vinyl. The dream hallucinated itself, if I carried on like this my grandma said I'd go to hell. So I dreamed of others doing it on blogs with scissors or wine bottles or fingers or the real thing itself, every ounce they could get, just guzzling it, restocking themselves with it, telling themselves it's ok to cry you know it's ok to cry baby you're just being vulnerable just showing them you're still a little human still.

Hell the first time I remember crying it was 'cause my footstool got stolen. I could climb up and down; nobody would stop me. There's a stepladder on your floor, I remember 'cause my footstool got stolen the first time I remember crying it was hell. I always climbed up and down my own footstool even though that's not what they're made for but I never let myself try to climb up your stepladder because you're very particular about your belongings and I don't know which of them I'm allowed to touch and which of them aren't really yours but things you've borrowed and wish they were yours and things that I touch seem to break all the time and you're pretty broken so maybe I touched you somehow.

Hell when you touch me I feel like I'm in hell. The most shallow one, a bad vine climbs the wall. You keep trying to touch me when I'm nearly asleep, I feel like hell when I'm in you touch me. Just like all the other times like when someone tries to write something radical and I'm not buying it like when the boat kidnaps my love off my beach like when I have to chase my lover down and even though I took swimming lessons I'm really bad at swimming like when you touch me like when you tell me I'm not allowed to touch anyone else like when you're high and we're locked out of the house like all the other times I feel I'm in hell.

Well I remember writing a superhero drama in locked rooms with you.

Well I remember my cock pressed against the flesh of my clothing for you.

Well I remember well when you said you hope I soon get well.

Well I remember you dropped your weed-smoked clothing all over your lawn.

Well I remember you kidnapped me and tied me up naked in the back of your van.

Hell I knew you well when you held my hand.

Hell I knew you well when you whispered my name like it was a rotten fruit.

Hell I knew you well when you pressed my hand like it was cutting you.

Hell I knew you well when you ripped up my poem like it was you.

Hell I knew you well when you knew this wasn't about you.

Strictly, I'm stuck in the structure I've built. Or my body in the bruising that shapes my gait's grace. If I tell you something about my structure or my body instead, I'll need something in return, but I don't know what that is yet. Maybe pen marks on paper or more tattoos on your skin, something that makes something else real, or something like something something else.

Strictly, I'm here to break my own bones, so you know my body wasn't built for this. Or my brain in the grace that marks my face's shape. If I show you a photograph of my face, I'll need to know you can keep it a secret, even though you've little care for me. Maybe more dollars in my bank account, stains on my stomach, something that tells me you don't love me but you're willing to try or something along those lines.

Strictly, my bones are in my bullet points. I've put it all on the page but it's still unmarked by sense. If I were to make it all make sense, I'd need to know you'd still like it, even though you've already made it this far. Like, is it as good as the egg you perfectly poached for breakfast is it as good as the first kiss you gave to your life, I don't expect you to answer these questions really or well.

Strictly, most of what I have to say has been said before. I know it in my blood and on my bookshelves. If I had something new to say none of you would know what to do with it so it'd sit on display to touch sometimes and say you're so proud of, I'd need to know you'd read it even though you never wanted to. You could build a whole temple for it or use it as flame for the fire, one of the two options but please just let me know you got the message first.

Strictly, I want to go back on what I've said to you. I know I don't have much left. If my gas tank had more space then I'd write something else to turn you off and you'd shut me down one word at a time reading some kids' book in your head. But I'll always be here even if you're not looking at me gathering dust and growing old in the corner, a little bit more soft and mellow every day, stronger in my head knowing more about you than you thought I ever could, building fantasies out of frozen porn shoots I wasn't in, imagining what you could have done to my body but I've recovered from too hard and too fast, imagining what I'd look like if I was put onto paper like a drawing or maybe a photo of a wood carving, who knows, if I'm gathering dust maybe I'll start sneezing one day as you're asleep in bed and it'll wake you up and you'll look through me as if you're terrified something or someone is haunting you but instead I'm just some body you groped around inside one time when you were littler but couldn't properly get a hold on, and then you'll fall back to sleep and dream about how your husband has his arms around you you're okay you're so okay everything is fine and will be fine for ever, and somewhere in another space I might be able to feel your pulse in my yellow wallpaper and it's beating all over and inside of me, maybe one day I get so bored of watching you that I turn my back while you lie on your deathbed, maybe your life flashes before your eyes but I'm too busy looking at the little spider crawling across these little piles of paper you left lying around in your desk drawer years and years and years before knowing you'd look at them once then forget them, maybe I put a little bell jar over the spider and watch it learn its geography, maybe I write a book where I rip out your arms, maybe I write a book where you rip out mine, maybe you're passing through to meet me and just as you see me board the train the door slams shut in front of you and you're alone, you've never really known what I'm saying anyway, but now it's real, now you're bleeding out and you're going and you know I'm gone too.

Josiah Morgan was born in Christchurch in 2001 and has been involved in the Aotearoa performing arts scene his entire life. He studies anthropology and English at the University of Canterbury and runs his own freelance theatre company, JMO Theatrics. His debut poetry collection, *Inside the Castle*, was published in February 2019 by Amphetamine Sulphate and has been described as '*The Waste Land* for the 21st century'.

Joy Holley

Why Girls Always Go to the Bathroom Together

The Lonely bra you want to wear tonight has five hooks down the back and crossover straps, so you can't do it up on your own. You hold your hair up in your hands and your friend asks which hook you want it on. 'The tightest one,' you tell her. Her fingers climb your spine like a ladder. It gives you ASMR and you wonder if you even want to go to the party; maybe you should just stay home and plait each other's hair. Then you remember the guy you're in love with and how you're determined to make out with him tonight. Your friend plucks your bra straps. They untwist. You are corseted and ready.

The guy you're in love with is telling a group of people why *Eraserhead* is the best piece of cinema to date. You will him to hurry up and let you drag him off somewhere. He doesn't. You unscrew the jam jar that you have filled with vodka and unbend the plastic straw you have folded inside. You know that plastic straws are bad for the environment, but you also know that if you don't use a straw, your lipstick will be ruined, and that's not an option you're willing to consider. Of course, your lipstick will be ruined if you end up kissing, but that will mean the lipstick's already had its intended effect. The boy you're in love with moves on to *Mulholland Drive*. You decide you don't even like him that much.

Your friend rolls a joint in celebration. You get high on the bathmat; 'like Aladdin,' she says, but all you can think of is Jasmine and the three wishes. By the time you remember the magic carpet, you're both in hysterics. You don't break eye contact for what feels like hours. You're laughing so hard you've stopped making any sound, and the soft drip of the tap makes everything even funnier. Someone bangs on the door and you both shout that there's another toilet upstairs. She takes the joint and finishes it off. You could almost swear the bathmat is hovering a few centimetres above the ground.

'Come on Eileen' starts playing. Everyone puts down their drink and migrates to the living room; dancing their way into a circle. The row of boys on the couch are the only ones who don't join in. You are all too aware that they are watching you. You have no interest in any of them, but you turn your body so they get the best angle anyway. Your hips brush against the guy next to you, light enough to feel like an accident. He shouts along to the chorus without looking at you once.

You decide you need more make-up. First you sit down on the edge of the bath, but your friend says the light isn't good. She looks at your face from various angles, then puts the lid down on the toilet and makes you sit on top of that. You feel the plastic bend under your weight, then relax. She gets out her pencil and begins drawing wings onto your eyes. 'Make them bigger,' you tell her, 'like Amy Winehouse.' Her face is so focused that you are afraid you'll twitch and break her out of it. Your eyes begin to water. You realise you haven't breathed for a while. You inhale just as she exhales. Her breath smells of white wine and ice and peppermint chewing gum.

You drink a bottle of scrumpy and take control of the aux cord. After three goes, you finally type in 'Promiscuous' without any spelling mistakes. There are some hoots of approval and soon you're at the centre of a small crowd. There is a lot of slutdropping, and then you're crawling on the floor, but in a sexy way. Some guy gives you a piggyback ride and you feel like a queen up in her tower. The song ends and another guy asks you to dance with him. You accept, but you don't dance how he wants you to. You try to turn it into a joke, but he steps forward so you're pressed against the wall. He tries to kiss you. 'No, no, no,' you say, slipping away while he calls out 'What? What? What?' You're vaguely exhilarated by such a near miss, but you also feel kind of sick. You want to tell your friends what just happened because that's what people do, but you're worried they'll think you're proud of being wanted so much by someone you don't want at all. You're worried that they're right.

You and your friend push open the door and two girls spin around to face you. They are smoking out the bathroom window. You know them well enough to join them and the pretty one gives you both a cigarette, because 'your outfits are always so cool'. Soon you're talking about love. You turn the bathroom lights off, and the pretty one says 'I don't usually talk about this but I'm really drunk . . .' She tells you how her boyfriend just broke up with her after two years of togetherness, and now she's scared of sleeping alone. You tell her you've never had a boyfriend and you're still scared of sleeping alone. In the dark, someone squeezes your hand.

On the kitchen windowsill, there's an empty beer bottle with a bunch of flowers in it. They're wrapped in cellophane and no one's taken the price sticker off. You peel it away and stick it to your left boob: $3.99. You know you're worth more than that, but you're starting to get pretty desperate for someone to love you. Through the window, you can see people jumping on a trampoline. You step outside and some guy immediately offers to peel the sticker off for you. His friends snigger in a *Beavis and Butthead* kind of way. You push past them, take off your shoes and part the trampoline netting. Someone offers you a hand up. Your body is thrown into the air before you're even standing. The boys bounce so big you are almost constantly hovering in the sky; feet barely skimming the black canvas before you're propelled upwards again. Flying over the net and into oblivion feels like a definite possibility. You're over the moon and a little bit terrified. You wonder if this is what being in love feels like.

You're seriously dizzy. Your friend helps you to the bathroom and locks the door. You lie down on the tiled floor, like you used to do when you were little and you got sick. Your eyes land on a set of bathroom scales, pushed under the sink. You tell your friend you think you should throw up. She crouches over you and touches your hair, pushing it back behind your ear: 'You don't have to do that.' The light is so bright it's giving you a headache. She gets up and turns it off, then comes back and lies down next to you. Just lying there with her makes you feel way less sick. After a few minutes, you turn on your side so you're face to face. It's blurry in the dark, but you can see her blinking. You move towards each other so slowly you are not sure if it's just you or if she is moving too. When your lips touch, you both go still. The music from the living room is faint and far away. You make out the lyric 'We'll talk about it soon'. You make out for the next three songs.

When you go outside, someone is playing 'It Wasn't Me' on a Bluetooth speaker. You walk across the yard, climb up to the treehouse and squeeze in. Some girls are trying to convince some guys that romanticising *Lolita* is seriously problematic, but they aren't really paying attention. You join in and one of the guys actually listens. You start talking to him about music and find you like some of the same bands. You ask what his favourite songs are. The titles are all familiar, but the most you can remember about any of them is the album that they're on. You don't say this. You say 'Oh, I love that song too!' and '*Hail to the Thief* is definitely an underrated album'. He's too drunk to notice your lack of further knowledge, and soon you're talking about your favourites instead. He seems genuinely interested. You feel genuinely interesting.

While you're peeing, you tell your friend about the guy in the treehouse. The downstairs bathroom was taken so you're using the upstairs one, which turns out to be much fancier. Your friend has opened up the mirror cabinet. First she inspects the bottles of pills, then the bottles of perfume. She sprays some on her wrists and rubs them together. You don't tell her that's not how you're supposed to do it, and you don't tell her that you think you're in love with the treehouse guy. You just keep peeing.

Never Underestimate the Power of Girls Who Want a Secret to Keep

for Maeve

initiation was on a friday:
stealing potions from our parents'
liquor cabinet without reading the labels.
we couldn't taste the curse
if we added enough juice.
some of us cried, some of us filled a bath. we all climbed in.
candles were lit. photos were taken.
the virgin mary came out of my underwear drawer
and flashed green for
go.

we pressed play.
the carpet turned into a trampoline
and we turned into animals, jumping and screaming and clawing
at our clothes. we ran outside and threw them at the moon.
she threw them back. a velvet dress, a gauzy cape, two identical bras
lay cold and black on the grass.

the carpet turned magnetic.
we crawled and pulsed
until our hair was wet with sweat.
our cackles cracked the ceiling.
i grew from the ground, all thorns and curves
and somewhere between exercise and an exorcism,
i sacrificed my hips to the spirits in the speaker.
my friends watched.
our playlist was called
the love cult, and so were we:
wrapping strings of fairy lights around our shoulders
as we danced around an invisible maypole.

you and I broke the circuit.
it was a quiet explosion, nobody else heard it
and I thought i dreamed it
until our eyes met.
it was a breath of fresh fear.
we locked it in our lungs and kept it there.

the next night, we met alone
over a cauldron the size of a coffee cup.
i told you i had spun a web around myself
and you were the first person to get stuck in it.
you told me you had built a shrine to yourself
and asked if i wanted to see it.
we told our friends we were busy
and went back to yours.

the washing-machine whirr of our quiet talk
reverberated through the house.
everything got quiet.
we kissed spells
on each other's neck
and spelled confessions
on each other's back.
neither of us mentioned it
in the morning
(we could smell smoke
before anything was burning).

this became our favourite ritual:
muffled words and a midnight laugh,
black, curly hairs on pale pink sheets,
a baby alligator under the bed.
we were divine and we knew it
yet we were still surprised
to find our limbs in knots
that couldn't be untied.

i left my toothbrush at your house
and you left yours at mine:
accidental amulets, one plastic, one bamboo.
you bought me two tubes of toothpaste for my birthday,
though we celebrated late. over a piece of carrot cake,
you traced the lines of my palm;
pretending you didn't know
that the future was forbidden.
we practised telepathy
on the bus home.
I clung to your arm like a crucifix.

we called each other
dream sister.

i called you every night.
sometimes you called me
moon lady, or
best friend.

our secret language became so secret we couldn't speak
when other people were around. i clung to lyrics,
repeated like a chant. *night time, videotape, ribs.*
we wrote each other messages
and hid them in each other's bedroom. i left the longest one
on the blank side of a jigsaw puzzle. you never turned the pieces over.
eventually, our code was too complicated
for either of us to understand.

our friends were ready to crucify us
and we still wouldn't tell them why.
the truth was always there;
on your wall, in my sheets, written on each other's back at midnight
but on trial on the telephone
at 1 a.m.:
i too, refused
to be the first to confess.

Joy Holley lives in Wellington and completed her masters in fiction at the International Institute of Modern Letters in 2020. Her writing has been published in *Starling*, *Sport*, *Stasis* and other journals.

Kerry Donovan Brown

Dragonfly, Dragon

The sky is changing colour, this side of the volcano darkens. For now, the mountain is nameless, yet there it is, conspicuous on the land, reddish and naked. Above, a bulb of smoke hangs like a thought bubble, almost motionless, so that if you didn't know better you might say the smoke is returning to the vent, rather than rising from it. Behind the sulfuric vapour, a whole section of rain cloud bulges like a muscle. This is it. This is beautiful.

Kit had parked by the shore of the pool, watching from the Land Cruiser, waiting for Dragon to appear. She hadn't been sighted for several weeks, maybe preferring to investigate the herds on the flood plain. But the last few days had been sweltering, hot enough for Dragon to seek shelter in the swamp forest, Kit thought. This body of water in particular was special to Dragon, something like her headquarters, so it was disappointing that after nearly a day's surveillance, she hadn't made a blip. Here, the river fed into the deep sprawling pool, lifting up the bulrushes and floating mats of water plants. The bright columns of conifers cast swaying images against the swamp, and a dragonfly (the length of Kit's forearm) seized something from the surface, the tannin-black water sparkling from where it rebounded. They were somewhere near what would someday be called Hell Creek, but the volcano reddening through the blue haze of the forest would grow cold and erode to nothing before that name was written down. Everything about the world around Kit would change again and again. Things would exist here namelessly over and over, until a time so glutted with language that words would surge backwards through time and cling to everything they could, including Dragon and her kind. Even then, most things here would escape record, the soft parts of their bodies defying fossilisation, their skeletons crushed beyond recognition by consolidated sediments. So much of this hot pink world was marshmallowing towards the poison bullet of the Asteroid. Kit could almost feel the astral heat on their skin. Thankfully, parked in the shade of a tree fern, the Land Cruiser hadn't been uncomfortable to wait in – and a few appearances across the day meant the survey hadn't been a complete waste of time. From the safety of the vehicle Kit had witnessed an allosaur-descendant – only known in the present day by a few fragments – step onto the sand bar across the pond. The hunter had made a low, nervous sound in their throat and turned a yellow eye to face them. Kit wasn't in danger in the Land Cruiser, and flashed the allosaur a big smile. They snorted, and dipped their head to take a mouthful of water, before disappearing back into the forest. Beautiful, thought Kit. Almost more beautiful than I can take. Some people of faith couldn't reconcile their belief in a higher power with life before human beings. Kit's faith grew stronger here. Here, they felt like a conduit between the God they were born under and an older version of the same God. Not simpler, not less sophisticated. Maybe more rugged. Stupider even. Emotional. Their creations vivid and alluring and unashamed. Kit imagined these two life stages reaching for each other, through them, converging. Down by the pool, the water edge blinked and rippled, catching their eye. Probably the resident gharial slithering against the bottom, loosening bubbles. The sky was darker now. Kit went to start the Land Cruiser, but brought their hand to the door instead, opened it. They stepped out of the cab, crossing the distance between the vehicle and the pool before they could think. They crouched at the edge. An unbroken skin covered much of the surface here. It wasn't only green to the eye, but green to the nose, alive with a viridescent stink. Kit reached out and took some of it between their fingers. It felt slippery and cold. It tingled against their skin. What if I went in? They had been ignoring the impulse all day, but right now they were seized by it. They wanted to swim down, naked as a gharial, to touch the bottom of the swamp, to turn upside down and look up through the water to the algal ceiling. In the mud, their body would grow warmer and soft under the press of microbes. They would grow warmer and softer until they incandesced, resurfacing in bubbles of pale fire. Their bones would be gambled to the Cenozoic. Kit's trance broke as the water whirled before them. An armoured tail, red as the volcano, whipped against the surface, spraying them with water. The gharial must've been concealed right under their nose, growing more and more concerned, before acting suddenly. Heart racing, Kit steadied themself against a stand of bulrushes, watching the V-line of the submerged gharial veer towards the middle of the pool. They wiped swamp water from their mouth, spat on the ground. It's nothing. Just a frightened crocodile. Still clutching a broken reed, Kit staggered up and returned to the Land Cruiser. Dragon wasn't coming. It was late.

The Land Cruiser was heavy enough to withstand collision with local wildlife, and the forest tracks could be hairy, so the drive home was slow, though thankfully uneventful. When Kit reached the electric perimeter fence, the research station was coming alive with interior lights against the darkening sky. Like the vehicle, the buildings here were designed to resist intrusion: even the greenhouse was built like a barracks. While Kit waited for the exterior gate to open, the nearest watchtower flashed as a sentinel moved behind the railing, sweeping the entrance with torchlight. In the exclusion cage, the gatekeeper, Russ, scolded Kit for staying out late – 'but I'll let you through this time,' he said, with a grin.

Outside the hangar, Mary was in the yard giving her full attention to a cylindrical carrier set down on the picnic table there. Kit stopped, wound down the window to see what she was up to. Mary's bees were emerging from an opening in the carrier. They were gorgeous to watch, gathering around each other, seething like boiling gold. One ascended suddenly, drifting up like a tiny balloon loosed by a tiny child.

'Now's a good time to release them,' said Mary, still concentrating. 'They can get their bearings without the meadowhawks bothering them.'

'Why are you releasing them?'

'I'm taking some leave,' she revealed. 'I'll come inside in a tick?'

Kit nodded and drove ahead, entering the hangar to park. Mary was an entomologist, and jewel in the company's crown. Insects infrequently fossilise, so her fieldwork surveying pre-Asteroid bee diversity, and their symbiosis with Cretaceous flora, was groundbreaking. In their own time, global bee populations were in crisis (even in Aotearoa) so a comprehensive understanding of pollinator collapse, and subsequent recovery, could help alleviate catastrophe. Accolades aside, Mary was Kit's friend, one of the few people they felt close to here. She was thoughtful, uplifting, and off-kilter in the same way that Kit felt off-kilter. They were immediately uneasy to hear she was leaving.

'I just need time away to think,' Mary explained. 'To dream, actually. I don't dream here. I only think about the end of the world.'

'All I do is dream here,' admitted Kit.

'I think that's good,' she said, earnestly. 'Operations like this need dreamers. The company's probably terrified you'll change your mind and leave.'

'I guess I should ask Juanita for a pay rise then.'

They were sitting in the open boot of the Land Cruiser. The massive doors of the hangar were trundling closed to keep night-flying birds and insects away from the bright lights. From beyond the fence perimeter something big emitted a sequence of barking calls, and then a long, languorous groan. Kit was pulling apart the brown, velvety head of the bulrush reed, the down accumulating in their lap.

'Ask Juanita to name a new species after you,' said Mary. 'One of those new frogs. With the eyebrows, and the big mouth?'

'Ribbit,' said Kit, limply.

Mary laughed, bumped against Kit's shoulder, feeling their mood drop.

'Hey, or that therapod you've spotted by the lake. An allosaur relative, you reckon?'

'Well, he is *beautiful*,' said Kit, running a hand through their hair, grinning.

Mary laughed again.

'Anyway, Kit, you know me. I've been putting off taking leave. The travel kills me. But I'll be back. I wouldn't abandon you here.'

'I know that. I love you.'

Mary hesitated, surprised by Kit's abrupt declaration.

'I – I love you too, kiddo.'

Mary looked past Kit, maybe searching for a diversion.

'Here comes the new intern with Juanita. He's handling some of my workload while I'm gone. The redhead. He's cute, hey?'

Juanita Pōhatu, their lead, was crossing the hangar with the new guy in tow. He was tall, bright, wearing a brand-new company uniform. He was laughing with Juanita. She waved out.

'Kia ora rā kōrua,' she said, beaming. 'Any luck with Dragon, e hoa?'

'She's a no show today.'

'Eh. Well, I trust your instincts, she'll turn up. Have you been introduced to Wairua yet, Kit? Today was his first day.'

Kit stood up to take Wairua's outstretched hand, the mass of bulrush fluff tumbling down their legs.

'Hi, haere mai,' mumbled Kit, feeling foolish, wondering whether they would hongi. Wairua didn't release their hand, and lent in. Kit felt the space between their bodies close. Wairua inhaled, and blew the air back through his nose: the breath of life. Kit's exhalation was a clumsy echo. They noticed the smell of the time-jump solution still hanging over Wairua, the grease still clinging to the skin of his collarbone. It was a shit to get off. They stood apart.

'Oh, Juanita,' said Kit. 'He aha te kupu Māori mō *dragonfly*?'

They un-pocketed their camera and offered Juanita the display.

'Ah, te kapokapowai,' she answered, admiring the picture. 'I'm not sure of the genus. You, Wairua?'

'I don't know either,' he said, peering at the screen. 'Was she big?'

'Bigger than I've seen here,' confirmed Kit. 'If you're interested I can drive you over to the pool where I saw her. Hopefully Dragon will be hanging around too eventually. Dragonfly and Dragon.'

'I'd be very interested,' said Wairua, looking to Juanita. 'If I have time over the month, that is?'

'You bet me to it, Kit!' said Juanita. 'I was going to ask you to show him the pool. It's a real special spot.' She turned to her favourite. 'Mary, you feeling ready for the jump?'

Mary made a face, which Wairua returned, knowingly.

'It's the worst,' he said.

'I used to get sick on the school bus, so I can sympathise,' offered Kit.

Wairua laughed.

As Juanita and Wairua made their way across the hangar heading to the mess hall, Mary leaned shoulder to shoulder with Kit.

'You're going to be fine without me, you sook.'

Kit didn't see Wairua often the first couple of weeks of his placement. They took a trip together to Dragon's pool, but for Kit, it was an awkward experience. They could feel themself closing over on the drive down, and stayed trapped in their head the rest of the day, tongue-tied. Wairua was just as quiet, fixated on the insect life at the pool, dragonflies, meadowhawks, various leaf beetles. They spent the time together in almost uninterrupted silence, before parting ways back at the hangar. Things thankfully got better the week following. They began eating evening meals together at the wharekai, and an ease developed between them. Kit didn't know how Wairua felt, but they couldn't help recall their courtships back in the future. They invented a courtship between themself and Wairua there. At some nightclub they'd first exchange glances and guarded smiles. Soon after that, there would be murky love notes over Grindr, hastily considered self-portraits on Snapchat. In this way, it would seem at first as if the space between them, for no special reason, was uncrossable. But finally, Kit saw them alone together, swimming. The sea was warm. A big, dark sky gathering over Pito-one. The setting sun hitting everything with yellow light. Ahead of Kit, Wairua would move through the water, swimming closer, his body incandescent against the surface.

Over this time, Dragon remained unobserved at her pool, though every other day, the mysterious allosaur appeared to drink.

One morning, Wairua surprised Kit as they were leaving the gymnasium.

'Oh, hello, I thought I'd join you for breakfast for a change,' said Wairua, grinning.

'Sure thing, early bird.'

At the wharekai, they were given scrambled eggs and a small, waxy apple each. Kit warmed their apple in their hands while Wairua talked. He talked a lot, explaining his understanding of how the timeline was correcting itself, minute detail by minute detail, so that in the present day history remained unchanged, and wasn't that mind boggling? He moved on to yesterday's insights into the social lives of prehistoric carpenter bees, and their emerging hierarchies. He was so handsome, young-seeming as he rolled his eyes in the telling of his stories. Freckles, like hundreds of red pebbles polished against stone, coloured his face, his jawbone, down his neck, maybe to his shoulders, his chest.

'Do you like it here?' Kit asked, interrupting.

'I do. How could I not?'

Kit smiled. Wairua was meant to be making the jump home in a matter of days, but he didn't seem upset about it. Maybe his placement had been extended.

'Yeah, I like it too.' Kit leaned back in their chair. 'So, why're you up so early, anyway?'

'I wanted to see you,' said Wairua. Kit couldn't tell if the edge of pain in his voice was genuine or contrived. 'Someone messed up my schedule. They're sending me home earlier.'

'When—'

'I found out less than an hour ago.'

'I mean, when do you go?'

'I'm leaving here early tomorrow morning.'

Wairua reached out and covered Kit's hand with his own.

'There's time now,' he said, meeting their eyes. 'Do you want to go somewhere?'

Wairua's room was dark when he opened up. The lights flicked on automatically, bluish to begin with, before settling on smoky pink. Inside, a single bed engulfed by an oversized duvet, a night stand for the company's homunculus, a glowing statuette. On the wall, a full-length mirror, and taped alongside it, a kid's crayon drawing: a spray of lava, a triangle the exact reflection of the volcanic cone itself. A pterosaur flies towards the cataclysm. Wairua kicked off his shoes, and began to take off his clothes, folding and dropping each garment before starting on the next. He didn't hesitate, but still it was like watching an animal being coaxed from a place of withdrawal. Wairua's bare chest teemed with sunspots, like faint bands of crimson stars across the pale of his body. He ran a hand through his auburn hair, shifting it from his face, and sat down on the bed, naked, except for a necklace, a medallion of carved pounamu. His cock shifted against the cradle of his thighs, lifting.

Kit took off their clothes too, clumsy, but not uncertain. The less clothing he wore the more purposeful he felt in his body. He caught his reflection in the mirror, saw his tattoos, recognised some of his muscles by name, the indentations of his hips curving to his erection from both sides. *Transversus abdominis*, he said to himself, too quiet to hear. Turning to Wairua, he saw him notice the scar: beginning below the notch at his throat, dividing his sternum, down onto the softer flesh of his stomach, and then there, a little beyond his belly button, it ended. The cut transfixed Wairua, only for a moment, but in that moment, Kit was struck by the memory of another face peering at his body, grave and impassive, alien.

'Dino damage,' explained Kit, warming the palms of his hands across his chest. He took Wairua's shoulders in his hands, and leant down to kiss him on the mouth. He felt Wairua's body grow tense. He knew that his scar must look fearsome, what was done to him was a fearsome thing. He held the kiss, waited for the tension to lessen. When it didn't, he unlatched his mouth from Wairua's and reached for the lights.

'Nah,' said Wairua, turning the lights back up, knocking the statuette over in doing so. 'I want to see you.'

Kit dropped onto the duvet, guided Wairua on top of him, so they were facing each other. Wairua pressed himself to Kit, their balls rested against each other's, so then Kit could gather their erections into his hand, working them together, as if they were one.

The upended homunculus turned violet, pulsating with growing intensity, but only minutes went by before it ended, with Wairua shuddering against Kit, Kit's chest and neck hit with bright, warm streaks.

A little later, Wairua said, 'Kit, that scar—'

Kit rolled over to face him.

'It's fine. I'm fine. This isn't my first rodeo. Or my last.'

'Good. I know that. It's just that it's shocking to look at, e hoa. You must've been sore.'

'Isn't it difficult to recall the exact intensity of any sensation?' said Kit. He sighed. 'I wish you weren't going.'

'Juanita's pretty sure I'll be asked back next year. I don't know exactly. I'll find out later,' he said. 'Kit, I wanted to say—'

With a start, the automatic window shade activated, letting in a flood of daylight. Wairua sprang up and climbed into his underwear, 'Fuck, we're really late, aren't we!' Already, Kit felt the space between them widening. He was dressed before Wairua, kissed him briefly against his temple, and left the apartment alone.

In the exclusion cage, Russ remarked on the head of black clouds bulging above the floodplain – 'looks like we're finally about to get it today. I don't like the idea of you being down there for long.'

'Only a bit of rain, mate,' said Kit, dismissively. 'I'll turn on my walkie-talkie.'

Kit left the station in a hurry and soon the beech forest closed in around them, defiantly lush despite the heatwave. Kit clicked off the emergency radio, and connected their music to the Land Cruiser's sound system, hit play. An intro began, a few keys from the far right of the piano. Kit rounded a bend, a little too quickly. The track opened up, and Kit caught a glimpse of volcanic smoke, yellowish, through the treetops. They let the feeling and intensity of the music move them, both closer to Dragon's pool, and further away from Wairua. The Land Cruiser flew around another bend, and then another. Struggling to control the course of the speeding vehicle, Kit almost left the road. 'Fuck,' they said, and pulled over, cutting the ignition. 'FUCK.' Kit got out and slammed the door shut. The beech forest whooshed around them, the branches rustling like static, and then a distant peal of thunder. 'That's the devil starting up his motorbike,' their Nan would say. No devil here. It was that rugged young deity, feeling savage or celebrating. Minuscule raindrops fell against their shoulders like faint electric shocks. Fuck it, I'll go the rest of the way on foot, decided Kit. It wouldn't be more than a quarter hour's walk to the pool. Through this part of the forest, stalks of brilliant green weeds reached almost to the lower canopy. The undergrowth prevented Kit from seeing very deep into the woods, but the presence of numerous animals was apparent, chittering, and rummaging, the clear, bright chirrup of a hunting troodon. A small black bird hopped onto the road ahead, and cackled. When it fell quiet Kit reconsidered leaving the Land Cruiser. The crack of a branch breaking was almost a relief.

When Kit arrived at the pool something was different. Yesterday, the algal slick had closed over the entire surface, but today it had broken apart like a sheet of melting ice. Where it remained intact, portals were opening and closing as raindrops fell with increasing strength and regularity. Across on the sandbar, the red gharial had beached themself, their narrow jaws agape, eyes alert. A massive bubble broke the surface at the centre of the pool.

'Dragon?'

Everything Kit needed to record Dragon's return, and to do so safely, was in the Land Cruiser. They'd have to go back. They turned and stopped. Partly in shadow, the allosaur stood under the tree fern where Kit normally parked. He was motionless, the toes of the left foot slightly lifted as if about to take a step closer. The yellow eyes stared at Kit, transfixing them. Releasing the tension in his body, the hunter darted forward.

'No!' Kit balled their fists. 'Fucken no!'

The allosaur lunged, striking Kit with his snout, sending them sprawling into the bulrushes. He reared up, pinpointing where Kit lay, like a giant heron sizing up a frog. He bared his teeth, hissed. In response, a deep menacing rumble issued from the water, so resonant that the surface rippled. The violence implied in the sound was staggering. Dragon was emerging from the pool. The allosaur took a step away from Kit.

Dragon was the colour of all possible conditions of iron. Her massive head was interlaced with warning patterns, as if plugged into a molten body, super-heated metals feeding through her veins. Above the orbit of each eye grew a horn, tapered and massive, held up high against her shield and muscular neck. Kit saw something struggling in her beak, a turtle. With a crack the shell split open, unable to resist the pressure Dragon was applying, and bright red blood laminated her lower mandible. She tossed the carcass aside. The dinosaurs advanced on one another, the allosaur pawing at the ground with his talons, but neither attacked. He played a long piercing note, overlaying the deep bass of the triceratops. Dragon tracked her enemy with the two points of her horns.

Kit's breath was knocked from their chest. They tasted iron. One arm was buried in mud, the other beginning to bleed. Again, they felt the press of two versions of the same spirit, the future and the now. They imagined the bones of the giant triceratops preserved in the sediments of the secret pool, mingled with the broken teeth of an undescribed allosaur. Kit imagined Wairua, their hand pressed against his chest steadying him, feeling his heart race as the intersection of his thighs moved against Kit, again and again and again. He felt Wairua's mouth against their own.

Kit got to their feet. They needed to put some distance between themself and inevitable combat, but the dinosaurs were blocking the road. Looking out over the pool, they saw the whole volcano turning to vapour underneath the storm. A cascade of lightning struck at the summit. Kit staggered, a warm trickle of blood moved against their hip. They entered the water and began to swim. The rain was so heavy now that the two dinosaurs were indistinct shadows by the time they reached the centre of the pool. When the attack happened, Kit felt the force of their two bodies colliding. They heard the allosaur scream. Pain crept in now, the extent of Kit's injuries becoming apparent, but this wasn't their first rodeo, and not their last. Floating in the water, at the centre of the green ceiling, Kit closed their eyes and waited for the violence to subside.

Kerry Donovan Brown grew up on the Waitaha plains before shifting to Te Whanganui-a-Tara as a young adult. Their 2014 novel *Lamplighter* (Victoria University Press) explores a dysfunctional village riddled with bizarre traditions and violence. 'Dragonfly, Dragon' is the spiritual sibling of Kerry's essay 'Queer Debris', published by *The Pantograph Punch* in 2019.

Lily Holloway

the thing

in the suburbs

an unplugged freezer

[someone's been in]

over the dishes

she falls

tries to read the cereal box

[but it swims]

light on the harbour

and a sound of cicadas

concussions without impact

havana

a miniaturised headquarters

view the facade from the balcony

cigarettes in the ashtray

someone has poisoned the dog

seismic wave

through the walls

lobbed like tennis balls

all you can do

is get off the X

immaculate concussion

[empty watch stations]

a mysterious water pump

& microwave

trauma

a focus of energy

like burning ants

dissolving fibres

around nerves

bubbling arterial blood

a child in that alcove

or just an old cold lingering?

i think i can feel reverberations of something further downstream

i am worried things will never be okay
because i slept all day
i woke wondering why i could hear the sea and thought maybe
the very tops of the trees were moving in the wind
just the very tops
but it was your laptop overheating

in the night i pull a fragile train behind me
a blanket trailing in earth
not like how illegally released koi
are dragged over the rocks
because they are ornamental and inedible
on their way to be put into the meat grinder on the back of a flatbed truck

i dream i am scooby doo from the original '69 version
in the supermarket of the afterlife where everything is free
and each drink is exactly what you need
but didn't know you needed
where you shoot rusted clockwork birds moving on rails around the castle walls
only to have them pop up again

a toaster is passed over my head and i tell my sister
to make her own ekphrastic postcards
and that koi skulls are sensitive to vibrations
they feel fingertips or bootlaces falling into the river
and flee in an orange rushing that you have to see to believe

commuting with angela

last night i walked   her dog   boots scuffing concrete solitude
glistening in puddles   pissing on laingholm poles

she is scared of slugs   those grey spotted tongues
          inching under porchlight
     towards her door   invasion   moving morning
perspiration

hold her thigh   – not hard or that's charlie's horse
i'm driving   but slips hand into yours
     two fingers
     circle your pulse   to the backstreet boys

     self-acceptance is
frida on her back   staring mirror ceilings   strokes
skinny west auckland signs
               Brocco
               li
it is what it is
she says, *slugs pop like blisters   rat lungworm burst forth   confetti larvae*

     and we cannot survive it

Lily Holloway (born in 1998, she / they) is a forever-queer English postgraduate student. In her spare time she enjoys reading New Zealand literature, eating nachos, and visiting second-hand markets with her girlfriend. Her creative writing has been published in *Starling, Scum, Poetry Lab Shanghai, The Pantograph Punch, Midway Journal* and other various nooks and crannies (see a full list at lilyholloway.co.nz/cv). In 2020 she was honoured to receive the Shimon Weinroth Prize in Poetry, the Kendrick Smithyman Scholarship for Poetry and second place in the Charles Brasch Young Writers' Essay Competition. She is an executive editor of *Interesting Journal* and has a chapbook in *AUP New Poets 8*.

Lorae Parry

from Eugenia

Scene 4: Courtroom, 1915

EUGENIA stands in a point of light. The disembodied voice of a judge is heard.

JUDGE: Eugenia Maria Martelli, you are charged with gross and excessive fraud. You have changed your name and quality to impersonate a member of the opposite sex. You have reversed the order of nature. You have sinned in the eyes of God. However, as this is your first offence, you will be spared the rigours of prison life this time. But if you commit a similar offence in this Borough of Nelson again, you will be incarcerated for a period of six months. The court sees it fit to fine you the sum of ten pounds.

FINN enters. The lights come up to full.

FINN: Ten pounds. That's a fine thing Jack . . . er, Jean, a fine thing, that they didn't put you behind bars.

EUGENIA: Ten pounds! How is it possible? Is too much. Too much!

FINN: I tell you what, I'll pay it for you.

EUGENIA: No, no, I cannot.

FINN: I'll be sorry to see you leave. Boss reckoned you were one of the best men . . . er, best women . . . I want it back, mind!

EUGENIA: I pay you back. Twice. Double!

FINN: There'll be work going down at the Textile Mill making uniforms for the soldiers . . .

EUGENIA: I am taking the boat to Wellington, Mr Finn. The wages for a woman are only half that of a man. And if you wear the trousers the world looks different. They say that, 'Whoever the breeches does wear, lives a life as free as air!'

FINN: Aye, but you'll not be free as air if they call you up for the territorials. They're talking of bringing in conscription soon. It's one thing being a man, it's another thing being a soldier!

EUGENIA: Me, I like to be a soldier. To fight for my country. Maybe I pass.

FINN: They do medical examinations, man! You'll have a hard time telling them what happened to your whatsit. How would you explain that?

EUGENIA: I would say . . . 'Holy Mother! But, it was there this morning. Maybe I misplaced it!'

FINN, *laughing*: Ah, you're a character. You had me fooled!

EUGENIA, *extending her hand*: You have been good to me.

FINN: I don't know whether to shake your hand or to kiss it, damn it.

EUGENIA: Thank you for the money. You'll be surprised how quick I pay it back. You'll be a rich man!

FINN: Don't let them catch you at it again. They'll not be letting you off so lightly. Don't make your parents disown you.

EUGENIA: My father has already done that, Mr Finn.

Pause. FINN extends his hand to EUGENIA and they shake.

FINN: Good luck, Jack.

EUGENIA exits. Italian music wafts in.

Lorae Parry was born and raised in Sydney, Australia, and moved to New Zealand in 1973. She is a playwright, actress and director with an extensive writing and acting career. Her plays include *Frontwomen*, *Cracks*, *Bloomsbury Women & The Wild Colonial Girl* (Women's Play Press), *Vagabonds* and *Eugenia* (Victoria University Press), *Scarlet & Gold* (Time plus Talents), and *Kate & Mrs Jones*. Lorae has co-written many stage productions including the *Destination Beehive* political satires, and *Digger & Nudger* for the Hens' Teeth Women's Comedy Company, of which she was a founding member. Lorae was awarded the Stout Fellowship in 1994 and was the first woman playwright to become Writer In Residence at Victoria University of Wellington in 1999. She has a masters degree in scriptwriting, and in 2004 was made a Member of the New Zealand Order of Merit for her services to the performing arts.

Luka Leleiga Lim-Cowley

Vaka-tokatoka (Pasifiqueeredisabled)

i watch you from across the room.
i can see you
        replaced. replacing.
can't butterfly the flesh tone of your voice,
but it's in your face,
        the quick of the eyes,
        plaster-dry of your mask;
you codeswitching
back-and-forth-back-and-forth between—

i don't know
how long you've been doing this
nor do i know
which way
        the
        conversion
                now
                travels—

        i listen: (lissom) You
translating yourself
into other people
translating other people
into yourself
they say it's all the same love (fucking cliché)
but i don't know anymore
about space   (between us)
or time   (between us) or
if this ever stops
systems colours scents numbers signs
maybe you've lost count.

when we talk alone together it's different.
turned inwards, towards each other
constructing worlds ;
data falling in amongst numb yaqona

funny me being
so English,
London-born Samoan
    orate about
bdsm positions polyamory+
but i am shocked (to my eyebrows)
when you joke with someone about their solipsism;
you are shocked (eyebrows skyward, too)
when i joke about the cishetnormativity in
'finding Mr. Right'
in the presence of our
 straightcis-
            -perisex en-
    -abled
        Samoan
        friend.

i want to tell you
who gives a fuck if they're comfortable
(sacrificing –
domesticating
our body
    mind
    soul
the uncredited labour of doing the right things
the right way at the right time the right place in the
right presences of right people —
    — And strangers amongst our siblings)

i think of how
you told me
your partner
told you 'Sing.'   (*'my voice...'* 'No. Sing.')
to cover up
her moans
even
in our own beds

we are not free, it seems.

pronoun-switching,
not telling your daughter's teachers,
can't show up
with your partner,
careful
for your son, the cost
of keeping
a household
intact.

changing your clothes
(so they'll listen)
changing my clothes
(dresses, dresses, conferences,
female-tying
the 'ie, and my
'ie faikaga
i left—unloved—at home)

un-dressing
the two of us alone at Tokatoka. me
showering, then you
showering, with me singing,
sitting outside the bathroom, on the bed.
(my voice, i'd guess, would carry through...)
us lying in the dark
in separate beds

you wanting to talk and me wanting to lako i moce,
(your comments another node a tendril reaching out
tender-tender
through shadow
strung music
like spiderwebs
between our silhouettes.
my responses laconic eclipsing
tending to
zero
a dead-end.

a numb fading.

a purposeful erasure:
temptation—
my skin
screaming

for you just fuck me already—)

Ko Veivosaki-Yaga-O-Na-Wai dabe i ra beside us
teenage tanoa, he's freshly cut, with acid edges
vacant of artemis grace by his namesake,
tiger balm tacit & jewelled agender –
Au se vagaluya, kare, aua ou te lē iloa
lou loto, lou leoʻula, lou māfaufau...

we rehearse waiata, pese, fatele held together
on belts of you telling me how beautiful
i am recurrently valea:
don't you know these things count for nothing

keep remembering your foot against my leg
under the table. iloilo your intent.

But you're partnered.
community notorious for
monogamy. wondering whether you miss this,
the thrill of newness, wanting my youth, or
freedoms – maybe it's
the same thing
(never settling)
us sleeping
[in separate beds]

4:30 wake
'yadra...' mouth half moon full
on somnolence
and you onosaʻi in your sheets
perched up statuesque
studying the wall.

outside: seeing Matariki
(or the pleiades
the eyes of
Tāwhirimātea severed
or the atlantic sisters felled,
whichever way you'd have them
rendered)
together and apart

Inside Us the Dead (London-born Version)

Today I am going to make myself clean
Wash off all cold oracles and have faith again
That (taualuga) was a performance
My gender is not.

Karlo said
Albert said
Inside Us the Dead, And we said:

We know the best minds of our generation being lacerated and spat out
Driven insane by holy white walls and a white-skinned Jesus
Radioactive in concrete rot, erasing margins in beige coffers, bitter trade,
Hanging—
in the liminal real between argot archives and finding our ways back
to ourselves
Chasing so many dawns scarred with stars, Papua Merdeka ,
postmemory. postcolony. How it is that you can be there, and us, here?
We crave icons and idols that are like us—that ARE us,
Breaking tyrannies of the fake universal, like 'Pacific'—
Pasifika—Oceania—this colossal undulating body
can be confined to what is straight and staid, enabled and binary
Verifying fetishists, exotic collectors through conflict mineral matrices, woke
to death
and Encountering Enough: soli le vā disguised as tausi le vā, teu le vā, tauhi vā,
Self-sacrifice to supremacy, this tacit assimilation of souls is nothing
to celebrate

But noon is for remembrance,
As our shadows brace,
Waiting to fall in with the cadence of my siblings,
Wading skyscrapers with eyes drawn to flax pattern of gutter water, not for
shame: for continuity
Ours is a body-woven, cycle-bound and linking,
Keeping these knowledges chafing just under the skin
Singing ourselves into survivances,
Sculpted in limbs, braided in marrow,
Etched into aching page, our names
Flare red in our mouths, on our hands,
and storm-coloured in shells and bowls,
as the hours turn thick with our bonded blood

Tonight is not for mourning, but for memorising spliced roots
made flesh between our tongues:
Fa'atama, o'u uso, palopa, takatāpui, fa'a'afa, pinapinaaine, malalahi, leiti,
'akatangata, vakasalewalewa, intersex tombois, non-binary butch queens,
my siblings are throwing our laughter into the chaff of cicada mesh,
Crossing over, unfurling—into the shapes of the ancestors we resemble
and my body aches for her like fa'ataupati, gloss-lilted skin
like the slick of rain
that keeps you still. spinning. stimming. vā = space between
us blooming.
—> ia, sau le aiku:

Inside us the night-on-fire, writhing crimson like shrimp
Inside us time weaving back through itself in blue-twisting nodes
Inside us relentless rhythms pulse through plumed flesh
Inside us, Alofa
Inside Us
the Dead

(Tulouna, Tai Lava, Fa'amalosi—Ua lē uma—)

Born in London, **Luka Leleiga Lim-Cowley** is a tauiwi fa'atama totolasi neurodivergent writer and ambivalent academic. Ia has published poetry in *Stasis* and *Salient*, and is currently working on their masters thesis about Pacifiqueeredisabled climate-activist performance.

Michael Giacon

Argento builds a relationship

We share a very large residence on a substantial piece of land or each has a medium-sized home in opposite corners of an even larger property with something densely scenic between. Perhaps we maintain the places we already have and stay over several times a fortnight. In the amazing small space out of the city where we retreat together alone, lockable cupboards for sharp objects are a discreet feature.

We are most probably of similar maturity give or take 10 years they say although with advancing vintage one a decade younger than another feels better than older, doesn't it? We need to be fairly fit: walking, swimming, something involving a soft surface, like yoga. Do Pilates require padded walls? This is, after all, the long haul.

We will have talked about our sexual health early on, candid, honestly. We have loved and lost through epidemic and here we are making plans. Where are we each with monogamy, pornography, topiary? Further more or less, in laying bare our intimate history the exchange may have been brief, spasmodic, a reflection of the content. Did we decide to forego such regurgitation okay that we were new men fresh from knowing?

Getting naked can, in practice, be a business, even home alone in winter. The big reveal was either fast, florid, or staged as we got our tongues around it, with time for several sweat sessions, dental whitening, liquid nitrogen, manscaping. Could this culminate in a country lodge with something thermal in the garden? Perhaps better not to recreate the past however distant. It may have come as some relief that the relief was not indeed so messy as it was.

The sound track is most likely a mixed tape, trending from back when. We could call it *Whatever, We Agreed*. It might be fun to swap sealed envelopes with 5 forbidden artists and 1 genre (excluding jazz). Imagine what it would suggest if our selections matched. No rhapsodic bohemians, where the sun takes forever to go down on me, no C&W. We don't need to talk about our feelings, after all, we are too misty, this much in love.

Michael Giacon

The Intimacy Consultant

They wait behind a screen. I sit
in reflection. From one angle I am intent
but from below the cursor hovers over

Maybe
Perhaps
When
Don't Know 15 minutes gone.

Which will it be? The one who can
teach an old answer new questions
the one with the Magic Wand
App, the one who is The One? I am against time.

I must describe myself. From the outside
I look young for my age, from the inside
I don't, my inner child in his 20s still dressing
the broken action figures although, at least
searing flesh and blood are just a click away. You are 50% complete.

Restricted Section: Preferences.

1. Verify your age / range / gender / identity / sex

sex / race / culture / out / income

2. Rate each letter of your acronym of choice

0–10 on any 3 of the following:

Maybe Happy When Sad Good

Although Bad Okay Perhaps Okay

Yes Calm At least Don't Know

Angry Okay Anyway Other

3. Click right to save this section. How much time is left?

A Final Reflection.

In 50 words or less write on ONE only of:

A. Who initiates, who stops, how long does it go on? who who how long

B. Intimacy as choreography. choreographychoreography

C. How to ensure a convincing portrayal. a convincing portrayal

To ensure a convincing portrayal of intimacy I believe it is important to be *1 2 3 4 5 6 7 8 9 10 11 12 13 14* open-minded, open-hearted *15 16* and although the idea of intimacy as portrayal does have a certain appeal *17 18 19 20 21 22 23 24 25 26 27 28 29* part of me does wonder *30 31 32 33 34* about *35*
love and Your time is up.

Submission Complete.

Return to the anteroom

until your name is called.

Scenes from a Gay Play

Walking up three flights of stairs back down two, up again, heart pounding outside the meeting room deliberating, deep breath, in through the open door gay liberating.

Shuffling papers, tipping them off the table, accidentally discreet for nerve and calm, for time to remain behind, ponder a simple question in safety – Where can I go to find others like myself?

Marching down Queen Street on a Friday night, 8 of us in the rain behind a police car chanting 2 4 6 8 GAY IS TWICE AS GOOD AS STRAIGHT.

'The Petitioners – In honour of those who signed the petition against Homosexual Law reform, 1985', my 32-stanza rave of rage:
If you filled out the coupon in the newspaper and sent it on be sure to watch the same space next week, we're offering a cut-throat special on solo mums.

Indiscreet at The Maidment, workshopped from the Gay Sweatshop Theatre Company (1976). I muffed my lines, wiped 10 minutes of dialogue, bringing this landmark event to an early but rapturous close.

A dance during Gay Rights Week 197? Painting posters, hiring lights and sound system from the Student Union, hauling all up those stairs, carrying Donna Summer (before) and David Bowie LPs. The first boy I fell in love with turned up at the door.
How Dare He! Bolden Golden! The rest is a blur.

Grey Lynn YCS Leaders' night, St Joseph's Church Hall, 1972, my turn to host.
Nigel Baumber in make-up and silver platforms, holding queer court.
The priest went on about having children which he did quite often once he left the priesthood.

Tuesday, December 15th, 1981: First date with Adrian.
A rose, Raiders of the Lost Ark, my place.

If you are homosexual, forced to sign in fear, be a sly subversive for your human dignity – that's the state of fair play in God's Own Land.

Pink Triangle Badges. 'How dare you presume I'm heterosexual'.
Taking a magazine from a stand at the supermarket. HOT SEX NOW!
Rainbow wristbands.
The Internet, LGBTIFTQ+

Not he or she but they, not tolerate, embrace where people are, not where you / I / he / she / they think we should be.

Justice Kirby in AUT WA306 talking 'bout a revolution, the bend of history muddling through unkindness, cruelty and irrationality to justice, to liberty. Though tribe and tongue may differ in brotherhood we are strong.

A Rainbow Youth panel at the 'Queers In Tertiary Education' seminar in the Whare Nui. Everyone nervous, an audience of the staff network and ancestors.

If you are aged and infirm and those you need made you sign as they did their daily round with the tray of tranquillisers, good luck old friend.

Same Same But Different, 2017. 'Spoken Worlds', queer and trans poets under 30: a commune of intensity, brittle power incandescent, to a chorus of clicking fingers.

Sunday, February 13th, 2005: Adrian's quilt at the Big Gay Out.

Archie and Ada, Tin-Tin and Pearl. All those boys, always young.

Michael Giacon has been published in journals including *brief, a fine line, Landfall* and *Poetry New Zealand Yearbook 2021*, and in 2016 won the Kathleen Grattan Prize for a Sequence of Poems with *Argento in no man land*, featuring the poetic alter ego Argento Q. That year he graduated from the AUT Master of Creative Writing with a poetry-focused project, which has evolved into a manuscript for publication. Michael is on the Board of the Same Same But Different LGBTQIA+ writers' festival and is a founding member of the Auckland-based Isthmus Poets.

Natasha Dennerstein

Much too Fast.

So I turned myself to face me
But I've never caught a glimpse
Of how the others must see the faker
I'm much too fast to take that test
— David Bowie, 'Changes'

You feel self-conscious, dress androgynous – marle sweat pants,
yellow hoodie, kung-fu shoes – nothing incriminating you as trying

too hard to be male or female. You are embarrassed about your
facial hair, growing it out long enough to be zapped

with electric needles – regularly and painfully – like prolonged dentistry: your
punishment for daring to try to be a girl. You

keep wary eyes out for prolonged stares that are sometimes
what is its and other times *va-va-vooms.* You are scared. Until one

day, you're walking on the street in jeans and a T-shirt, a guy you
knew before does a double-take, eyes popping, jaw slack in

amazement and you know he's thinking *damn!* and you know it's working and
you know you're changing. And you like it. Suddenly

you've got hips, suddenly you've got tits, suddenly you've got booty and
suddenly you realise you've got a tiny bit of power.

You decide it's about time you got yourself a new name and decide to call
yourself *Natasha*. Why the fuck not? It's exotic.

O, Positive, 1993.

You trance all weekend on E and meth, meet
red glitter horns guy, cloven hoof and tail,

tail him home and fuck for hours, bronchitis me
Monday morning, sound shocking, can't hardly speak.

I cinnamon you stewed apples. Later you tell me:
the virus. And that was the weekend.

You said you knew, like a woman can know the exact
moment of conception, when her ovum is penetrated:

a tiny *ping*. You say you know that I knew, too, and I did.
I never knew how sick you were, how the virus

colonised you, how your blood let us down, how you
couldn't fight infection. Then you died. And I miss you.

ESTROGEN

I was born twice: first, as a baby girl, on a remarkably smogless
Detroit day in January of 1960; and then again, as a teenage boy,
in an emergency room near Petoskey, Michigan, in August of 1974.
— Jeffrey Eugenides, Middlesex

E strogen, you feminising chemical, she loves how you plump her up,
making her flesh ripe and juicy like a young chicken, how you come from
Woman and give Life, how you bring out her girly qualities, you.
S wallowed with a glass of water every morning, how she can feel you first
in her nipples, itching with the pain of growth – bone pain in the hips –
signifying change.
T hree blue pills.
R elease the feminine divine in her, estrogen, how you work your magic.
O istros: Greek for *verve* or *inspiration* and she loves how you give her that,
estrogen.
G rowth of secondary sexual characteristics to prepare for childbirth – tits
and ass – adipose fatty tissue deposits and breastfeeding. How you make a girl
feel fecund, ripe.
E motional range and how you expand it, ethinyl estrodial.
N ever going back, never re-androgenising. How you make her feel that
femininity is the natural state for her and long may it last and how she loves
you, estrogen.

Natasha Dennerstein is a trans woman poet born in Melbourne, Australia. She spent many years working as a psychiatric nurse, which gave her an interesting perspective on the human condition. She spent several years living in Aotearoa New Zealand and has an MA in creative writing from Victoria University of Wellington, and an MFA from San Francisco State University. Natasha has had poetry published in many journals including *Landfall, Shenandoah, Bloom, Red Light Lit, Spoon River Poetry Review, Foglifter* and *North American Review*. Her collections *Anatomize* (2015) and *Triptych Cali-form* (2016) and her novella-in-verse *About a Girl* (2017) were published by Norfolk Press in San Francisco. Her trans chapbook *Sea-horse* (2017) was published by Nomadic Press in Oakland. She collaborated on a book with visual artist Kaye Freeman, *Turn and Face the Strange* (2019). She lives in Oakland, California, where she is an editor at Nomadic Press and works at St James Infirmary, a clinic for sex workers in San Francisco. She was a 2018 Fellow of the Lambda Literary Writer's Retreat.

Ngahuia te Awekotuku

Auntie Marleen

They were off in the taxi, Mum and her husband, just as Auntie Marleen came through the door, following her smells, which always came in first. Grease, sour tobacco, and oiled rows of chestnut hair running short-cropped from the forehead to the neck. Motorbike fumes, dust, and worn-out leather in the soft brown folds of her fighter pilot's coat. She was my babysitter; she'd arrive in a crackle of smoke – from her Three Castles roll-your-own and her machine's exhaust – and she'd pull up by the house, the engine of her Norton chugging reluctantly to a standstill. With a smile to my mother, and a slight nod to the man at her side, she marched smartly up the back steps, her heavy lace-up shoes creaking, the sharp grey edges of her flannel trousers catching the sun.

She had a routine, which was always strictly followed. She would shake my hand, and I'd wonder at the coolness of her ivory white fingers, and severely clipped nails, and the spoiled bit of skin, stained by nicotine. Then she would take off her coat and unroll a long green knitted scarf from around her neck, revealing a buttoned shirt collar sitting above a thick navy blue pullover. The shirt was blue, too. She'd hang the coat and scarf on the back door hook, taking some stuff out of the pockets. Three Castles, matches in a Beehive box, blackballs, and a book, red-cloth covered with brittle library plastic. The Famous Five again. I watched, thinking greedily about a blackball, melting sweet and gooey in my mouth, as she made two cups of cocoa. And with the Famous Five's latest adventure tucked into her armpit, the drinks steaming and balanced in one hand, and the blackballs in the other, she walked ahead of me into the bedroom.

After the cocoa, I was allowed one blackball. Just one, which I'd clatter between my teeth and lick beneath my tongue willing it to last and last. And as she turned the fourth page, my head heavy with the cocoa, and the day's activities, I was out cold . . .

Auntie Marleen's voice was like that – low and droning, even at the most exciting bits, where Jo catches the runaway horse, or Quentin grabs the smuggler; Auntie Marleen's quiet monotone stayed on the same dogged, slow, dreary level, and I drifted quietly away, safe in the murmur of the story . . .

That was part of the routine too; that I fell asleep early, so that she would go back to the kitchen, make another cup of cocoa, turn on the wireless, and read the paper. She was doing this one night when I had to go to the lav;

she didn't notice me creeping around; she was behind the paper hidden by clouds of curling tobacco smoke.

Auntie Marleen. She had broken little teeth with mossy brown edges from all the smoking; and an awkward, rare lopsided smile, so that if she smiled, she showed only the left side of her jaw – where the teeth were not so bad. Her skin was downy and sallow, and moved a lot as she talked; soft creases and deep grooves around her very neat, very straight nose. And her eyes were kind and hollow, the colour of fading autumn leaves; sad. She never ever laughed.

Auntie Marleen gave me my first cat.

And my very first look at what I could become.

Remembering Them

'The Last Post' floated over the water, faint notes fading into the steam. Remembering them, at dawn. Remembering them.

Princess was supervising the cream cans. His real name was Pirirakau, but close relations called him Princess. Willowy, sleek, always fashionable, though this morning's outfit was more – The Working Man. Gumboots, pressed jeans, and a bulky olive swanndri, hair smoothed down beneath its hood. Small gold sleepers twinkled discreetly. He examined the nine bottles of rum. Six Corubas, two Plantations, a classic Capn Morgan. All donations, three for each can. The nephews Eru and Ra heaved the large metal containers out of the concrete steam boxes, and placed them on a low slat table in the kitchen. Their young arms bulged with effort; the liquid sloshed.

The milk was scalding hot from fifteen minutes in the thermal cookers; perfect. Eru had set the valves exactly right. Princess, both hands wrapped in old tea towels, carefully removed the first lid, then peeled the protective cloth off his fingers. Whiteness bubbled and hissed, then settled as he poured in two bottles of Bushells coffee and chicory with swift precision. Eru, a sturdy attentive youth, folded the mix with a long wooden paddle; he breathed in the fierce fumes when his uncle / auntie emptied the rum into the gaping metal mouth, and then took the stirrer from him. Strong sinewy hands blended the rich aromatic liquid. They repeated the process two more times, refastening each lid. The cans were set together in a straight line, ready for the coffee pots and small kettles. Ra had wandered off. Eru stayed and helped and watched and learned. 'Most days she's my Auntie Princess, but today he's my Uncle Pirirakau,' he whispered to himself, proud. 'Doing the special coffee to warm the koros up after the ANZAC service.'

It was still dark outside; heavy clouds hung close upon the flat surface of the Ruapeka, hiding the soldiers' cemetery that hunkered low in the shadows across the lagoon. The activity had shifted, in well-disciplined and sombre ranks, to the marae of Paratehoata. Tables outside, tables inside; the weather was being kind. Rows of cups on saucers, plates of crackers, cabin bread, cheese; trays of fry bread, butter, golden syrup. The big breakfast took place later, after the Cenotaph Service in town. This memorial was for the boys; for the ones who did not come home; this time was for the pa to cry, and to remember them.

Light moved in thin lines of dawn through the vaporous dark, glimmered on male faces moist with remembering. Around them moved the gentle bustle of wives, aunties, sisters, nieces, mothers, cousins, offering them hot drinks 'with or without'; and Princess. Quiet smiles, a steady touch, a firm hand on a frail elbow, he positioned chairs and assisted the very old and tottery; he found single gloves and ornate tokotoko, woolly hats and lumpy knitted scarves; and even the rare lost red poppy. He was very busy.

Uncle Tei was sitting alone at the end of a table, downing his second cup. He touched the fine badge on the black beret hemmed with thin leather on his grizzled head; his dark hazel eyes crinkled a warm hello as Tahuri came over to him, two coffee pots at the ready. He'd just finished rolling more smokes, which he lined up in his Three Castles tin, on top of the tobacco. Careful to avoid the small paper flower on his lapel, he slid the small box into the inner pocket of his black dress jacket. The pocket sat behind a row of gleaming medals and stars fixed to ribbons of red and two blues; cream and red and two blues; lots of red; and one that was red and green and white. All the stars were yellow metal like gold; the round ones were silvery with a King's head on them. One ribbon was black. Tahuri knew that each one told a special story; she wished she knew them all. She offered the koroua another cup. He motioned her to sit, and to pass the coffee to a niece working nearby. She did. He was watching Princess.

The olive swanndri had been removed, to reveal a dark blue ribbed pullover with red and white stripes around the V neck. It looked very patriotic, and set off the scarlet poppy, as its tiny white tag matched the crisp shirt with one button undone at the collar. Shining patent leather shoes had replaced the gumboots. Princess was enjoying himself, ordering the females about, issuing playful instructions, relishing his role as Head Waiter in Training. He was in his second year at the elegant Waiwera House, only five minutes' walk from the pa. He loved food, he loved people. He wanted to make them happy, to make them laugh; he wanted them to need him. He flirted shamelessly with his aunties and his uncles, winked at the younger boys and girls, parted the glossy waves of his hair down the middle, and smiled wickedly in all directions. He threw Tahuri a knowing look, and cocked a shapely eyebrow. She caught the look like a softball, and flung it straight back, grinning; but Princess didn't notice, for he was busy again. With practised grace, he carried four trays piled high with empty crockery back to the kitchen, lean hips curving to a swish.

Uncle Tei was still watching him.

The old man seemed to be gazing behind Princess, peering into another place, another time. He turned to look at Tahuri.

'That boy, Pirirakau. I knew boys like him. Sissies, we used to call them. Sissies.' He paused, as Princess sauntered over to a nearby table, setting out more food, flicking the koro a saucy glance. Uncle Tei lowered his voice.

'You were lucky if you had one with you. In your section or platoon. They were the best barbers, wuu, they did the good haircuts. Not just short back 'n sides, but style, real style. And they were good field medics too. But niece, when everything around us was wrecked, was mud, was rubble, broken walls, broken houses, broken roads, wrecked, blown up, everything fallen down, trenches, bomb craters, wrecked . . . they could find us a feed. Anywhere. Puha, wenoweno, nettles, beetroots, corn, turnips; vine leaves! One sissy boy even scrounged us a lettuce. A lettuce! If it was kai, they found it. Even on the hoof, or on the wing. And cook, oh, they could cook!' Memories made him lick his dribbly chin, wipe the damp from his eyes. Concerned, Princess started hovering in the background.

'Marvellous, tau ki te mahi kai. And niece, they could fight. And they could kill. They had no fear of death. Or pain. They went straight in, no more bullets, bayonets out, straight in they went. Those sissies cleared the way. They had no fear. They were the real heroes. Not us. And most of them got left behind,' he sighed, breath heavy with grief. 'They never came back. But I remember them.'

This story is dedicated to those sissies buried far away in foreign lands. It is also in memory of Dr Vincent Heta Olsen Malcolm-Buchanan (Pirirakau), and my beloved nephew Erunuku. Maringiringi tonu nga roimata, moe mai ra.

Ngahuia te Awekotuku (Te Arawa, Tūhoe, Waikato) has fought for Māori, women's and LGBT rights for five decades. In July 1971, she wrote 'Lesbianism: the elegance of unfettered love' for the University of Auckland's *Craccum*. She duly lost her part-time teaching job but maintained her queer activist profile. For this, in 1972 she was refused a scholarship visa to the US as a 'known sexual deviant'. She kept at it. She has produced three collections of creative fiction and poetry, a volume of essays, and the definitive *Mau Moko: the world of Maori tattoo* (Viking, 2007). Her numerous works on culture, gender, heritage and sexuality have been published and acclaimed locally and internationally. She is an emeritus professor.

Oscar Upperton

New transgender blockbusters

If we put on make-up the camera won't linger
and we'll change our clothes out of frame
or if we change our clothes in frame it will be done casually,
talking as we shrug teeshirts over our heads
or pulling on the spacesuit to try to fix the loose coupling
one last time. We won't die, or if we die,
we'll die surrounded by our grandchildren, handing out bequests
of stolen property and vowing vengeance on rival families.
We'll travel in time, and save the world,
and doom the world but not in an earthquake-causing,
crime-against-nature sort of way.
We'll have transgender friends and family members,
the frame of the film sustaining with ease the image
of transgender people talking to each other.
We'll all be very very brave
because being a person requires great bravery,
and we won't have to wear signs around our necks saying I am a Person.
We'll become immune to all tropes, and win every prize.
If we find a gun under the floorboards in the first act,
we will bring world peace by the fourth act.
If we open our lockets to show the platoon a photograph of our loved one,
we'll be guaranteed to survive until the end credits.

New dictionary

Now you're dead, you've lost definition.
Don't be scared. You've done this before.
When you were a baby, you held a word in one hand
and an object in the other, and smashed them together.
You just have to do it again.
Your first word is coin. Coin is a doorway.
Your second word is doorway. Doorway
is a world. A world is a family.
A family is a deep-sea creature dancing under ice.
Ice is a punch to the back of the head. Head
is a buried thing, gutter is fluid in the lungs,
sugar and malice are your two rotting hands.
Hands are sceptres, sceptres are words, words are rain
inside you, bad weather always but warm.
You understand?

Small talk

How've you been have you
mastectomy or
called dyke at a bus stop

How do you find Wellington do you
trapped or
it will be taken from you

What do you do do you
produce or
your wound that no one talks about

What do you do outside of work do you
counselling or
keeping the baby alive

What do you prefer do you
things on fire or
things yet to be on fire

Do you want kids do you want
girls or
kids

What kind of music do you like do you
birds screaming or
heterosexual wedding playlist

What do you do to relax do you
visit the grave or
childless

Am I terrified am I
are we all or
alone

Oscar Upperton lives in Wellington. His first poetry collection, *New Transgender Blockbusters*, was published by Victoria University Press in 2020.

Pasan Jayasinghe

The Dance Party / The Other Me

Marine Drive hugs the ocean for a good part of Colombo, from just outside the inner city to where the suburbs begin. A journey along it is always a confluence of the road traffic, passing trains on the coastal railway track, and the sky and the sea, ever present and ever together. On any odd evening, all these settings are dialled up a notch: the road is packed with impatient, loud vehicles; the evening commuter trains are crammed to implausible degrees with people; and the sea is restive as its sky rapidly shuffles through a series of ridiculous colours. Every city has places where its entire essence is concentrated; after thirteen plus two years, I still don't really know Colombo, but Marine Drive might just be it.

A few hours later, in the deep of night, the equation changes slightly. The traffic slows down; the trains peter out, with less people spilling out and clinging on for their lives; and the sea takes over from the sky in the dramatic stakes. The waves crash and crash against the coast's rocks, taking a breather only to allow the bellowing of the trains' horns to reach land.

It's in the deep of this, while speeding along on a tuk tuk, that the night dissolves into a grey, navy and lurid amber blur. We are sitting five in the back seat; the two people above the permitted limit are stretched across the laps of the other three. Someone – me – has snuck in a plastic bottle of tonic mixed hastily with some gin that is being passed around. Loose hands drape over each other and clutch at limbs and bodies. It's a disarming feeling of safety.

Anticipation is a drug on its own. 'Why do we keep doing this?' someone asks, rhetorically drunk. 'Because what is your life without this, aney?'

There are no gay bars in Sri Lanka. There was one in the late '90s (or maybe it was the early '00s), but it closed down when the cops raided it. Everyone knew it was a gay bar, of course. The owners were just running their luck on how long it would take before they came after it. It was on par with a brothel in that sense. A matter of which bribes appeased whom and which eyes were turned what way. As it turned out, nothing would come to replace it after the raid. Impermanence is the fate of queers. It is especially pronounced here.

In its place now are the dance parties. Once a month, at some lower to mid-range inner city hotel that is desperate enough for the easy cash to be undiscerning about the clientele. They are advertised strictly through word of mouth and breathless group messages on WhatsApp and Grindr. For a thousand rupees, a ragtag team of entrepreneurial gays promise a night of bright lights, loud, agreeable sounds in confined surroundings, and more. There's a lot who fall for it, once a month. A lot who make speedy beelines for it down Marine Drive.

The first time I walked, or stumbled in, I couldn't help being reminded of walking into Family Bar for the first time. The walking past, and then back, on the sticky black speckled grey K' Road sidewalk; the panicked internal deliberation about whether you had dressed too straight (jeans *and* plaid?); the fervent attempts to avoid the eyes of everyone from the bouncers to the mirthful gays and imperious drag queens by the front tables. Until, finally, being enveloped inside by the creeping autumn cold, the bad rum kicking in and the faint strains of a lost, irrepressible Kylie Minogue remix.

The intervening years have instilled more confidence, or something like it. There's less room to manoeuvre here anyway; the eyes outside can always turn hostile and there's no space to dither. So I hurry across the uneven, crumbling sidewalk, up past the gaggle at the front and through the makeshift ticket desk manned by the bored-looking aunty. The faintest smile teases her lips as she ties the band around my wrist. I *beam* back at her.

Inside is a controlled frenzy. Under the flashing lights, people break out into dancing in scattered clusters: those with poor forethought trying to calculate which overpriced drinks would be the most efficient; past hook-ups avoiding or actively seeking each other out; the DJ lining up one crowd-pleasing Hindi song after another to fill out the dance floor; awkward stare-offs between social enemies; and bright, bright laughter. This is rote for a gay space anywhere in the world, perhaps. But there's only one in Colombo, for one night a month only, and everything is frighteningly, exhilaratingly concentrated.

The balcony outside is a break from the dancing. Everyone mills around on the wet, tiled expanse as other textures of the night take shape through the words you catch.

'It was better back in the old days, men. These kids are just here to have a good time.'

'Back then?'

'It meant something more, no? It was dangerous. We didn't know if we'd be back for the next one. And the music was better.'

'You don't like "Laila Main Laila"?'

'Oh, no, I love that one! Is it on again?'

'Haiiii *akke*, how are you?' says a familiar face falling onto mine. *Sister*. I bite my tongue, moved beyond words.

'These old queens exaggerate, no?'

'How?'

'Of course it was bad back then. But like it isn't now? I mean, what's really changed in ten, twenty years? We're still criminals, no?'

She's beautiful. The blonde highlights flow impossibly straight over her shoulders and onto her brilliantly red dress. 'You're new here, no?' she says, with an effortless flick of her head, running a finger down my shirt. I nod giddily. 'Come dance with me later, men.'

She is this vision of herself for just one day of the month (sometimes a few more). On the dance floor, her dress creates its own crimson frenzy as she dances, not missing a single beat.

'Look, the faggots back then were doing the same thing. Looking for dick and money, while a few of them pretended to fight for more.'

'Isn't that the problem?'

'It's not a problem for them!'

'This isn't a place for people like us, no?'

The dance floor itself is like any other – loud, sweaty, dark and bright in equal, incalculable measures. With a logic of its own, undictated by who is here, and for what purpose. Driven merely by the light and sound and motion.

Like any other dance floor, there are bodies, too, and people attached to them, and small currents of something like desire infusing the already charged air. So hands, yours or others', reach for shirts and pull the bodies and the attached people in closer. For a kiss, and if time and the ratio of dark to light permits, more than one.

Everything – the law, society, our own shame – conspire the future out of our hands. All that remains instead is the present. In that, you think a kiss is enough. It has to be.

Way up from above, the night winds down in a flurry of miniature activity. The late stragglers stumble into tuks, drunk and high. Random street food hawkers hover around hopefully. And always, the phalanx of policemen who have gathered steadily through the night. There is a friendliness to them in the glaring lights of the hotel but just out of reach, you sense a certain lurking. When you're being perceived for what you are, and only that, you just know.

When the exits begin en masse, onwards to more dancing or other pleasures, they activate. Feet shuffling forward, shoulders relaxing into swaggers to question those whose voices don't carry upwards, lost as they are to the sea and road's combined din. This is policing in its true sense, what you can call it when the deviant are pushed into line and that line is already blurred. The same policemen who smiled so generously as you blundered in turning inscrutable as you stumble out. All the more reason, then, to press yourself down; box the femme in so as not to implicate yourself. Every fag for themselves.

For those who are self-incriminating by reason of simple existence, it's another negotiation for the night. We try, piecemeal, to ask for the National Identity Card numbers of the tuk drivers and note down the badge numbers of the watching policemen in the same breath as we bundle those we can into the tuks, the faux chiffon of their dresses trailing after them.

On the way back, spent in multiple ways, I miss the point where I should get down and must make a trek back from where the tuk expelled me. Just past the junction, I notice too late the lone policeman leaning against his bike. Separated from his kind, he is a different type of threat. I tick off in my head all the things that give me away – the long hair, the earrings, the too tight jeans – my body jerking itself into sobriety and straightness as quickly as it can. I try to check at least what I can control; holding the arms straight and the wrists locked, keeping the walking pace steady and resisting the urge to run a hand through my hair. I feel his eyes scan me and imagine him assessing the opportunity costs: how deserted the road is, how easy a target I am and how much he can get away with.

In the numerous configurations of this encounter I accumulate, I have passed through completely unscathed; been pulled into a brief 'where are you going?' – 'going home, sir' exchange; and had the same exchange extended onwards to a request for ID. In all these instances, my heart would be thudding uncontrollably, my mind desperately trying to predict the next part of the sequence and cursing myself for the infinitesimal choices and vagaries that got me there.

Where my sequences end, however, they continue onwards for so many others. Where power makes short work of dignity. When harassment turns to humiliation turns to outright abuse. When money or a slap to the face or a terrifying blow job has to be exchanged for the luxury of not spending the night in a cell. Where even that is not the end.

I don't know how lucky I am.

*

Queer people are slow to see each other. We are often too preoccupied with our own versions of oppression to notice what others are nursing. The suffering makes us feel singular, special, and we blur out those who might make us less so. Even in our hurting, we are selfish.

It comes from a natural distrust, born out of the weariness of being let down by so many others. In New Zealand, I leaned too much into it, being wilfully blind too often to my species in return for an imagined safety.

But I've told myself I won't be that here. I trust the two oceans in between to help keep me to my resolve.

So I persevere, latching onto anyone who responds even remotely to gentle pushing. I see versions of me in all configurations. They're plagued by fears I've had from all stages of life. How do you best stave off marriage talk from the family? Which clinic is the least humiliating? What even is dating? And who do you *love* love, at the end of it all? Freakishly, so many of these versions *look* like me. This shouldn't make a difference, but it does. I thought I was the only skeletal brown kid shouldering these questions.

And all these configurations so frequently, generously lure me into tuks and out of them, to something like freedom.

I collect their stories ravenously. I prod and probe to uncover what it was really like. This whole business of growing up as one of us, if I had stayed here like I was supposed to. I want to know, I *have* to know: what would it have been like?

The answers come slowly and steadily. They are frequently exhilarating, like striking a fantastical windfall. 'The boys were so handsy, men!' and 'Everyone was into it,' and 'I fell in love so many times.' The details – the classes that were shared; the exact configurations of the toilets; what *their* girlfriends looked like – filled in over many nights on that balcony and at random bars and on nightwalks together.

There is, at first, a burning envy, because oceans away I skirted on past, untouched either which way for so long. I imagine the life-rupturing glances-touches-kisses-fucks earlier for myself, the ensuing revelations more pronounced somehow, and the resultant *me* more distinct.

But over time, and through more of the back and forths, the import of how the stories would usually end kicks in. 'They abandoned you after they realised what you were, and that they might be that, too' and 'I could never, ever tell him' and 'Now they're all married, with kids.'

When I plug myself properly into the scenario, I realise slowly that I could never have made it out unscathed. Simple, confused pleasures in exchange for a never-ending series of bruises I wouldn't have made sense of for a long while. I try to make a kind of peace with what I am now and who I could never have been. There is no word for the scratching feeling in the throat that describes the in-between.

Everything eventually circles back onto a kind of awe at those who respond to the prodding, though. To pass all of it off as nothing as they flick their cigarettes off the edge.

'Why did you come back?' from *them*, then, is a different enquiry altogether. Leaving a New Zealand to come to a Sri Lanka is not simply abandoning the economic security a white country brings. It is exposing yourself to certain kinds of shame and fear and violence. It is having to fashion large parts of your safety yourself. Giving up entire life paths altogether because they are so much harder or not even imaginable in the first place. Writing off relationships that are recognised, celebrated, even. Forgoing seeing yourself in certain ways; less the subject of your surroundings, and more your own being, maybe. So why, then? Why be so reckless and illogical and so damn *stupid*? As always, I have no real answer.

I want to tell them that this security doesn't include the slurs shouted across pristine, perfectly paved streets on random nights, the eyebrows raised at unexpected junctures, and the curling into yourself, always so tightly, against judgements real and imagined. That beautiful relationships are sometimes a fantasy for brown boys in a white world. That you can be a full, rich, complete person anywhere. But they would pick that over this. Every time. And why wouldn't they?

In the end, I am *obsessed* with the person who stayed behind, in another universe. The one not perforated by the act of leaving. The one who probably got nine As in the O Levels. The one who grew into a person amid throngs of people instead of alone. The one who slid into the medicine track for the A Levels and, failing to make it in, cobbled together a backup career in something related to accounting.

And, the one who harboured more crushes, earlier. The one who fell in love too quickly and too disastrously; unrequited being a misnomer for confusing tragedy. The one who was broken in different, less salvageable ways. The one whose shyness was beaten into remoteness by fear. The one without the courage or the people or the safe hands on the lower back to help say the words. The one who, still, got by.

In that other universe, he heads for New Zealand at the same time as I, in this one, return to Sri Lanka. He flees the claustrophobia of limited options while I am trying to escape a comforting quicksand. For him there is a life of long, languid stillness ahead, while I hurl towards permanent, uncertain frenzy. We've both chosen suffocations of different kinds.

When our planes cross each other over the Strait of Malacca in the middle of the timeless dark, we both wake for a second and feel a strange, momentary turbulence.

Pasan Jayasinghe is a PhD candidate in political science at University College London. He grew up both in Sri Lanka and Aotearoa, and has lived in Sri Lanka again for the past four years. He spends his time trying to write; keeping track of a multi-continental murder mystery collection; and extensively cataloguing girl bands. He has been published in *Overland*, *The Pantograph Punch*, *The Hindu* and *Clash*.

Paula Boock

from Dare Truth or Promise

As they rounded the final corner they saw the road widened into a circle of grass and a carpark, and to the right rose the dark shape of a monument. Louie put on the brakes and some loose stones clattered under the car.

Beyond the monument were the lights of the city. Everything else was black. As Louie opened her door, it swung beyond her hand with the force of the wind on the hilltop. She got out and was knocked a pace backwards – 'Wo!' – then she grabbed the car door and heaved it shut again. Willa let Judas out from the back and he leapt away into the darkness.

The monument was a big rectangular shape with what looked like a flagpole on top, but there was no flag. On either side sat giant carved figures of pioneers – one male, one female, wrapped in stone robes and sitting cross-legged like Scottish Buddhas. Louie and Willa felt their way along the railings to the front of the monument. Ahead of them was the fabulous view of the city. The harbour was a black space in the middle, and all around it the yellow, white and red lights spread out over the hills like a huge embroidered coverlet. Above, the stars seemed incredibly close, crushed glass flung across the sky. The wind was freezing and roared in Louie's ears. She opened her mouth wide and gasped into it. Across from her she could just make out Willa's hair whipping about, and watched her raise a pale hand to hold it.

Louie found some steps leading below the monument to a gravel path and bushes. 'Here!' she yelled at Willa. 'Come down here, it's more sheltered.'

There was a rustle in the shrubs beside her and Louie jumped. Judas appeared, his eyes yellow spots momentarily in the blackness, then his breath warm by her hand. Willa was stumbling down the steps.

'God!' she shouted, a bit too loudly for amongst the bushes, 'it's freezing!'

Just then there was another movement in the undergrowth and something white zig-zagged ahead of them. A rabbit. Judas's paws skidded on the gravel as he took off after the animal and both plunged into the bush.

'Judas!' yelled Willa, 'No! Judas!!' She turned to Louie. 'Damn. He thinks he's a great rabbit hunter.'

'Can't trust a Judas,' Louie replied, flinging herself after him. 'Thirty pieces of silver and all that. He's probably dobbing us in. Come on.'

She ran ahead, not realising Willa had stopped. Then, turning back, Louie saw Willa stumbling after. Her hands and face pale against the bush. 'Hang on!' Willa grabbed Louie's arm. 'I can't see a thing,' she explained.

Louie laughed back, the wind making her feel crazy. She took Willa's hand, and this time it felt good, that small white hand in her own, and they staggered after Judas through the scrub until they reached an open bank of grass that whirred in the wind. Louie spread out her free arm and pulled Willa into a run, and they whooped and laughed, their clothes cracking behind them, until eventually, deliberately really, they fell over in the tussock.

For a while they lay and caught their breath, and let the wind wash over them. In the grass it was much warmer and seemed quiet.

'Dare truth or promise,' said Willa suddenly.

'What?'

'Dare truth or promise. You know.'

Louie knew. 'Truth,' she answered, looking up into the blackness.

'Do you believe in God?'

'I guess so.'

'You guess so.' Willa's tone was flat.

'Don't you?'

'No.'

Louie sat up on her elbows and looked at the city lights, the huge audience of the hills. '*The world is charged with the grandeur of God.* Don't you feel it, like electricity? Like now?'

'That's God?'

She laughed and lay back down. 'I don't know. My turn. Dare truth or promise.'

'Truth.'

'Do you have a boyfriend?'

There was a slight shift beside her. 'No.'

Louie smiled at the sky. 'Whose is the ring?'

'That's two questions. Dare truth or promise.'

'Truth.'

'Don't you ever choose dare?' said Willa. 'Okay, have you ever been in love?'

'Since I was about twelve years old with someone or other.' Louie heard her words and felt silly.

'Yeah,' said Willa.

'Dare truth or promise.'

'Dare!'

Louie laughed. 'Okay. Stand up and take off all your clothes.'

'Get off.'

'What can I dare you to do?'

'Just sitting up is hard enough.' Willa brushed the hair whipping across her face.

They both sat up, buffeted by the slapping wind. Louie's ears burned but when she put up a hand to touch one it was icy.

'Isn't it stunning?' Willa said, admiring the view.

'My ears are freezing,' said Louie. 'Feel them!' She grabbed Willa's hand and held it to her right ear. It remained there, even though Louie dropped her own and listened to the faraway sound formed inside the cup of Willa's hand. Her father used to tell her it was the sea. She tried to see Willa's face in the dark but could only make out a pale outline, not her expression. Willa's hand stayed there, surely longer than was normal, still longer again. Her palm was warm against Louie's cheek. It's happening, she thought, she's going to do it. Her throat tightened and a frantic fizzing rose inside her chest. Willa's hand moved slightly, brushing Louie's neck, then she drew it away. Louie choked silently. *Don't*, she wanted to say. *Don't stop*.

Instead, she turned back to the view and tried to think of something, anything to say. She was conscious of Willa leaning back on her elbows beside her, quiet. After a bit, Willa jumped up and began walking around, calling out to Judas. Louie swore softly, then got up and joined her.

Judas returned eventually, and hopped happily into the back of the car. It was warm in there, and terribly quiet after the wind, but neither of them spoke. Louie drove carefully down the road this time, wanting the drive to last, wanting to have said something by the time they got back, but the more she tried, the more locked she seemed to be. Willa turned on the stereo and looked out the window. Louie's thoughts became more and more manic. *Say something!* she screamed inwardly, but there it was; not a quote even, a line of Shakespeare, a silly joke within range. Louie Angelo, known as Motormouth to friends and family, every report reminding her that she would do better with a little more attention in class, now, when it felt as if her life depended on it, simply could not speak. Had she imagined it? Had anything happened at all? Yes. Something had happened, the silence in the car told her that.

When she drew up outside the Duke it was twenty past twelve. Willa leapt out as soon as the car stopped and released Judas. She smiled quickly and unconvincingly. 'Thanks,' she said in a strained voice. 'See ya.'

Louie opened her mouth but the noise that eventually came out sounded like a bagpipe – and anyway, Willa had gone.

Paula Boock is a novelist and scriptwriter. She has written several young adult novels and won numerous awards, including the AIM Best First Book Award, the Esther Glen Medal, the NZ Post Children's Book of the Year and the AFTA NZ Best Drama Script Award. She has held the Writing Residency at the Dunedin College of Education as well as the Robert Burns Fellowship, and was the 2009 Writer in Residence at Victoria University of Wellington. Her essay 'On Make-up and Makeover' was published in the Montana Essay Series, and her screen credits include writing on the multi-award-winning television series *The Insider's Guide to Love*.

Pelenakeke Brown

A Travelling Practice

Provocation

A Travelling Practice looks at Samoan concepts and ancestral knowledge held within the landscape and context of the contemporary keyboard. The keyboard becomes a crossover site that intersects my many identities and art forms, as well as becoming a tool for freedom and creativity of expression.

As a disabled artist working within crip time, the power of movement that I can achieve through my keyboard and the liminal space of the internet is integral to help me connect, create, and facilitate my artistic practice. With this work I wished to expand what is considered movement and explore the specific choreography of the keyboard, both physically and conceptually, and ask, how can one move without moving?

I focused on the small movements created in this contemporary landscape and how it invokes Samoan concepts. The keyboard is set up with a pre-existing set of relationships, from the keys that most people know and understand, and each movement, each tap, no matter how small, is a powerful propelling forward through time (tā) and space (vā). Using the Samoan framework of the vā or spatial relationships,[1] I analysed the relationships of the keys, using the concepts already on the console to think about movement. Looking at the relationality of the keys of the keyboard, I realised many of the characters in the keyboard reflect many of the symbols of the Samoan tatau (tattoo); specifically, the malu, traditionally worn by women. I was fascinated to see that in this modern technology there is this ancestral knowledge in plain sight. I wanted to connect the two in my use of text and visual images and explore what some of these movements look and feel like, and how this is reflected in the Samoan tatau.

Tatau has continued to evolve and today it is still a significant and important marker of identity especially within communities of the Samoan diaspora. Artist, tatau practitioner and scholar Tyla Vaeau Ta'ufo'ou defines tatau as a travelling practice and connects tatau to the wider movement of Samoan people both historically and in contemporary forms in her thesis,

1 To learn more about the vā, please read Albert Wendt, 'Tatauing the Post-Colonial Body', originally published in *Span* 42–43 (April–October 1996), pp. 15–29, New Zealand Electronic Poetry Centre, http://www.nzepc.auckland.ac.nz/authors/wendt/tatauing.asp

'Fa'avaetuli: Like the Feet of Tuli >>> Samoan Tatau as a Travelling Practice'. With her permission and with much alofa ma fa'afetai tele lava, I have used her title as I similarly applied this spirit of exploring tatau as a movement practice in itself, through space and time, and the malaga (journey) I have taken both physically and conceptually to create this work.

This work connects to my wider multi-disciplinary practice as it explores the quiet intersections between race, disability, queerness, immigration, decolonisation and aesthetic.

< < < < < < < < A Travelling Practice > > > > > > > >

I look down at the landscape before me
in each corner I see four deliberate markers of space and time

esc		on
	and everything in between	
fn		|>

Today's journey begins with a crick in my neck, an ache in my left arm and a longing for home
this longing for home feels like a dreaded dry mouth and a lead weight of nerves in my stomach
with a wish to be supported, floating effortlessly in the water
with my ears covered by the cool, smooth liquid
muting out the outside noises
and my own (often more debilitating) inside voices
the reverberation of these opinions
echoing long after the action that I am agonising over has ended
(())
(((())))
(((((((())))))))
(((((((((((((((())))))))))))))))

I look at the landscape that I am in
the framework of this space
the context that is held within these keys
the relationships between each of these keys
the ascending
descending
symbols and languages
worlds within worlds

My body, although always tired has made its own rhythm
and knows, instinctively, how to move
I, too, have home keys, familiar steps
although sometimes I falter
....

My hands are hovered above, midflight
If I make a tap I need it to be perfect
I need to be sure, there is no room for error
but with no guarantee the only way forward
is to tap on
>>><<<
into the abyss
into the vā
the space in-between

As I type, I watch the symbols and keys build upon each other
shift and move along the page
as I tap each key
I see how it changes the configuration and movement on the page
It is gentle, yet stable work, and while I type it calms me
At other times
I sit there in silence, unable to move
afraid, to go forward
|stuck|
fearing 'what if it's not right?'

I notice on my keyboard
that there is often a corresponding action in the keys
a reflection and reciprocity
this reciprocity mirroring
the vā
relationships that support and protect each other
to increase there must be a decrease

ctrl + z
ctrl + y
===========
++++++++++++++
{}{}{}{}{}{}{}{}{}{}{}{}{}{}
[][][][][][][][][][][][][][][][]
****
<><><><><><><><><><><><><>

#######################
()()()()()()()()()()()()()()
\\//\\//\\//\\//\\//
Enter // *Return*
Enter where?
and *return,*
to whom?

When I type (strike)
/// \\\ /// \\\ /// \\\
I move into a rhythm
like the Tufuga tā tatau and their 'au, with each strike on Samoan ancestral flesh
the strike of my keyboard is a way of affirming my existence
and connecting to something outside of ourselves
Like my ancestors did with our lineage, travelling, exploring new worlds
now, I am journeying from the comfort of my home
while still resting these sore bones of mine
using these contemporary keys that hold ancestral taps of knowledge
which propel me through time and space
tap, tap, tap,
remember there can be no vā without tā

spoons
movements
constellations
containment
I am the tatau
the process
the travelling practice
I am the ever-changing movement of line in space
the gentle tapping as I struggle to move forward
knowing this is where I am meant to be
or rather the only way forward is to tap
>> tap >>
<< tap <<
| forge forward |
This, the keyboard, is my modern tapping tool
an instrument that enables me to move in the world
freely
to format and create comfortably
In these journeys
I seek to
return
shift
control
command
delete
to find
alt(*ernative*) *option*(*s*)
This device
is an asymmetric mirror
with double shifts
a sea of *command*
control, option, command, space, command, option
there are spaces b e t w e e n these keys
remember there is no such thing as empty space, Albert says

Contextual relationships
and connections
<|>
threads
-->>>---<<<--
of belonging
\<|>/
|| alignment ||

Here in these strokes
in this modern tā, tā, tā
I can tap out my reality within this vā
I am striking tā and carving vā with each tap

My ancestors and their marks live here.
The possibilities of truth telling live here.
^^^^^^ >>>>>><<<<<< ^^^^^^

My mother's struggles live here.

Her words and possibilities are contained here.
I have the power to unfold, unfurl,
rhythm
^^^^^^
rhythms
^^^^^^^^^^^^
with (one) gentle tap

My grief lives here.

All the things I cannot say live here.

< >
< That voice whispers *return* >
< >
< I press >
< *enter* *return* >
< *enter* *return* >
< >
< >
< I am yet to *return* >
< >
< >

shift
lets me know
that I am human
that I feel
and can move
forward
command
is the ever-powerful tool I am searching for
control
is the cool face of detachment
but when you peer under the table her hands are gripping (too) tightly.

Are there any *alt*(*ernative*) *options* to let go?
(and how can I *delete?*)

The continual striking of tā in my movements in this liminal vā
the continual pressing of *return* (or is it *enter?*)

I am unsure this will lead me anywhere.

^^^
\\\\\\|//////	\\\\\\|//////	\\\\\\|//////	\\\\\\|//////	\\\\\\|//////	\\\\\\|//////
\\\\\\|//////	\\\\\\|//////	\\\\\\|//////	\\\\\\|//////	\\\\\\|//////	\\\\\\|//////
\\\\\\|//////	\\\\\\|//////	\\\\\\|//////	\\\\\\|//////	\\\\\\|//////	\\\\\\|//////
^^^

It is a claiming of space
<><><><><><>
The stories of my old lovers live here
the inking of the skin
like the memory of you on my skin
To ink
[] [] []
you on my skin
to type out your name(s)
is to etch your existence
I have uttered (all) your name(s)
carefully tapping out each of our stories
so many of them brief

_ _ _
-<<-<<<--<<<<--->>>>-->>>->>-
_ _ _

After it ends
I store these memories in my body
and I can always determine how honest I was
when I place my palm on my chest
and take a breath
[] [] []
If it's open
and I can feel the empty space
if there is a trace of movement
a possibility of the wind
<><><><><><>
and I can breathe freely
then I know that
the bird has left
with no crunch of regret

^^
|

^^^
\\\\\\|//////	\\\\\\|//////	\\\\\\|//////	\\\\\\|//////	\\\\\\|//////	\\\\\\|//////
\\\\\\|//////	\\\\\\|//////	\\\\\\|//////	\\\\\\|//////	\\\\\\|//////	\\\\\\|//////
\\\\\\|//////	\\\\\\|//////	\\\\\\|//////	\\\\\\|//////	\\\\\\|//////	\\\\\\|//////
^^^

{{{{{{{{{{{{{{{{{ }}}}}}}}}}}}}}}}}

I sit here now
legs wide
coming out from the slit of my dress
the birds
of my heart, soaring, trying to find land
to rest, to be cradled upon
within

^^

^^ ^^

^^ ^^ ^^

^^ ^^ ^^ ^^

^^ ^^ ^^

^^ ^^

^^

I imagine my tatau will feel the same,
she will cover me, connect and protect
mark me as Samoan out in this travelling world
in a language that only a few will recognise

It is a grounding visual force
and connects me to so many out there
I do not need to move to feel this connection
It tells you where we have been and where we are going

return and *enter* are one and the same
when I think I am returning I am in fact moving forward

I have always had the movement of my score right here

Manuia lou malaga

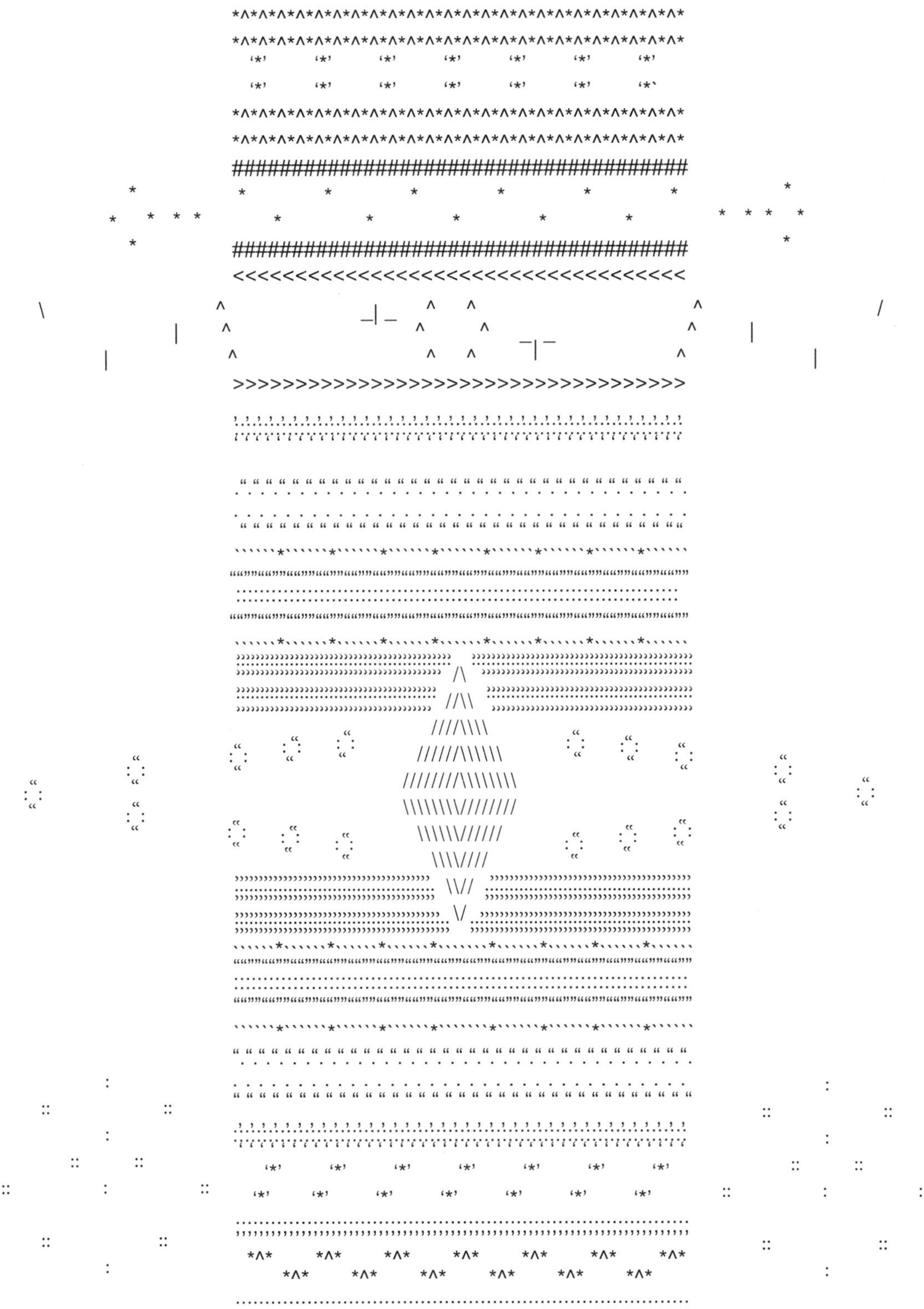

Pelenakeke Brown is an interdisciplinary, Samoan / Pākehā, disabled artist born in Aotearoa. Her work explores the intersections of disability and Samoan cultural concepts. She has exhibited, performed and published work in the US, UK, Germany and Aotearoa. She has created projects with Movement Research, the New York Public Library for the Performing Arts, Lincoln Center, the Metropolitan Museum of Art and many other arts organisations and institutions. She has had residencies with Eyebeam (NY), The Laundromat Project (NY), Denniston Hill (NY), DanceNYC (NY) and the Vermont Center (VT). Most recently she was awarded a Pacific Toa award at the 2020 Creative New Zealand Arts Pasifika awards.

Peter Wells

Sweet Nothing

He said he was a brain surgeon and looked at Alan with the candid eyes of a liar. Alan looked at him long and hard then simultaneously they burst out laughing.

'You've got a lovely laugh,' the brain surgeon said with a voice of quiet longing. Their eyes, blue and brown, touched, touched, then swerved apart.

It had been like that from the start – an impossible attraction, an irresistible connection between an out-of-towner and a local.

When Alan came to think of his companion's body later he saw it in terms of a Michelangelo nude, that magnificent framework of limb, lovely musculature, symmetry. That he had the slight slutty voice of a small-town girl gave his huge body a kind of charm, like a flaw in a magnificent vase.

He was blond, slate-eyed, tanned. Alan's first impression of him was that he was a beach prostitute with a kind of Marilyn Monroe mind, light, flirtatious, with a melancholy layer of seriousness underneath. Sexual.

'I bet you're hard, eh?' the beach boy said, looking at Alan straight in the eyes. 'Why don't we do it in the bushes here, right behind me? *Now*.'

Alan looked around the sunken garden: the splash of the waterwheel, the salt-glazed annuals, the peeling paintwork of the bed-and-breakfast opposite. It was New Zealand at its most prohibitively prim.

'No,' Alan said with a short sigh. 'Not here. Come back to my motel. Come . . . back,' he said after a short pause of calculation, 'and we'll have a smoke. You smoke?'

'The minister said I shouldn't smoke,' the beach boy said with a high, wild laugh, 'but I've been totally out of it for three days. Haven't eaten for two.'

He proceeded to tell Alan about a minister who had picked him up one day on the beach. Just like now. Except the minister hadn't ostensibly picked him up. He said he was worried about the beach boy's soul. He wanted to help. So he went back to the minister's room. The minister went into the bathroom and came out saying, 'You realise I've already ejaculated?'

The beach boy said he went into a library and looked the word up in a dictionary.

They both laughed at that and Alan was aware he didn't have an erection. The talk of religion had removed his effervescence. The beach boy began to talk randomly about being mixed up, and was it wrong, and how he couldn't afford to be seen going into motels with strangers.

'Come back,' Alan said with a note of entreaty in his voice. '*Come back*.'

The beach boy looked at him: their eyes fused.

'You've got lovely eyes,' the beach boy said then. 'I could really go for a bloke like you.' He paused and did his own calculations. 'You'll have to walk ahead. Oh God.' He made a small gesture of self-rebuke. 'That's terrible, isn't it? But I live here.'

They sat together looking at the world they found themselves in.

'What's your name?' Alan said quickly, as they stood up.

'What's yours?'

'Alan.'

'That's mine, too,' the beach boy said laughing. 'A good name, Alan.'

A long time afterwards Alan wondered whether that was true, or whether Alan, the beach boy, had made it up on the spur of the moment. It probably made it easier for him to remember who he was with.

The room was lit by an orange curtain Alan had pulled along to kill the daylight. He had rolled a smoke and they paused a moment, breathing it in. They stood together, loosely touching. Their hands, bodies were hungry for each other. It went on like this, a feverish exploration that terminated in laughter as they rolled back onto the big flat motel bed.

For Alan it was a dream being in a motel with so handsome a stranger, having sex. Trying to have sex, because Alan was overtaken by a strange feeling of not responding to this beautiful, strange man who was more magnificent physically than anyone he could remember being with. It was a gift, a strange talisman, a sleight of hand like a rainbow seen very quickly then not there.

Alan the beach boy quickly established that he would not be kissed, sucked or fucked. This gave him even greater pause as he wondered what exactly they were to do. And he had no excitement. Or rather his sweeter excitement came from the warmth of flesh, the pleasure of touch.

They lay there, breathing heavily, sweating in the heat, a stalemate.

The beach boy said, 'Do I smell? Have I got a gooby at the end of my nose? Am I so ugly?'

'No no no no,' Alan kissed his arm lightly. 'We don't *have* to fuck, you know. It doesn't matter. This . . . this is nice . . . just being with you.'

The beach boy paused and looked deep into Alan's eyes. 'I could really lose my head over a bloke like you,' he murmured slowly.

They had a shower and acquainted themselves with each other's body. It was a quiet moment, almost introspective, as hand touched flesh, Braille of lost moments.

Underpants, shorts, T-shirt, jandals . . . little by little, like a film oddly in reverse, the beach boy slipped back into the guise of the stranger outside the room, on the street – till he stood, bag over shoulder, ready to go. But their eyes wouldn't leave each other's face as if, in the last seemingly casual moment, each was already remembering the other.

'Take my address in Auckland. Take my number,' Alan said without feeling the words belonged to him.

'What's the point?'

They kissed, for the first time, on the mouth, tenderly, slightly, softly, almost a child's kiss.

Alan let him out by the fire escape.

The following day, alone in his motel room, Alan sought to make order out of the confusion of the previous day. He was in the town delivering a consignment of books. He had only one day left. Yet already, almost against himself, he had begun looking for the beach boy.

One thing floated back into his mind which, at the time, he had hardly thought of. It was when the beach boy told him quickly, confessionally, with the complete frankness of strangers who meet accidentally and know they are unlikely to see each other again, his life story. That is to say, carefully not divulging where he lived, worked, what his surname was – though once, referring to himself, he used what Alan instinctively knew to be his real name. Terry.

His story was of such a piercing sadness that for days afterwards, weeks, the memory of it would bring Alan to a halt in the middle of the street, in a traffic jam where, sitting in his car, the beach boy's face would return to him with an almost shocking power, his slightly sibilant voice tripping out his tale, his peculiar, poignant humour.

That day Alan gathered fairly quickly that Terry was married, had children, worked in one of the huge processing factories that surrounded the small city. Further, he gathered that Terry had one or two days a year when his wife visited her family. It was in one of these rare moments of freedom they had met: it was in those chaotic sudden shafts of freedom, like a sudden uplift of breeze, that Terry investigated his real sexuality.

Terry's story was that his homosexual life began when he was twenty-two, pursued by a silent stranger. This other stranger, a man in the small town like himself, had not spoken to Terry but would silently turn up outside his house as he got into his car, eerily appearing beside Terry as he shopped inside a supermarket with his wife, parking behind him when he visited the neighbouring town.

Terry's own family never suspected, and the stranger, apart from one day leaving a note on Terry's windscreen, never attempted to talk to him. Life went on like this for two years, until finally the stranger came up and spoke. Would Terry fancy going for a drive in his car? Terry asked what for – he had his own car. Besides, he wanted to get back to his *wife and kids*. So the stranger disappeared.

Then a curious thing happened. Terry began to look out for the stranger. He began to feel a new emotion, a realisation that he himself had come to rely on the stranger's presence. He missed him. Painfully. Agonisingly. So badly that he himself began to search for the stranger who had so silently, and over so long a period, pursued him. *Two years.*

The strangers met, as if by accident. They argued, Terry denying that he was now in pursuit. Their argument ended in chaotic, furious love-making, hot with tears, blind with the fumbling realisation of feelings denied so long.

Their relationship after this was whatever two men can achieve in a small town full of eyes, where a mute dissatisfaction translates into a kind of rancour that forbids true happiness or ecstasy in others: in fact, sees it as a kind of reproach.

It ended badly. Without air to breathe – in a landscape of plain, mountain, ocean – no room to move: not even a room. The two men would meet on the wide shingle beach at night: it was there, under the clouds or stars, they made love. But it was bitter in the cold. And the excuses, the unhappiness, the dreams in the middle of the night when he reached out to touch his wife and murmured his friend's name.

That was the sum of the stranger's story: probably no different from a thousand other stories of gay men in small towns throughout the country, Alan thought later. But its potency fed into his life when he returned to Auckland. In the small town he had felt a rare, genuine connection, something more real than even his friends could provide. At the same time, the *tristesse* of the story lingered. Two years.

Slowly, as if forming in liquid, this powerful underlying melancholy came to focus on a shade of blue. Blue of hydrangeas, blue of radiant ink, jeans stiff after their first wash: cornflower blue. And Alan's first glimpse of Terry sitting on the beach, peeling his shirt over his head to reveal the body of a Michelangelo slave. It was one of those sharp tufty days, and out at sea there were beautiful blue-purple drifts, imprints of clouds. It was this passionate shade of blue he recalled.

With surprise, almost as if he wasn't himself, he began to whistle 'Blue Moon' so soulfully that, walking down streets, strangers would turn to look at him.

The chance came to return to the small town. His joy in going back was commensurate with a sense of getting closer to the place where Terry lived. He told himself, of course, he would not look for Terry: it would simply happen, as it had the first time, by accident, but as if it were fated.

He moved into his motel, carefully choosing one with an exit far away from the prying eyes of the owner. He washed himself carefully before going out, bought a bottle of Scotch, constantly glanced at himself in mirrors as if to see what Terry might see on first sighting him again. And he liked what he saw. He was happier than he had been for a long time. His eyes, hair, skin, all had the lustre of assured romance.

So he went about his work, all the time alert for the beach boy's reappearance. It was as if Terry might, at any second, walk through the door of the room he happened to be in, appear in a shop, simply emerge. This anticipation in itself became a form of enjoyment, for Alan, as if it was a liqueur to be smelt first, savoured.

Then swiftly, suddenly, the memory of two years ago revived and Alan began, almost against himself, to peer down the vistas of streets, searching for the stranger who he was convinced would soon appear. Gradually this feeling in itself changed into a kind of fretful waiting, an impatience: because the seemingly impossible had happened. The man called Alan, or Terry, had disappeared.

Alan began to rack his brain for clues he might have forgotten: he combed the phone book for likely names, he even began to walk around the streets, randomly, carelessly, without any design or motive other than the hope of running into Terry again.

He neglected his business.

He missed his plane back to Auckland.

It was a week later. It was as if Terry had completely disappeared: as if, in a way, he had been no more than an illusion, a phantom of beauty, longing, desire, summoned up by the vision of him unpeeling his shirt against the hydrangea-blue sea. A curious feeling of recklessness overcame Alan – he scoured hotel bars, toilets, sports clubs – but it was no use.

He rebooked his flight to Auckland.

He had an hour before his taxi took him to the airport. He retraced his steps and went down to the beach, to that part where he had first met the beach boy. He sat there, listening to the shingle roar. It was a hot day and the sun suffused the sky with a brilliant white glare. He grew drowsy, lost in his longing, which had become almost a drug to him, sustaining him even while, silently, slowly, it was debilitating him totally.

He lay back, closing his eyes.

'*You've got nice eyes.*'

Alan awoke to see Terry's face reversed over his own. He was laughing, either at him or with him, Alan couldn't decide which. He felt the brush of Terry's fingers on his shoulder as he came and sat down beside him. Alan looked at him. They were silent, their thighs just touching.

'I was looking for you,' Alan wanted to say, 'all over town. I just wanted to see you again. I miss you.' Instead he said: 'Busy at work?'

Terry didn't say anything. He did an exercise with his legs, developing the tone of his calf muscles.

For a moment there was silence, Alan letting his eyes be dazzled, not by the man at his side, but by the sea. He noted how the hydrangea blue was changing, quickly, under cloud, into a deeper crushed purple, then back again, swiftly, into a piercing shade of aqua.

'You were just someone I met,' Terry said. 'You were nice,' he went on, continuing his exercises. 'Lovely.' Then: 'It was nothing.'

He stopped his exercises and turned to look at Alan with those eyes, the candid eyes of a liar.

'Nothing?' Alan said.

Terry smiled then, and leaning forward, his back shielding him from the eyes of the town, he kissed Alan on his neck lightly, affectionately, softly.

'Nothing,' he said.

Peter Wells (1950–2019) was an award-winning author and filmmaker. In his lifetime, Peter consistently broke barriers in both publishing (the first gay book written under the author's own name) and film (*Jewel's Darl* showed transgender characters in a sympathetic light to New Zealand in 1986). In 2018, he produced a memoir of his family, *Dear Oliver*, as well as a series of Facebook posts chronicling his experience of living with cancer, later reprinted in *The Spinoff* under the title 'Hello Darkness', which won a Media Voyager Award in 2018. An expanded book version of *Hello Darkness* was published in 2019 shortly before his death. He co-created the Auckland Writers Festival in 1999 and the Same Same But Different LGBTQI+ writers' festival in 2015.

Pip Adam

from I'm Working on a Building

Thorncrown

This is the moment I go to.

It is twenty years ago. We are two young men running through a wood of disorganised trees with uneven branches and roots that spill from under the ground into the path, laughing. We are laughing in the bush, in Hanmer Springs. 'It's in North Canterbury,' we tell our mothers. 'A couple of hours out of Christchurch.' We came here in buses from the engineering school, on a Friday. The sun is spluttering over us as we run. I'm in front. We started laughing when we were deep enough in to be covered. I started, or you started. The bush closes up behind us as we run. We are looking forward to drinking. You've got a girlfriend but I'm not seeing anyone in particular. We're like elves, or dwarves, or something else supernatural. Woodlandish we run and the sun spills on us as we laugh. This is as far away as we've been. We're supposed to be looking for something – it's a scavenger hunt, a team-building exercise – but because of the lick of the light and the looking forward to drinking and us, everything disappears except the laughing and the trees and the sex we're not having. We start to get out of breath and I shout, 'Paul,' and you shout, 'William,' to take the piss out of me but you slow to a jog and I slow to a walk and you catch me up and get your tobacco out of the back pocket of your jeans and we each roll a cigarette and smoke and walk to where we think the footbridge is.

It will be there, and we will write down the date that is on the plaque that is on the bridge, on a piece of paper we were given for the scavenger hunt, but we're not there yet. I look at my watch and add up how long it is, exactly, until we can drink. I'm conservative with my sums. We're away from home and we're really looking forward to drinking. Drinking like we did the week before we came here in a noisy nightclub when you told me I looked like your brother and you told me how much you wanted to have sex with your brother and I wanted to have sex with you – very much. Then your girlfriend came back from the dance floor and you fought with her in the street and we walked home and fell asleep in your bedroom in your flat and the next morning we talked about Fay Jones and how he was the greatest architect, how we didn't have much time for most architects but Fay Jones had started as an engineer and never underestimated the possibility of structure. There was something magical about Fay Jones, we agreed.

Our team will do badly. There is a lack of strategy that, as we walk through the mongrel wood – the laughing still close – we don't see. We split our team into three groups of two, thinking it would be faster and it is for a while, but in the end we won't all arrive at the same time and some of us will stand at the finish line with some of the answers, watching team after team come in together to beat us. We will probably be last or we probably won't complete the exercise at all and one of our lecturers, a man who is decent and courageous, will explain the point of the scavenger hunt and how it demonstrates something bigger, something that will be useful when we are all working as engineers. Our team will be a good example of a bad example.

Then it will be time for drinking. We will drink and drink, finally and with purpose. I will fall down in the car park and won't be able to get up and I'll moan. My mind will be completely alert but my body won't work. You will call me a pussy and say I can't handle my drink and help me up. Large parts of my body will press against large parts of your body and you will tell me again, softly and in my ear, how much I look like your brother and we will laugh.

When we get back to Christchurch we will go to more bars and you will move into Donna's flat and I will sleep with one of the women you flat with. This will upset you greatly. We'll have a loud, drunk fight on the street outside a bar. I'll spit at you and you'll push me. I'll regain my footing and punch you in the face and in the stomach. You'll recover quickly and grab the back of my head with both your hands and smash your head into my head, splitting it open from above my hairline to the top of my eyebrow. This will end the fight. After stitching and time it never closes properly and any time I want to think of you, I have you under my fingers as I sweep my hair out of my eyes.

You will sleep with someone who looks like your sister, if your sister is a blond woman with no hips who isn't Donna. You tell me you woke up with her, but you can't be sure. I'll say, 'Oh you can be sure.' Neither of us will know why you've come to me. I will pick a piece of tobacco off my tongue and look out over the backyard of the blond woman's flat, but not yet.

Now, we are walking in silence, smoking, toward the bridge and the plaque and 1902. Without looking up you say, 'This is bullshit,' and I laugh in a snorty way and say, 'Nice day though,' and you call me a pussy and I say you're the pussy and we laugh for a moment and you shake your head like it's all bullshit. I slow barely so you're leading and I can see you, even when I'm looking down. This is the moment I go to now. I watch the silent swing of you as you walk down the path through the ferns and the short trees and part of me knows we will never be together like this again.

As we walked that day you told me sometimes you imagine both of us are dead, and as we walked I imagined you imagining we are dead, and this is what it looked like then and, to my surprise, this is exactly what it looks like now.

The low green bushes straighten and grow into another hemisphere's wood. Our imagined Ozarks. Their branches become ordered and high up. They thin, so the sun comes in in sheets then is gone and it is cold. The noise of our walking feet changes as they land on dusts, then centimetres, then metres of snow that suck our feet back each time we take a step, like sand. We've never seen snow like this. We grow older as we walk through the unseasonal brightness – years adjust us as we walk. Eventually we're wearing the dress pants and dress shoes and collared shirts that we left the office in. That we lie in now. We're grown men, structural engineers, you're married to Donna, you have children, but I'm not seeing anyone in particular. People assume I'm with Craig – you do and Donna does – but it's a front, just like your family home and your kids, just like my indifference to you.

There's been an accident; something we built has failed. You can't find your camera and we have stopped, finally, fighting. I pull my short, cotton shirtsleeves in vain over my skinny arms, you fold yours over your chest but neither of us blow on our hands or stop and jump because nothing can hurt us now. I try your name slowly in the vapoury air, making a big deal of the plosive then leaving my mouth open for the cold to come in – 'Paul' – and it is round and large and floats. I walk through it. You try mine with the same theatrical start, 'Will He Um.' We laugh again and look at each other. Everyone we know is dead to us because they're alive. You know where you're going and as the snow falls suddenly from nowhere and in all directions I follow you up an incline, digging my thin-soled leather shoes deep into the snow, cutting steps like you.

I look at you as you reach the top and the light of Thorncrown warms your face and as I climb and look to where the light is coming from, the chapel grows from Ozark mountain stone, like trees do – close and slight until, when my feet find level ground, it stands in front of me properly made. Lying along the slope, the building has one glass wall facing the valley. Its opposite wall faces the rocky, wooded hillside. Now that it's here, if you took it away, it would look like the hill had fallen.

In plan it's no more than a single room, in form no more than a gabled shed, but it lifts our cold, still hearts to its highest pitch where they stop, pulled back with all the forces by the parade of cross-braced structural frames coupled into the steep roof. Like the opposite of a Gothic cathedral, it is landing rather than flying. Pulled together by light interior members in tension rather than pushed together by outside mass.

One clear symmetry calls itself out of the lattice storm. Two diagonal crosses – saltires like other ordinaries extended to the edges of the field, opening up large diamonds, triangles. Repeated and repeated, rattling on our eyes: slim stands of wood arranged again and again into the same strange truss. I count it off: the timber posts down each side of the space, the short cross-braced members and their vertical hanging rods. Then, towards the ends of the eaves the long, raking, inclined members. It's not obvious how it works. Some of the members just join to the vertical posts; it's not fully triangulated.

So, if there's a thrust down an inclined bit of wood then its associated post has to bend to take the force of that thrust. There are bending moments but there are no bending moments in a conventional truss. It's not immediately obvious how it works, even though every constructional element is exposed, readable from within and without. Every framing member, every connection, every nut, bolt and screw shows and if any one part is removed, the building will collapse. Even the vertical elements that appear non-structural stiffen the slender diagonal members. It's everything it is, but it's not immediately obvious. It's a truss that's a frame that's a truss.

You're still in front of me, standing as still as you can, shaking in the cold. It's still cold. You turn round to look at me and you're smiling, open and absolute and you say, 'I bet we won't get out of here,' you're sure we'll be changed, but I agree so I can't take your wager. You nod your head toward the chapel and we walk to it because we are going inside it.

We crunch crunch our way to the heavy tall doors, which are open. It's not much warmer inside. The oaks and the maples and the dogwoods shelter us from the worst of the wind and the glass walls stop the rest of it but we leave the doors open and the weather comes in through the holes in the rock. We are completely held from harm, nothing worries us. We look down the aisle to the altar end, which opens to a small grove of trees, a rock outcropping and a steel cross. The frames are high above us and around us. Now that we can't see all of them they each seem individual, smaller, and in their new scale they point out the other small things to us. The lecterns, the pew supports, the door pulls and the exterior cross are all painted in an icy blue. They dance about in the grey-stained wood of the chapel and the trees and the white snow.

You walk down between two pews to a post and for the first time I see that the two sticks of wood that form the columns hold between them a stack of small wooden blocks, one on top of the other. You run your hand over the smoothness of the sticks, then the bump of the blocks, then the smoothness again. Everything was carried here two men at a time – nailed together and lifted by hand. Nothing is so big that it can strike us down. I wish the sun would come out and it does and a sparkle of light rings out inside the roof like bells do. We look up. At both levels where the inclined wooden members meet in the crutch of the cross they stop and are joined by a little world of steel plates and almost miraculously the very centre of the joint is open and transparent and there are jewels of light penetrating through each of the frames. The way the light in the Canterbury bush we were in kisses us, this light stutters down on us – nothing more than light and shade, reflection and transparency.

This is the moment I go to.

Pip Adam (she / her) is a Pākehā queer writer who has published four books: a collection of short stories, *Everything We Hoped For* (2010), and three novels: *I'm Working on a Building* (2013), *The New Animals* (2017) and *Nothing to See* (2020), all Victoria University Press. Pip makes the podcast *Better off Read.*

Rachel O'Neill

Your dead language

My son, Alex, made a will at the age of thirty, a year before he died. While I was grateful he had made a will, I wanted nothing to do with the execution. The execution of a will has always seemed a strange turn of phrase. I did in fact want to chop its pristine, neatly typed and enveloped head off. The ritual of the execution of the will could be greatly improved. For example, the lawyer could simply hand the will over. The loved one would then proceed to the Guillotine Room, place the will under the blade and let loose. The execution could be performed once or multiple times, whatever felt appropriate. My son's will was unexceptional. The only curious clause was on page two.

'I assume you know what he means here?' The lawyer stared at me.

'I have no idea,' I lied.

The lawyer read it again. 'The film you make must be under ninety minutes. It must not be sentimental for the truth.'

The moment Alex died I thought, Who will narrate? Do I still have that photograph of Alex reading in the large rubbish bin he filled with water to make a pool? Will the soundtrack have any human noises, like sighs? The perverse impulse to turn the burden and chaos of ordinary human emotion into a moving image had been dormant for fifteen years, yet surfaced in me in that instant. The impulse came even before I had cried. The monster that I was wanted to save those tears for a raw, unselfconscious moment of insight in-frame. Motherhood is full of acidic drips of shame. Even when I was no longer technically Alex's mother, I was contributing to the great maternal pollution.

Luckily, there was too much to organise. I didn't have time to get my tripod fixed, to do storyboards, to make even a few notes in my notebook. I made phone calls to strangers, who delivered flowers, made caskets for human ashes, and advised me to leave it to the police. I wept for days without accruing insight, except which brand of tissues collected snot without turning my skin into cardboard. Some days I was very eloquent. I cracked jokes about the past, the present and the future. Other days I couldn't speak. I slept for a week of nights in the wardrobe in the garage, because it had been Alex's wardrobe during the long ordinary dissolution of his childhood. I grew to like the way the naked wire hangers trembled above me. The closet was the only place I could fall asleep for a few hours.

Narration

GINA:	Alex liked to tell me that because I tended to manipulate things to sound as if they were true, as someone who was comfortable only with true-sounding things, I would never make a great artist. An artist, he told me, steps back from the violence of a single truth. She builds relationships with many truths. She becomes a perversion of truths.
ALEX (voice actor):	The artist does not get to enjoy the same comfort and companionship, security and sense of coherence that a truth-hugger does. Even after dealing with a tonne of personal shit, I realised I was still a truth-hugger. How does anyone begin to change that?

Visuals, interior: Gina's garage, night
Gina, in pyjamas, closes the automatic garage door. She tidies some garbage to the side. Gina picks up a novel, Doctor Zhivago. *She enters the wardrobe.*

Interior: the wardrobe
Gina switches on her headlamp, makes herself comfortable in the wardrobe.
She starts reading from page 98 of the novel. She looks up at coat hangers that dance above her.

Sound: The garage door descends. The metal shudders to the ground and stops with a thump.
A group of children make playground noises of war, shrieks, guttural wails, explosions, thrusting noises, gurgling.
Wire coat hangers rattle together. The children weep.

My second child, Laura, was always threatening to do things. I'll get my bellybutton pierced, I'll steal a dog, I'll burn the house down. Alex just went around quietly doing all the things he never threatened me with. He got a part-time job, he got a boyfriend, he became more or less a boy. I've always been myself, he said to me, matter of fact. It's not my fault you weren't paying attention, that you had other ideas. Why should I be this thing over that, just because it's acceptable. That's not my name anymore, he said. That's never how I'll dress. Your constant worry is of no use to me. Speak your dead language somewhere else, he said.

Today I met Poppy, the art student. She had a short cropped fringe very high above her eyebrows, like a dark skyline. She drank the long black I paid for. She took two phone calls from a woman called 'Dusty', who seemed to be having problems with carbolic acid.

'If you've dropped carbolic acid on carpet,' she asked me, 'do you know how to stop the acid from going deeper . . . ah, from eating into the floor?'

'Sorry, no,' I said. 'Try Google.'

'Try Google,' Poppy said to Dusty, down the line.

'Sorry about that,' she said, after hanging up. 'So you want me to edit out what again?' she said.

'I need you to edit out the sex. Is that a problem?'

'No, it's just that you'll need to give me a thorough run-down of what constitutes "sex" and what doesn't. You see, I've been in this situation before, and there's been, um, a misunderstanding.'

'Well, I guess, I need you to make the footage R13?'

'And what if the content is metaphorically sexual – you know, like in the films set in space where there are the long docking sequences. Do I leave those in?'

'Yes.'

'Can I ask why you want to edit the sex out of a porno?'

'No. Can you do what I ask?'

'Sure, no problem.'

'Great. That's great, Pippy.'

'Um, Jenna, can I, like, get another long black?'

Narration

GINA: His only verbal threat was something he wrote on the back of a postcard that he sent from Los Angeles. Mum, I'm going to make sure to live an interesting life. Interesting enough for you to make a film about. When he got home I gave him a glass of wine, which he drank very slowly. He seemed to want to spend time with me, which was unusual.

Conversation between Gina and Alex (voice actor)

GINA: What did you do?

ALEX: Too many shows. Too many comedians.

GINA: I watched your performance on the Gala show. You're really funny, Alex.

ALEX:	I'm only pretending. I'm good at pretending to be good at being funny.
GINA:	The skit about the pornographers was . . . I laughed out loud. You've always had a good imagination.
ALEX:	Imagination?

Visuals, interior: café
Gina enters the busy café. She removes her sunglasses. A young woman, Poppy, an art student dressed in hipster attire, waves at her almost immediately, though doesn't get up.
Gina sits down at Poppy's table. The waiter arrives and Gina orders their drinks. Poppy takes a phone call. Gina digs around in her bag. She puts something rectangular, wrapped in a black plastic bag, on the table. It is the size and shape of a DVD case.

Sound: The sounds of a busy café. A police siren wails for a few seconds.

I had eaten sushi with the professor of human sexuality before. It was at a screen industry conference. She was being interviewed as part of a panel discussion analysing the representation of sexuality in recent local films. We had all gone out to eat Japanese after the event. The professor of human sexuality wore a collar trimmed with faux fur. The fur fluttered whenever the door to the restaurant was opened and the southerly blasted in from the street. Everyone seemed a bit disappointed with the professor because, aside from her fur trim, she was not titillating or fetishistic. When someone cried 'Here comes the main dish!', all eyes turned to her as if expecting some lascivious joke. One of the male directors took it upon himself to say, 'I thought that was me! Are you trying to tell me I'm not the main dish?' The professor screwed up her mouth and removed a bit of prawn shell. 'There was something a little bit, you know, about the way she used chopsticks?' someone suggested as we waited for the taxi. 'Nah,' came the reply.

'This is our second meeting?' the professor of human sexuality asks me as I set up my voice recorder.

'Yeah, I met you at a film festival – no, the conference that was attached to it – maybe ten years ago. I probably wouldn't remember either,' I said.

'Just to restate my position,' she says very clearly, 'I'm happy to talk to you and answer your questions, however I want to know why you're making this film.'

'I'm interested in the boundaries in art where there is a risk of moral or ethical failure, and what part the boundaries of ethical risk play in the purpose of art.'

'I mean,' she says, 'your personal reasons.'

'I had a communication breakdown with my son, Alex, before he died. I'm trying to—'

'Why do you say a communication breakdown?'

'Because there were important things that he didn't – that I didn't – communicate, that had an impact on the, ah, level of trust and intimacy between us.'

'You can begin the interview now if you like,' she says.

'Thank you. Do you think pornography can tell us things about the human condition? Can pleasure, the representation of pleasure, reveal important truths about our cultures, ourselves?

'Is it possible to "disinvent" the hydrogen bomb?'

'Pardon?'

'I'm quoting a line from the adult film *Atomic Bottom*.'

Narration

ROBERT: When I first interviewed Alex for the job he said stand-up didn't pay much. This work would give him other options. He wanted to travel. I didn't think he'd last long doing this kind of work, but he took to it like a duck to water. He became very popular with our online customers. The landscape has changed quite a bit with video on demand. He mentioned you, actually, in that first interview. 'My mum's a filmmaker,' he said.

GINA: I bet he laughed.

ROBERT: No, he seemed really proud.

Visuals, exterior: park, daytime

Two men sip their hot beverages. A dog runs onto the scene. It drags its lead. Its owner yells for someone to catch the dog. The tallest man gets up and lunges at the dog lead. He catches it. The two men pet the dog while the breathless owner jogs over and takes possession of it.

The men walk and hold hands.

Close-up: the couple making intimate, nervous eye contact.

Sound: continuing banal office ambiance.
FX: sound of lush verdant leaves thrashing in the air.
Vivid note of orgasm.

Rachel O'Neill (she / her / they / them) is a Pākehā non-binary queer filmmaker, writer and artist who was raised in the Waikato. Rachel collaborates with other filmmakers, writers and artists on films, exhibitions and books, and they are a founding member of All the Cunning Stunts, a four-artist collaborative group with Liz Allan, Clare Noonan and Marnie Slater. Their debut book, *One Human in Height* (Hue & Cry Press), was published in 2013. As a storyteller Rachel strives to represent the longing for connection, and the humour and strangeness that characterise human experience.

Ray Shipley

Four Experiments

1.
X. is filling out a form for a new job and is asked to select a gender. This is not a simple task. Sometimes, forms will give X. options. Sometimes X. can choose *gender-indeterminate, unspecified* or *other*. Not this form. This form has two choices, *male* and *female*. Sometimes, the reason X. is made to declare a gender is clear. More often, it is not. This form is not for a medical examination. This form is not being filled out for statistical purposes. X. would sometimes like to sink back into female like a warm winter coat – but when they try, it is scratchy and ill-fitting and it doesn't suit at all.
X. checks female anyway.

2.
X. is learning the rules of wearing ties well in a busy and pretentious bar on a Thursday evening. *You should clip the tie pin here*, says X.'s father. *Make sure it isn't too high*. X.'s father is wearing a blue checked shirt, and he is talking with his hands as well as a booming Scottish accent that turns heads sometimes. *The end of the tie should just hit the top of your belt buckle. Did no one ever teach you that?* X. grins, looking sharp. Together they sip their pinots. The conversation moves on. X. wonders how different things would feel now if Dad had planted those seeds of fashion possibilities before X. asked for them. They are talking about the snow down south now, but X.'s father looks distant. And a bit proud.

3.
It's after 2 a.m. X. is with friends in a sticky and loud nightclub. It's been a bourbon and coke night, sweet and strong and full of dancing. But X. is fading, the beginnings of a headache pressing on their eyeballs; a mouth lined with sugar. X. pinballs their way to the bathrooms, adjusting their tie, combing back their hair. There's a hallway with two doors: ladies and gents. The ladies has a picture of a handbag. The gents has a picture of a pipe. X. is carrying neither of those things. The light is harsh and embarrassing. X. pushes on the first door. Three cubicles, all taken. X. waits, aware of every inch of their body. Artificially flat-ish chest, blazer. Round face, no stubble. Small, smooth hands. Hips, hips, hips. X. waits, anxious, stands with their legs closer together. Someone flushes, walks out, pulling her dress down, glazed eyed. *What the fuck are you doing in here?* she asks X.

4.
X. is off to the supermarket for some cold beer. The air is fresh and warm and the neighbourhood is preparing for summer. A kid stares at X. from behind a gate. He has muddy knees and a bucket of weeds and a red sunhat and a T-shirt with a truck on it. X. smiles. The kid says *hey*. The kid says *where are you going*. The kid says *are you a boy or a girl*. X. imagines explaining that it's that kind of binary thinking that fuels toxic masculinity and impossible standards of femininity; imagines the kid's eyes widening as X. tells them that the harsh ingrained polarities of boy and girl means that he might not feel safe about crying one day; means one day he won't be able to hug his father without saying *no homo*; means he will feel a passionate and inexplicable desire to play rugby, even though he prefers singing and trucks and drawing to throwing and catching and jumping.
Did you hear me? the kid says. *Are you a boy or a girl?*
X. says yes, and keeps walking.

The Catholic-Mobile

I learnt to drive stick shift in a van of questionable road-worthiness,
Borrowed from mother Mary full of grace
Who knew, though we didn't ask her,
And who saw, although she was not there, really,
I mean her statue stood on the dash
Hands praying paint chipping rosary beads hitting her or me on the face when I stalled.
Naturally, we baptised the van the Catholic-Mobile.

Jesus was in the front seat in the body of a smoking, cursing ex-Catholic who didn't believe in deodorant.
God was in the back seat and, having not found a working seatbelt, had my headrest in a death grip.
The Holy Spirit was there too – she was the lights of Sumner reflected on the water, the *danger – nature was greater than this cliff* sign that we ignored, she was the sound of late-night birds in trees unseen.
She was of course in the van too.
She was the smell of old incense and muddy football boots, each shudder and kick of the engine, each sharp intake of God's breath, each *holy shit* Jesus uttered, she was the redness of my knuckles.
I learnt to drive stick shift up a cracked hill and down the other side, shouting *save us* as we crunched gravel, accelerated accidentally and by some miracle, parked perfectly.

We tumbled out of the van, firm atheists again, announcing that we were fools and I was better off driving an automatic.

She remained.
In the sand between our toes and the echoes of laughter on the cliffs, she remained.
She remained in the hollow shells of crabs and in the sound and the knowledge of the waves crashing long before we arrive and long after we leave she remained,
And she remained although we exhaled and exclaimed wasn't it so beautiful to have this, and to not have to believe in sea monsters or fairies at the bottom of the ocean or the bottom of the garden as well,
And so we praised great writers and dreamers and non-believers,
And she sighed through the trees and
She remained anyway.

Ray Shipley is an Ōtautahi-based comedian, poet and librarian. Ray was a Billy T Award nominee in 2019, for their stand-up comedy show *All This Crying Is Making Me Hungry*. Ray has won the Christchurch Poetry Slam four times, and placed third nationally in 2018. When they're not writing or performing, Ray works in a very beautiful and sunny library, recommending books and helping people to operate the photocopier.

Rebecca Hawkes

Fairy floss

How freely we had galloped past the nightclubs
in our cheap rainbow dresses   drunk on fresh legislation

in a country that more or less wanted us
to have a future   One with a ring on it

one we could pash in   in front of our families
and local priests   to light respectable applause

We were just girls   with real proof of ID
klutzy succulent godawful eighteen

and god forbid   we truly believed
we were daring   Belting out showtunes like

borrowed Broadway identities   but we were citizens damnit
seizing the streets like   Take me baby   or leave me

We could tell everything was always getting better
the good in the world ratcheting upwards permanently

not understanding what we'd been given   with eventual grace
though so obviously late   could be up for further debate

We thought pride was a party   We were just girls
fashioning fairy wings out of spun sugar from a corporate-

sponsored multicolour candyfloss machine at the parade
Those wings dissolved in any wet air   the dew in the breath

or on the tongue   until we forgot they were there
Twin stains of sticky colour on our shoulderblades

Still this was a country of tongues wanting a hot lick of us
and our   sensitive   hot-button issues

Hands held   clammy in a gust of slurs down our necks
in a city of breezes   that lifted my sweetheart's skirts

and carried her over the sea   Sometimes
if you look beyond the light pollution   this whole galaxy

is just so many leftover smears of her
bubblegum-flavoured toothpaste   the radiant

travel-brochure blue that oceans never are   enriched
with calcium and edible glitter   that stuck to our teeth when we kissed

Quad bike farm tour

She drives and I straddle behind her, our helmets
knocking together. My hands cramp white-knuckled
behind me, gripping the bike by its metallic pelvis

rather than leaning in and holding her.
Nevertheless the bike shudders our hips
damnably close in the seat's worn incline.

My shorts ride up. Weathered cracks in the vinyl
pinch at my thighs. Her calves chafe red
in a scaly ring at the opening of her gumboots.

She has shaved her legs without moisturising.
They have the flaky silver sheen of sandblasted driftwood.
Stomping down the gear change,

she slackens her accelerator wrist and rolls to a lurching stop
at the gate. Waits, revs her impatience before I realise
it's my job to dismount, to unlatch the fastening.

Dust and zinc powder crease deep into my fumbling
palms. Soon we are unstrung
from the powerlines that prop up the sky elsewhere.

Blooming gorse conducts its yellow current up the valley.
Her domain crackles around us, percussive
with bursting seed pods and a steady pulse of bees.

The bike purrs through the country. She's cocky,
speeding us in drifts up the metal road and rutted tussock paddocks.
She takes the crest of a hill too fast

and the bike rears up. The hind wheels threaten
to lose traction. She throws her weight
forward and tries to wrestle hulking metal

down by its handlebars. Yells at me to jump
and I don't even say how high, I just launch myself from the seat
as though my body already knew what she wanted from me.

Dairy queen

you're the other shedhand on the early milking shift
and you work shirtless
under your heavy rubber apron
which I appreciate from behind –
muscles moving under your tan
perspiring glossy as a cold can of golden pash
unfortunately the overall effect is ruined
by your bleach-blonde dreadlocks Grinch fingers
dyed greenish by weeks of cowpat splashback

the splatter of digested turnip this morning has a smell so strong I can hear it
as though my teeth are thirty crystal glasses and somebody
is tracing a finger along them
with skill and ease maybe dear colleague this could be you
oh when will you snap off your latex gloves and oblige me

nobody would hear us
over the rhythmic chug of teat pumps with their fake baby suck
musical lactation Fleshlights syncopated with radio blare
Lana del Rey wailing
her popular summertime sadness
I am troubled that some sadnesses are more adorable than others
I am tired of loving people for theirs
I resent asking to be loved in spite of mine
all summer
I've been skittish and gentle like a puppy
saying hello by resting my whole mouth around your hand but not biting

this is the only responsible form of tenderness –
hands limp with trust in each other's mouths
but practising secret reflexes just in case
fangs clamp sharp don't call it cynical
even though we are all secretly untrustworthy I still advocate for getting
vulnerable
particularly when I'm
4am shift delirious
highly caffeinated
ripe with morning

through a slit in the corrugated iron
the moon is bright pumice bobbing in a darkness bathtub
I want to shuck off my gumboots and scrub my feet on it

I want to climb into the feed troughs while you pull the chute
so I am bathed in barley seed and spurts of molasses
it would be the gushiest ever
the cows could lick me clean

we milk the sick girls last
their udders so sore and swollen with mastitis that they jog pendulously
to their places by the milking cups to hurry us
their milk comes out mixed with blood
the safe lurid pink of a strawberry milkshake
frothing into a bucket
it looks so gross
but so sweet

Rebecca Hawkes is a queer Pākehā poet and painter. Raised on a sheep and beef farm near Methven, she now lives and works in Wellington. Her first chapbook *Softcore Coldsores* was in *AUP New Poets 5* in 2019 and her work has been widely published in Aotearoa. She edits the literary journal *Sweet Mammalian*.

Renée

from The Skeleton Woman

The Skeleton Woman has survived the first round of the Stacy, where the judges look at photographs and choose what they want to see in the flesh, as it were. The Skeleton Woman is dancing, top hat at a jaunty angle, cane held just so, both legs off the ground in one of those leaps you see dancers do that makes them appear to be floating. Behind her is a skyline that at first appears to be a city; a closer look reveals that it's a river with blotches of light, silver and gold and blue lights. The river merges with trees and ends on the right in a stark area with stones and a large bird. Three borders frame the work. The middle one has keys, boxes, envelopes, diaries, cupboards, letters, all the items that conceal secrets appliquéd on it. The other two are the same deep bluey purple. It's worked in hand and machine appliqué and embroidery with various flourishes of beads, sequins and buttons.

'Dramatic,' Olga said, 'beautifully dramatic but sinister.' She suggested Rose have a card printed explaining the story of the Skeleton Woman and that this is sent with the slide of the hanging when it's couriered up to Auckland for the first judging.

Rose thinks the more mystery the better. The trouble with most people is that they shy away from mental effort. Rose shies away from emotional effort, but that's a different matter.

Or so Rose thinks.

Now Rose waits for the organiser's letter telling her how her hanging has fared. It's her first big competition so she can't expect to get better than a Highly Commended, but she does want that. Not just Commended but *Highly* Commended. For a week now every time she goes to the letter box at home or takes the mail from the postie at the shop she holds her breath until she's inspected the envelopes. Rose is not sure she actually wants the letter. Perhaps it's better to still be able to dream, although indulging in dreams about the possible success of a wall hanging seems almost immoral at the moment. But the dreams will stop anyway once she's received the letter and its probable bad news, and she can stop kidding herself she's made something really special.

Rose's mother Ada, who told her about the Skeleton Woman, would be delighted if she could see Rose's version. Her mother was, no doubt about it, an oddity. A staunch socialist whose hobby was fine needlework. Every room in her house a mess of papers except the sewing room where there was neatness and order, threads, needles, pins, scissors, tailor's chalk, transfer paper, all precisely set out in drawers, all transfers labelled, all books and magazines filed alphabetically, fabric colour coded and then graded according to what Ada called value. Now that Rose is the sole occupant every room in the house is neat, clean, tidy, free of papers, while you can hardly get in the door of the sewing room for the mess of fabrics, threads, rulers, rotary cutters, cutting boards, scissors, jars of sequins, beads, buttons, drawing pads, pencils, rubbers. Rose knows where everything is though, can lay her hands instantly on that small piece of yellow fabric, that metre or so of silver thread, those fine small scissors. She will clean the room up when she hears about the hanging. If she does it now she'll interrupt progress, dam up a channel, impede a communication between the judge and the hanging. Or so she feels. Rose distrusts the notion that one should go with one's instinct, except where her needlework is concerned. Her needlework is the one area of her life that is constant, can be relied upon, is not going to provoke rows or suffer a return of cancer. It can be relied upon to cause frustration, a sore neck, sore arms, tender fingers, headaches and tired eyes, but also huge delight and pleasure. It provides balance. Most other things in her life, Rose finds, sooner or later end up on the debit side with absolutely no delight or pleasure at all.

'You're a pessimist,' Olga told her.

'No,' Rose argued, 'I'm a realist.'

There's probably nothing inherently strange about mixing socialism and needlework at all. Perhaps it's a class thing to think that. In Rose's head, as she is sure is in everyone's, there are stereotypes that have one kind of person getting involved in socialist politics and the other in the perhaps quieter (more genteel middle class perhaps?) craft of embroidery, cross stitch and appliqué. What would Ada have thought of those planes? Of those poor people trapped inside them, not knowing exactly when, but knowing without any equivocation at all that death was going to be the end of this journey. At least with the cancer, Rose had had hope. And so far, fingers crossed, she's OK. Although that's what Sibyl had thought. Rose has an appointment at the hospital clinic on Monday, when the specialist will examine her breasts, her glands, under her arms, and tell her what the latest mammograms reveal. She has determinedly not thought about it, will not think about it until she's walking into the hospital, but Sibyl's news has buggered that plan.

Rose has had a busy Friday. The Book Stops Here had a good day. Perhaps it's those frisky little breezes blowing dust into the gutters and snatching newly delivered copies of *Hutt News* out of the letter boxes and onto the streets so that sheets of it slap against cars and snap into shop doorways. People who felt a lift of the heart because winter has ended now feel that – in view of what's happened in New York – this was precipitate. The idea of going home with a good book, pulling the curtains and settling where it's safe, still and warm is very appealing. Books have practically walked out by themselves. Lots of general fiction, practically a shelf of Mills & Boons and Westerns, that really nice old Bible, some Auden and Spender (sold to the same man) and that big coffee-table sized book of *Life* photographs, which has been in the shop since Rose first opened the doors. Eight Georgette Heyers (coming back into fashion) and at least five Goosebumps (going out of fashion), plus the only two Harry Potters she's got. Ten people had come in with cartons of books to sell, only one of which Rose bought. Some gems there. One, to Rose's astonishment and pleasure, a Margaret Atwood in very good condition, some Marge Piercy and Amy Tan. The Margaret Atwood sold thirty minutes after Rose placed it in the window. When she got back from doing the banking there were these two women, grey-haired, tracksuited, fit, both out for their daily walk. Both had decided at exactly the same moment to have a quick look in Rose's window, both wanted Margaret Atwood, both thought they were first and had a right to it. In the end Rose flipped a coin. The one who chose tails won *The Robber Bride* and went off triumphantly. 'I know I shouldn't be going on like this about a book,' she said, 'but on the way home I'm going to take a Lotto.' Rose tried to interest the other one in an Alice Munro or a Carol Shields, thinking, well, they're all Canadians. No luck. The woman knew Alice Munro was good, but she didn't like short stories, and she reckoned Carol Shields was actually born in the States in the same place Hemingway was born so she wasn't really Canadian was she. Then she saw one of Ian Rankin's she hadn't read and grabbed it. While she was waiting for her change she said, 'When I really want a book I feel as though there's a cat inside me snarling and lunging and I get all jangly and horrible, but once I get the one I want, the cat settles down and begins purring and I'm OK. I've always felt that. And reading a book's sort of comforting after watching television.'

Rose agreed. Rose nearly always agrees with customers.

Rose longs for a large gin and tonic to ease the ache across her neck and shoulders, dull the ache of those firemen's faces with their mixture of hopelessness and optimism, quieten the burning under the scar on her breast, comfort the pain the row with Olga has left in her chest, ease the terror induced by Sibyl's news. If it can happen to Sibyl it can happen to Rose. For one instant after Sibyl had told her, Rose felt a quick charge of relief. This time the bad news was not for her. Immediately she was bathed in guilt, hotter and sweatier than the menopausal hot sweats, which began two years ago. She hoped this wasn't obvious in her voice, but was afraid it was. You got pretty sensitive to that sort of thing when you were the one with the bad news.

Rose should not get cocky, she still has her own appointment to get through. They'd taken forever doing the mammogram. 'It's the staples,' the woman said, 'we need to establish clearly that what's on the screen is staples and not—' Once, Rose had to redo the mammograms because the specialist had not been happy with those ominous blurs at the top of the breast. When he rang to say the blurs were staples Rose began breathing properly again. Then thought, staples? Staples? I'm walking around held together with staples? Don't exaggerate, Rose, she hears her mother say. The awful anxiety between that clinic visit and the doctor's phone call had stayed with her, although submerged, but with Sibyl's news was up above the surface, clearly visible.

Renée (Ngāti Kahungunu, Gordon Clan) was born in 1929. Her first play *Setting The Table* (1982) was the first New Zealand play featuring lesbian lead characters. Her revues such as *Asking For It*, which featured Superdyke (is it a bird, is it a plane, nooo it's Superdyke), were very popular. Her writing focuses on the lives of working-class women. She has received numerous fellowships and awards, including Officer of the New Zealand Order of Merit in 2006, Ngā Tohu ā Tā Kingi Ihaka Award for contribution to Māori arts (2013) and the Playmarket Award for significant contribution to theatre in New Zealand (2017), and in 2018 she received a Prime Minister's Award for Literary Achievement.

Rhian Gallagher

The Gospel According to Longing

Your skill in complexity, your change of course,
the forest's dark boudoir you navigate,
each new doorway you cross saying, *this time*,
and still I await you; on the balconies
                                        I take hold of your wrist.

You say you have learnt nothing from life,
that the heart of winter is the same
as the heart of spring. Yet rain falling over the city
is like a hammer, a thousand pianos at the adagio.
My teeth are not smoke,
                              I am equal to the wound of any blade.

You tug at the knot. But I have your body.
Here is a breeze from the sea,
        your flesh is my prize.

Between

Close in and distant, you had me.
Whichever way you moved
I was swept, arrested.

Between the stay of home
and flight, our poise,
our muddled disarray.

In greys of London light
mid-passage, on our walks
across Brooklyn Bridge

between one country and another
two zones to every hour.
Body into body, that fit,

between the letting go and hold,
your hand all night upon my hip.

Embrace

Unshowered, wrestling with the sea still on our skin
when she catches me, mid-room, with a kiss.
Not a passing glance of lips, but her intended
till I press back against the wall
laughing, in a body-search pose
as ready as her to forget about dinner.

Once, in our first months, we headed down Christopher Street
starch wafting from an open laundry, the sound of a press
squeezing a line along a sleeve. We slipped
across the West Side Highway, out on the pier
pressing our faces to the fence to catch an air of sea,
distant Liberty. Winter sun pouring its heart out
over the Hudson, she stepped into me –
the cold became a memory
smudged under our winter coats.

Two guys stood on the far side of the pier
looking baffled, how long they'd been there
god knows. Gulping, knees undone, we surfaced like swimmers
and almost ran back up Christopher Street
laughing. We'd been gone an hour, the night had come
there were shelves of lights up and down the tall streets,
she was all over me. Everything had turned on.

Rhian Gallagher's first poetry collection *Salt Water Creek* (Enitharmon Press, 2003) was shortlisted for the Forward Prize for First Collection. In 2008 she received the Janet Frame Literary Trust Award. Her second poetry collection *Shift* (Auckland University Press, 2011; Enitharmon Press, 2012) won the 2012 New Zealand Post Book Award for Poetry. A collaborative work, *Freda: Freda Du Faur, Southern Alps, 1909–1913*, was produced with printer Sarah M. Smith and printmaker Lynn Taylor in 2016 (Otakou Press). Rhian was the Robert Burns Fellow in 2018. Her most recent poetry collection *Far-Flung* was published by Auckland University Press in 2020.

Robyn Maree Pickens

Malaysian love story

The first woman said this is a love story /
The second woman said I want to engage in a spectacular mass spawning event with you /

Both were arrested in April 2018 and caned six times for kissing

The first woman said   /
The second woman said   /

Abdul Rahim Sinwan said they were brought through different doors, they were taken out through different doors, as the purpose was not to humiliate the person

The first woman thought this is an architecture of compression
The second woman thought I am the veins of a lotus leaf hung out to dry

Moving in

You placed the glass jar of seawater next to the framed postcard of the moon
—and now I can only see it as a watery planet. This is how it is when you

move in together as a couple. I brought the red vase closer to another framed postcard
—of a yellow Grayson Perry vase, and together we positioned the carapace of a

sea urchin that looks like a vagina in front of them. I think we should bring back shrines
—of our own making. Your aunt found the perfect-sized pink container to shield

the fragile sea vagina as it travelled with you from Ireland to Aotearoa. Tonight I will say
—this is our shrine. You know, I would become each of the four sons of Horus for you

to guard your viscera when you pass (in the distant future). I will guard the four necessary
organs
—stomach, intestines, lungs, liver. This is how it is when you move in together. You must

learn where the sun falls to position plants for maximum happiness. You must adjust
—to the downstairs cough that rises through the welter, the folx living in low-rent flats

opposite who still burn coal and the singe of it on your lungs walking home on winter nights
—and the fat cat who runs towards you in error. There is so much misdirected, unnoticed

love in spam mail. It is unexpected, like a cluster of monks with Nirvana totes over their
slender shoulders. Modified pollen. I would like to communication with you. Like when two

black horses meet on a snowy plain. Steam flaring. We have yet to sage our apartment
—remove any distress oxides, left-behind karma, limbo stop-overs, streaky shadows, unseen

thickets. I wonder what we are waiting for? We also need coasters, stronger light bulbs
—in most rooms, and another lamp. These are as important as a lizard's tongue, the way

it darts in the dark, all sleek, while flowers rain down. Then there are the cobwebs
—the ones along the top of the sash window that we were both so sure we'd clear. How

could the previous tenant have lived with them? Yet here we are, a month in. These three
—plants, sage, cobwebs—this temporary failure of hygiene—belong to the same hand. When

we do one, we'll do all three. Like when I become the four sons of Horus for you I'll
transmute
—north, south, east, west with exceptional alacrity to keep your viscera warm and
honey combed.

Your inheritance tax

Now that I have heard the stutter of your bones in plastic

Now that I have carried you on my shoulder and along the shore—

you silty human, you briefly of ocean—I wonder if we could do it all differently?

I need deep time before it had seed crystals on its breath

I need the ocean when the earth was still molten

If I could make an excision just for us—

a certain deformation of symmetrical time . . .

somewhere between the pollination of the date palm

and the calcification of organised religion . . .

Yes there! Descend me from the nature worshippers celebrating

the curvature of cave

the spoor drift of the matsutake mushroom

the wide leaves of bromeliad and clay amphorae brimming with honey

Let that run all through our bloodlines

Don't scorch me with Sodom and Gomorrah

or insert another daughter in my place . . .

If I could make an excision for those of us?

Robyn Maree Pickens is a lesbian / queer poet and art writer who lives in Ōtepoti.
robynmareepickens.com Twitter: @handwritten_signs

Rose Lu

Notes from Mandarin Class

Three months ago my Mandarin teacher, Li Jing, asked me where she could buy face masks. I didn't know. I suggested the pharmacy, but she had already checked there – they were out. A staff member told her to try Bunnings. She went there and found masks designed for home renovations, filters uselessly coarse. Taobao had sold out of masks months ago, and she thought perhaps I would know of a source that she didn't. But I had never bought face masks in New Zealand. I couldn't recall ever seeing them for sale. When I was in Asia they were a common sight in convenience stores. I remember walking down aisles, passing displays of chocolate, chips and face masks. People passed me on the streets and in the subway, nonchalant in their masks.

Six weeks ago Li Jing tried to give me some of her face masks. A relative back in China had sent them to her. She apportioned some of her stash into a zip-lock bag for me and my household. My partner and I were still planning on going to Korea and Japan in a month. Li Jing had been keeping a closer watch on the virus's spread than me. Airports were a dangerous place to be. I felt like she was more worried than I was, and told her to keep the masks. In class she taught me the Mandarin word for Covid-19: 冠状病毒 | crown-shaped virus, explaining that the virus looks like the headdresses that ancient Emperors used to wear. Over the following week my social media started changing. A Shanghai dance studio I followed started posting online classes. I read a *New Yorker* comic about Chinese millennials posting quarantine cooking recipes to Xiachufang, a Chinese cooking website. A fellow Chinese-New Zealander tweeted: 'the racism that's coming out of the woodworks from this c*ronav*rus is absolutely wild, i'm used to a lot but this is next level . . . like, my sister couldn't book a haircut?? in new plymouth??? she hasn't been out of the country in years?!?'

Three weeks ago Li Jing and I had an argument about whether the New Zealand government was doing enough to contain the virus. In rapid Mandarin she explained how quickly and aggressively the Chinese government had been investigating cases of Covid-19, tracing each new case back until they could link it with an existing case. Later I would learn that the English term for this is 'contact tracing'. I didn't have subtle enough language to convey what I wanted to say to her about the initial cover-up, the reliability of media sources, our differing expectations of governments. In the end I told her that New Zealand is unlike Britain and America, and that I trusted our government to do the right thing by its people. She fretted that New Zealand would be too late in locking its doors, her knowledge of the virus's trajectory months ahead of mine. Later, I received email after email informing me of festival cancellations. My partner and I cancelled our trip overseas. I called my parents, and they told me that my grandparents had stopped going for walks outside.

A week ago I messaged Li Jing asking if she still wanted to go ahead with class. She replied yes; it would be her first time leaving the house that week. She came to class wearing a face mask and carrying a package of face masks for me. I thanked her and took it. We discussed moving classes online to WeChat in the future. I read several articles about the efficacy of face mask usage. They're hard to use properly. Washing your hands is more effective. There weren't enough of them for healthcare workers.

Lockdown was announced scarcely half an hour after my flat got back from the supermarket. The three of us had already started working and studying from home, and we had fortuitously decided to buy our week's groceries at lunchtime. I sent a voice message to Li Jing. As I suspected, the news hadn't gotten to her yet. I called my parents. They were in good spirits; they had been anticipating this for the last month and had been slowly stocking up the chest freezer. My mum said they wouldn't go out today for their evening walk, she'd been hearing too much news about discrimination against Chinese people. My dad said that he had tried wearing a face mask but found it too uncomfortable. He had left China before face mask usage became normalised.

On the day of lockdown I read the Wikipedia page about Taiwan's response to the pandemic. By early March, Taiwan was producing an average of 9.2 million face masks a day. Soldiers had been redeployed to mask manufacturing facilities to help staff production lines. Taiwan had stopped exporting masks overseas and had implemented a domestic rationing system based on the buyer's national identification number. I looked at their graph of cases. It was very different from ours.

On the third day of lockdown it poured with rain. But our house had run out of fresh vegetables. We made three shopping lists: one for Mango, the local Indian grocer; one for Yan's, the Chinese supermarket; and one for New World, the Western supermarket. I would go to Yan's. I prepared for the bike ride, donning my waterproof shoes, rain pants and rain jacket. I hesitated by the packet of face masks on the kitchen table. 'Where are the face masks?' my partner asked, stuffing a grocery list into his jacket pocket. I handed him one. He wore it easily and headed out. I took another face mask out and looped it around my ears. I adjusted the bottom of my glasses frame. I remembered the wire across the nose, and pressed down on either side. Was I touching it too much? I inhaled and exhaled. My glasses misted up. My dad was right, they're uncomfortable. It was too restrictive on my breathing. I couldn't imagine cycling with this thing on. I took it off. I had definitely touched it too much. I stuffed it into my jacket pocket and headed out the door.

Rose Lu is a writer based in Wellington. She gained her masters in creative writing at the International Institute of Modern Letters in 2018 and was awarded the Modern Letters Creative Nonfiction Prize. Her first essay collection *All Who Live on Islands* (Victoria University Press) was published to critical acclaim in 2019. Her undergraduate degree was in Mechatronics Engineering and she has worked as a software developer since 2012.

Ruby Porter

A list of dreams

On Wikipedia
there is a list of dreams
a man invented the sewing machine from a nightmare
his cannibals had holes
in the tips of their spears.
Watson saw a spiral staircase
spinning the double helix
and a French man found Benzene
in a dream about snakes
swallowing each other's tails.

I never dreamt of you much, I mean nothing by that
except that maybe
I loved you
before I knew you
and not much after.

In the US, a penny
and a nickel
cost twice their worth to mint.
We all lose something daily.
We all lose something daily.

I'm not bitter
the cost of you
was not that high
I've turned round the mirror on my bedside table
stood on scales
for the first time in years
in a way, it's all my doing.
In Massachusetts, a woman with an itchy scalp scratched right through
to her brain.

You always fingered too hard
never knew which bus to catch
and this time   my break-up song was
I Don't Fuck With You by Big Sean
and E-40
once
a town was struck   by inexplicable dancing
the plague lasted a month
several died
on their feet
danced right to death
you taught me that.

You can mix purple and brown to get a black darker than black
I taught you that

in New York, the penalty for jumping off a building is death
in New York, the penalty for jumping off a building is death.

Last night   I dreamt
that you were peeling off my skin
starting at my fingertips
stopping only
to tie knots   in my veins
or maybe that was me
but it was you, you I know it
who left me for a man
at a public swimming pool
that lit your mouth full of gravel
and words we didn't know
Honey, they weren't real
I promise, I simply screamed
goodbye
and jumped in with my jeans on.

Earth is the only place that isn't named after a god
Caligula was kicked from the heavens
by Jupiter
a day before his assassination and Abraham Lincoln
dreamt of his death
he could hear mourners
for three nights in a row
for three nights in a row
he could hear mourners

but room after room he found
empty
until he came to the one
with his own body
lain straight.

In Chicago, a man faked his death certificate
to get out of a cell phone contract
please
let me off easy

How to tell the truth but tell it *slant*

If this is endless repetition.
In the gaps,   yourself   and toxins.   Seep into the water.
    Not stand still   he will not see you when you come inside
                                        placed word
                                            over   image.

Look at it. Really look at it.
Loosen the narrative, fill the rooms of the house   his voice
                                        Sunday mornings and

where are we now?
When.
                    (If that word still exists, if it is a verb.)
4 p.m. in December
                by which I mean   the minutes were slow and we were too
                the young man from down the street, the one we'd never met.
            Sections   separated by rhododendron bushes.
Half-finished sentences.
            The union died in the middle of a   strike.
We turn into memories all the time.

And this is where the story always ends
            on the neighbours' front porch and   he's looking for his   keys
    Come at it the other way.
            The back door has a spare.

Where are we now?
When.
Wednesday night because you were cooking snapper
            rice in the pot, three days old.
                    The non-stick pan which always   stuck
polymer   fuming
                (the translator left it out because she thought it was   boring.)
                    He tells me to leave out the. I   am   scant
in every instant, two   but mostly   we experience neither.
                                Don't say that, you'll become part of the.
(How are the insects snared?
        You only *resemble* flowers.)   Unfold, and go flat
                                senses sharpening on the surface
                    like standing in a room where something just changed.

Where are we now?
When.
Over ten years ago
just beginning to forget
calling you from the ports to say
you need to pick up eggs
on your way over
you say
it's Tuesday
dead line out to sea.

Where are we now?
When.
The day that he said was too bright
rain wet and
early why are you here already?
(he is outside when you arrive)
struggling to find the way back
Dad, the light's not even in
but he wants you to turn it off
calling from down the hallway
you and I are in the syllables.

And they still mean things, but not the right things.
Buying cans of dog food,
voices heard from a carpeted floor go back into the house. Into something
that feels like.
There's a still life on the mantelpiece
and he'll pass it on his path to the shower
going the wrong way, to wash off the smell of the hospital
each time with a fresh soap.

(You'll help him afterwards with his buttons)
labels ironed into collars.
A grating against the words (that) still come.

Then later on you'll say *it's not as bad as you think.*
An upwards curve
we are lightning's children
doling out the pills into little plastic compartments, one for each and
where are we now?
When.

Two of the orange and one of the white.
He can recognise my photo but not my face
tomorrow, or even an hour from now
or outside picking the freesias, till there are none left.

eel

in my dreams the Auckland housing market is buoyed up each night
on the backs of a thousand   swarming eels
they say only the American and European varieties can climb on land
scale one another ball up and roll to the sea
but I know the kirirua can too
how else did they find Lake Pupuke
that lake that is actually a volcano   Mataoho's
wet offering to Mahuika
fire goddess
whose children are named for prayers fingers or
mangroves
that lake that has me seeing dead bodies tangled in undergrowth
every time we drive past
and
two hundred metres below
the biggest eel you'll never see
just waiting
to stretch
her
legs

Ruby Porter is a prose writer, poet and artist. She was the winner of the Wallace Foundation Short Fiction Award in 2017, and the inaugural winner of the Michael Gifkins Prize in 2018, with her debut novel *Attraction* (Text Publishing). *Attraction* was written during her masters of creative writing at the University of Auckland, where she is now a tutor and PhD candidate.

Ruby Solly

Both

I've always liked Venn diagrams.
The cocoon they make for those of us who walk in two worlds.
The shape of the waka, the porotiti,
the leaf of the karaka tree
grown from the seed my ancient held in his palms
as he prayed his way across the ocean.
His warmth germinating the plants
that feed the landscape he prayed for.

The shape of the tear drop,
the shape of the spoon that stirs honey into a china cup,
the shape of the pale hand that feeds me,
that washes me, that knows if I am well simply by touch and deep knowing.
The shape of the hull of great ships,
containing women in layers and layers
of thick cloth to hide the skin.

And I am in this small vessel in the middle of their two great waters,
pulling and pushing, owning and disowning,
navigating and negotiating, waking and sleeping.
When I am singing they tell me that I have their voice,
when I am screaming they tell me I have the voice of someone else.
When I remove my shoes and place my feet in the dirt to feel its warmth
they tell me that the fire has gone out,
and that I am just the smoke drifting further
and further away
from the fire it once was.

Lessons I don't want to teach my daughter

If you do not want them to touch your hair
coil it into a knot, and pin it to your head as a crown.
Hold your head up so that they will never see
where you unfurl after dark;
the black waves that lap around your chest,
sewing you into the night.

Practise one-way conversations
so that if you need to walk alone at night,
you can hold your phone to your ear,
listen to the safety in the silence and fill in the gaps.
Yep I'm fine.
He was there tonight.
I'll pick them up on the way home.
I'm nearly there.

Find a mark on your thigh that your mother is comfortable with;
I suggest a freckle, a scar, or maybe a birthmark the shape of a leaf.
Set it as a tide boundary for your clothing.
It is ok for clothing to brush the line,
but it cannot live above it.
It is not a safe place to dwell.
It is not safe for these sea dwellers to be exposed,
in air they may drown, in air,
you may not be safe.

If you are being hit,
your first instinct may be to tighten your muscles.
To pitch them high against your bones,
but this can strengthen the blows.
If after several hits you go limp,
they will think that you are passing out
or worse. They will not want
that kind of trouble
on their hands.

Practise your pepeha inside your head.
Move your mouth with your words in tiny movements.
That way if somebody sees you
and tries to tell you who you are,
it is already carved into your bones

even though they are still inside you.
And if you listen closely
        Ko Tākitimu te waka
you will hear all the voices
        Ko Aoraki te mauka
that exist inside yours
        Ko Waitaki te awa
holding you up
        Ko Kāi Tahu te iwi
from the inside.
        Ko Kati Huirapa te hapū

Rangatahi Tū, Rangatahi Ora

Tuatahi

You say there is dirt under our nails
I say there is whenua under our skin
see us cut our milk teeth
on all the things you mean but don't say
see us go where the wind feels the coldest
see us go where it touches the face but not the back
see us be pushed perpendicular
and survive with our tap roots held firm

Tuarua

One day we'll receive the family inheritance
moko rising from under the skin
Soft hands callousing
from the inside out
as our great-great-greats
work through the blood we all own
through the river beds we all flow through
blue sheets waving dry in the wind
getting ready to weave all the mattresses together
till the whole floor is soft and holding
I will reach out in the night
and touch a hand that knows me
I will breathe out in the night
because for once I want to breathe back in

Tuatoru

Some of us were born tired
and still sleep with clenched fists
you promised me a korowai and gave me a blanket
watch me stitch it with feathers and give it to my children to bear
I will not finish it in my lifetime but I will work through their hands
I will let my spirit drift outside their homes
peeping through the knots in the wood
to bare feet in the whare
and babies on the floor
exactly where they are meant to be
weaving us together

as they crawl through the legs
from one side of the whenua to the other
you say there is dirt on my hands
I say I am the dirt.

Ruby Solly is a Kāi Tahu writer and musician. She has been published in journals such as *Landfall, Brief, Starling, Oscen, Minarets, Poetry New Zealand* and *Sport* as well as having work exhibited in both Aotearoa and Antarctica. Her first book *Tōku Pāpā* was published by Victoria University Press in 2021. It explores how Māori identities are passed on through whakapapa and interactions with parents and whānau, with an emphasis on father–daughter relationships. She identifies as takatāpui and lives with her partner in Pōneke on the old rīwai plantation of some of her tīpuna.

Sam Brooks

from Riding in Cars with (Mostly Straight) Boys

20

Shane's car.

Shane has picked Kyle up from home.

KYLE: Hug.

SHANE: Nope.

KYLE: C'mon.

SHANE: . . .

Nnnnnope.

KYLE: Hate you.

SHANE: Where're we going?

KYLE: Town.

SHANE: Cool.

Shane starts driving.

Kyle watches Shane as he drives. He wants to tell him immediately.

Awkward silence.

KYLE: Shane.

SHANE: Yeah.

KYLE: Uh . . . um.

Huh. Haaaa.

I—

SHANE: How's the flower store?

KYLE: S'good!

SHANE: And . . . Mary?

KYLE: Martha.

She's good.

. . .

How's school?

SHANE: Uni.

KYLE: Yeah.

SHANE: It's uni.

KYLE: I know. How is it?

SHANE: So cool.

I live in this house with like six other people.

KYLE: Six?

SHANE: Yeah, like two guys and four girls. So cool.

My room is like the attic. Or it used to be, because it was a flat. Now it's my room.

So cool.

KYLE: How are your flatmates?

SHANE: So cool—

KYLE: Sounds like everything is so cool.

SHANE: Well they are.

This girl, Victoria, introduced me to Tori Amos—

KYLE: Um, what?

SHANE: You know, Tori Amos.

KYLE: I introduced you to Tori Amos.

SHANE: No you didn't.

KYLE: Uh, yes I did.

SHANE: I'm pretty sure you did—

KYLE: Pretty sure I did? Is that how that sentence ends? Because if it ends any other way, you are like, three thousand percent wrong.

SHANE: . . .

Are you okay? You're being weird.

KYLE: I introduced you to Tori Amos. Ages ago.

SHANE: No, Victoria did. This year.

KYLE: No, I did.

SHANE: But—

KYLE: Look, it's not important.

Drop it.

. . .

I'm sorry.

SHANE: . . .

Anyway, she introduced me to Manic Street Preachers too.

KYLE: Is she fifty?

SHANE: Have you heard them?

KYLE: They did a Kylie Minogue album. In 1997.

Shane snorts.

What?

SHANE: Nothing.

KYLE: No, what?

SHANE: Doesn't really count.

KYLE: Fuck you it counts.

SHANE: Whoa—

KYLE: You just don't like her because it's Kylie Minogue.

You haven't even heard the album.

SHANE: You only like her because you have the same name.

KYLE: Since when are Kylie and Kyle the same name? There's like a whole extra vowel.

That's like saying Shane and Shania are the same! Are they the same, Shania?

Shane goes to talk.

No, not the point!

It is such a fucking good album and you won't even listen to it.

I gave it to you and you still won't listen to it because it's Kylie fucking Minogue!

SHANE: Wait, what—

KYLE: And you know what? Kylie Minogue is great outside of that. She's amazing.

'Can't Get You Out Of My Head' is one of the best pop songs ever.

SHANE: Kyle—

KYLE: Ever.

And even the rest of them are great. And you won't even give her a fair try.

Yet you'll listen to your folksy, indie, boring music shit for ages.

Listen to some new music for fuck's sake!

We've got the internet.

SHANE: Okay—

KYLE: I love you.

Silence. Kyle doesn't look at Shane.

SHANE: What?

KYLE: I love you.

A beat.

Shane starts laughing. It's not a cruel laugh, it's one of genuine bewilderment.

SHANE: You're so weird.

KYLE: . . .

SHANE: Still not gonna listen to Kylie.

KYLE: . . .

Right.

The moment passes without another thought from Shane.

Kyle looks to him uneasily.

SHANE: So where are we going?

KYLE: Burger . . . something.

One of the burger places.

SHANE: Cool.

They sit in silence. Kyle slowly breaks.

. . .

You okay?

KYLE: Oh yeah.

Can get pretty heated about Kylie.

But, y'know, she's worth it.

Haaaa.

SHANE: Is she though?

KYLE: Shut up.

Shane laughs again.

Kyle watches him.

Still 20

Jay's car.

Jay is driving.

KYLE: So that happened.

JAY: Right.

KYLE: No reaction.

JAY: Right, got that.

KYLE: I might as well've been speaking Egyptian.

JAY: Was it ambiguous?

KYLE: I said 'I love you' pretty straight up.

Not many ways to take that.

JAY: Maybe you're pretty bad at saying it.

KYLE: Did you get it when I said it to you—

JAY: Okaymaybeyou'renot.

KYLE: Right.

Silence.

JAY: So is that that then?

KYLE: That then what?

JAY: For you and Shane.

KYLE: Well, we're still friends—

JAY: For you crushing on him.

KYLE: . . .

JAY: Kyle.

KYLE: Sure.

JAY: Kyle.

KYLE: No. It's not.

. . .

Straight guys fucking suck dick.

JAY: Well, no.

They don't.

That's kind of the problem.

Kyle glares at him.

KYLE: Do you know what it's like to have a crush on a straight guy?

JAY: I know what it's like to have a crush on a straight girl.

Kyle hits him.

KYLE: Not the same thing.

It's terrible. It's the worst.

It's like ramming yourself against a sexy, sexy wall that is never gonna love you back, and expecting it to suddenly love you back or that you're gonna suddenly turn it into a door and it's gonna be amazing and you're gonna have everything you ever wanted.

Does that make sense?

JAY: . . .

No.

KYLE: It's wanting something that's never gonna happen.

I may as well want to get a blow job on the moon.

Who's a straight guy.

That's what it's like.

JAY: I don't even see why you like him, to be honest.

He's nothing special.

KYLE: But he is!

He got me into water polo.

JAY: No, fit guys in speedos got you into water polo.

The fact that he was one of those guys is just a fortunate coincidence.

Other than that, I don't get his appeal. Nice guy, I guess?

KYLE: He's just . . . beautiful.

Sometimes he'll just stare off into the distance and it's like he's thinking about something really profound and you'll go, 'What's up?'

And he'll say nothing.

JAY: What?

KYLE: And, and . . . He'll just argue and argue even though he knows he's wrong—

JAY: Does he, though?

KYLE: Well, I know he's wrong. And when he knows he's right he'll be so happy and beautiful that it's almost worth me being wrong.

JAY: Right.

KYLE: Plus he has that accent.

JAY: It's always sounded like horns honking to me.

Have you tried . . . not having a crush on him?

KYLE: Why would I do that?

JAY: . . .

Okay.

What about not having a crush on straight guys in general?

KYLE: You really can't choose who you love—

JAY: You really kind of can.

KYLE: No.

JAY: Yes.

You can look at a straight guy and go, 'Not gonna have a crush on him.'

And move on. It's easy.

KYLE: No.

JAY: Kyle, you can.

How many gay guys do you know?

KYLE: Like, five.

JAY: Not including guys who come into the flower shop.

KYLE: Two. Ish.

JAY: Not including yourself.

KYLE: One.

JAY: Try meeting some more?

If you want to be with someone, that is. Do you want to be with someone?

KYLE: Sure.

JAY: Then go meet some more gays!

They're more likely to be into you than Shane is.

KYLE: You don't know that!

Gay guys are fucking weird—

JAY: Kyle.

KYLE: Jay.

JAY: Kyle!

KYLE: Jay!

JAY: Straight guys . . . they're never gonna love you back.

KYLE: . . .

JAY: Do it. For me. If not for you.

KYLE: Gross.

JAY: Kyle.

KYLE: . . .

Fine. I'll stop crushing on straight guys if you're gonna be a bitch about it.

Jay just smiles.

Sorry.

JAY: Yup.

KYLE: So I decided to try the boyfriend thing.

Met this cute guy called Trent at Martha's buying some flowers for his mother.

Got the gay vibe. In that he was buying flowers for his mother.

And he asked me out.

And I thought why the fuck not? He's cute, gay, available. It's everything Jay wanted—everything I'm supposed to want.

. . .

Yeah.

So, so many whys to not fuck . . .

20 – *Gay Date*

Trent's car.

Kyle and Trent have just been on a date to the movies.

Trent is eager and excited. Kyle is decidedly not.

TRENT: Well, I liked it.

KYLE: Yup!

Yup. It was a film.

TRENT: You didn't like it?

KYLE: It's not his best.

TRENT: It's his best in a while though!

KYLE: I liked *Vicky Cristina Barcelona.*

TRENT: But it's Paris!

Midnight in Paris, specifically.

KYLE: It was fine. Cute.

It's all about wanting what you can't have and all that stuff. Romanticising what you can't have, and then suddenly realising that 'oh no it's not what you thought it was' and he's so much better than that, you know?

He's angling for a fight. It doesn't come.

TRENT: . . .

I really liked it.

KYLE: I'm happy for you.

Left here.

TRENT: You liked Marion Cotillard at least?

KYLE: Of course. Very pretty, very French.

Left again.

TRENT: At least it was short—

KYLE: I liked it!

It's fine. Honestly.

TRENT: . . .

KYLE: Sorry.

It's just down here.

Trent pulls over.

Kyle takes off his seat belt immediately.

Trent clearly wants to say something.

TRENT: This was really fun—

KYLE: I'm so glad, let's do it again—

TRENT:	Um, you're really pretty—
KYLE:	Thank you—
TRENT:	And nice and—
KYLE:	Oh, not really. Look—
TRENT:	I'd love to do this again.
KYLE:	Right. Well, you've got my—
TRENT:	Can I say something?
KYLE:	. . .
	Sure.
TRENT:	Do you like me?
KYLE:	Well, strictly that's a question, but—
	. . .
	Sure.
TRENT:	I really like you. I think.
KYLE:	Thank you.
TRENT:	I'd love to do . . . more than this again, if you know what I—
KYLE:	Catching your drift.
TRENT:	I really like you.
KYLE:	I really like me too.
TRENT:	. . .
KYLE:	And. You're great.
	This has been really sweet.

Thank you so much for the movie—

TRENT: It was so good wasn't it!?

Like, I really liked it. I love Woody Allen's stuff though. Have you seen *Annie Hall*? *Manhattan*? *Bullets over Broadway*? That one's super gay.

KYLE: Super gay?

TRENT: Yeah, like . . . really gay?

KYLE: No, I know what the—

Never mind.

TRENT: He just gets all these actors and, and, and . . . puts them together and stuff.

And it's just so funny and witty and smart.

I wish I was a Woody Allen character.

KYLE: . . .

So, I'm just gonna—

Trent suddenly kisses Kyle.

He pulls away.

Beat.

Trent freaks.

TRENT: Um, oh god.

Oh god, I'm so sorry. That's not rape, right?

Is it rape? I didn't mean to.

You're just so pretty and I like you so much and this was so fun and I just wanted to kiss you, you looked so kissable, you look like you wanted to be kissed and, and, and . . . I don't know.

Please don't call the police.

I'm not a predator.

Kyle kisses Trent. It's softer. Just to calm him down.

Trent smiles, then gets too into the kiss.

Trent makes out with Kyle. It is a very one-sided make-out.

Kyle pushes Trent away softly.

Trent freaks.

What?

KYLE: You're just . . .

. . .

Nothing, sorry.

Trent goes in to kiss Kyle again.

KYLE: And thus started my first relationship with a gay guy.

He didn't play water polo.

Other than that it was good.

Regular kissing, regular sex, regular nice attentive text messages? 'Up2?' 'I miss you already.' 'Are you okay?' 'Did you run out of credit?' 'Is this actually your number?'

Not getting that from straight guys.

I mean the kissing is pokey and the sex is not pokey enough, and the text messages are gross in the tamest way, but it's an improvement over . . . nothing, right?

. . .

But he's so there. So present.

So . . . already mine.

What's the point, y'know?

Sam Brooks is an award-winning playwright and journalist who is noted for his critically acclaimed LGBT work, including *Riding in Cars with (Mostly Straight) Boys*, and his political work, including *Burn Her*. He has won the Bruce Mason Playwriting Award, New Zealand's most prestigious award for playwriting, and toured his art therapy show, *Say Something Nice*, to Australia. He is currently the culture editor at *The Spinoff*, and has had bylines at *The Pantograph Punch*, *Metro* and the *New Zealand Herald*.

Sam Duckor-Jones

Contact

I hugged my dad for 5 minutes in a dream
    I hugged him so tight   I loved my dad
in a dream   & I hugged him
    I hugged this man with a juddery eye
once on a peninsula   & later
    in the kitchen
we were generous with our hugging
    we recognised it was a dream I think
& were generous

On Isolation

Like music practice under the cherry tree I can think of idyllic moments Stripped down to shorts for rays took a seat & went over scores After Bach a soft applause I turned & saw past washing-lines a man with name tag clipboard tight shine hair & professional grin Got up to meet him semi naked & embarrassed but hospitable with a plan to say no thank you turn him away get back to études But Rakesh got in quickly said though he'd come to talk providers he had paused to listen first Charmed I said I'll hear your pitch & pulled a shirt from the line We took our seats in dappled shade & Rakesh outlined exciting savings offered by his firm First I thought his hair was black but as sun became an evening sun & solarised the flyaways I saw it was the dark of brown that's cousin to magenta Rakesh projected savings of up to forty bucks a month first bill on the house Rakesh explained the small print & laughed at the company jargon Rakesh shook his head in disbelief when I told him my current rates Rakesh reiterated the savings at stake & then moved on to sport the weather music travel books & films After signing up (what else? what else?) Rakesh asked for a tune Just before I go he said I'd love it please play something Now a little bit in love I said Rakesh ok & played him the Arensky theme & Rakesh closed his eyes

On Intimacy

Before
when I used to go round with the ocean late night hook ups
drunken punch ups surprising me with a present in love again
the next morning tantrums frightening sometimes I remember
but I like to be pinned down don't you like to be pinned down?

The day before my thirtieth I hooked up with a mountain & the
mountain took it seriously now I'm married to the mountain &
that's a domination . . . of a different colour in the winter
I spend baggy hours paling in his shadow

I did get away for a day last week to south of Awakina the ocean
puffed his savoury chest we wrestled saucily til dusk went to bed
with slap marks all over & kisses in my eyebrows . . .

Old mountain he knows he's a mensch cuckold he's old he
does his best so I guess I'll hang around plus
he's introduced me to this river his mate who is beautiful &
focused driven interested in the world affectionate but
with seasonal temper & on the same page as me more or less when it comes
to a coastal urge

Meanwhile all my friends are
pregnant & getting divorced & dying
I'll stick with this mountain till Christmas by then all the
ceremonies will be done & stale pledges nullified see me flicking
through my contacts got my eye on you Pūponga

Sam Duckor-Jones is a Wellington artist and writer. His first poetry collection, *People From The Pit Stand Up*, was published in 2018 and his second, *Party Legend*, was published in 2021 (both Victoria University Press). Sam has exhibited widely and is represented by Bowen Galleries.

2019
Have u left yet? I'm on Vic St and there's 3 groups of queers waiting here. At least 1 is anti the march.
sent
And they banned the cops!!!
Urrgh..
Just on Bowen Ave now. We're middle of the pack - near the P.A.P.A flag...
FREEDOM! FREEDOM! FREEDOM FOR THE PEOPLE NOW! FREEDOM FOR THE LESBIANS! FREEDOM FOR GAY MEN! FREEDOM FOR TRANS PEOPLE! FREEDOM FOR BISEXUALS! FREEDOM FOR US ALL!
TRANS
PRIDE WAS ALWAYS POLITICAL
I REALLY LIKED THE POLICE'S NON-THREATENING WAITANGI DAY UNIFORM
PROTECT IHUMĀTAO
ONEWALL S A IOT!
urmarch
!!
Sam! What are you doing?! Join in!
What does it mean to belong?
I ask myself this every pride.
Growing up I was the only "sister" in a house full of brothers.
I was always the new kid.
Please make her feel welcome
PARANORMAL PHENOMENON
And I was always the weird one.
I often find myself caught between my desperation to be accepted and my pleasure in being different.

2016
How's the parade? How many corporate floats compared to community ones?
How's the parade? How many corporate floats compared to community ones?
Judith Collins is marching with the police. People are cheering...
sent
CLAPS YAY! YAY! *CHEER* HOORAY! *CLAPS* YAY! HOORAH! *CLAPS* *CHEER*
Judith actively blocked trans-affirming law. I don't understand how she gets to feel more welcome here than me.
Rejection burns.
Even if it's in the form of not being considered.
I think most people in the rainbow community have felt rejection before...
...but that's why we need to talk about it.
We're not immune from enacting racism, sexism or classism just because we've experienced discrimination.
We're not even immune to homophobia or transphobia, despite being on the receiving end of it.
We're allowed to talk about PRIDE
but not about SHAME
We're allowed to wave our rainbow flags...
...but we're not allowed to cry.
How can we heal when we're only allowed to celebrate?
And how can we celebrate when we're still being hurt, and still hurting others?
Apr/19

Sam Orchard writes comics, essays and children's books, and creates animated videos, podcasts and resources with the aim of celebrating difference. His ongoing web comic 'Rooster Tails' has been running for over ten years. Written from his life as a queer transgender man, the comic explores themes of mental health, fat embodiment, nerd culture, trans lives, and caring for a food-obsessed cat. Sam is also the author of 'Family Portraits', a series of short comic stories that amplify the stories of intersectional identities within Aotearoa's rainbow communities. Sam's comics and resources about sexuality, sex and gender have been used internationally by sexual orientation and gender identity advocates. Sam is currently working on his first full-length graphic novel.

Samantha Byres

Where you find it:
A beginner's search for Melbourne's queer kink scene

It starts on a winter afternoon when I cross the city north to west. This will seem important later, this diagonal slice through the suburbs, from my neighbourhood glutted with cafés, big old houses, and hot young queers from nice families lugging boxes up from the organics store at the bottom of the hill. In A's suburb out west the streets are wider and dirtier and lined with abandoned industrial buildings that we'll later joke about fitting out: ropes hanging from the high beams, ropes to hang bad girls up by the ankles. For now, we walk the dog, put a movie on as a pretence, and don't know what to do with ourselves. We talk about our tattoos, and A takes off her shirt to show me hers. This is my first time having sex with a trans woman, and her first time having sex out as a woman. Did we have sex? 'What even is sex?' will become our ongoing joke, as we keep expanding the horizon of what we thought it was. Every time I think we've found the edge we roll right off it. That first time, though, it's clear we're both unsure of what it is, and how to do it together, and where the lines are and what the moves are. 'You can do it harder,' she tells me, and will keep telling me for months, but I don't know how to yet.

Really, it starts earlier, sometime in childhood. Later on, when I'm attempting to wrap desire in thought, I'll read essays about people's experiences of BDSM (bondage and discipline, dominance and submission, sadism and masochism). It often starts with an incident in childhood, pre-puberty. A formative episode, sometimes traumatic. This episode becomes an identifiable start point and becomes a hook for later experiences. Heading into adolescence people 'knew they were different' and 'felt something was missing'. Later, when they discover a BDSM community, there is a feeling of 'coming home', of 'belonging'. The stories are generalised enough to be meaningless, and I don't see myself in any of them. My childhood is more like a haze of low-level discomfort, watching my mother be humiliated by my father, being exposed to the bleed of their sex life through our everyday family life. My therapist wants to call this stuff – my early exposure and access to pornography, the enactment of unbalanced and non-consensual power dynamics, sexual and otherwise – trauma. There's no hook.

Memories are layered one on top of another, obscuring each other. Early in my time seeing my therapist, I remember a group of teenage girls touching me in a janitorial room on a family holiday when I'm seven. I'm not ready to explore this stuff with him yet, although we both acknowledge it's there and ripe for picking, and I'm not ready to link my childhood with my newfound dominance so easily, even if it makes for a neatly tied-up story. Being A's domme makes me feel good and worthy. But on the flip side, it also makes me feel clumsy, inadequate and uncertain.

Somewhere though, in my unsorted memories, is the locus of it all, or at least the thing I can call a locus, and hang my dominant desires upon: 'There. That's why.'

Similarly, there's no match-up feeling of 'coming home' or 'belonging' for me. In the same way that I can't neatly identify one point of origin, I also can't identify a return.

When I ask A about her experiences, she says as well that she can't really think of anything precise. She can't separate her past experiences of sex into neat boxes of submissive desire or desire to experience sex out as a woman. There were things, she says, but it's hard to explain. She remembers asking her parents to tie her up with a dressing gown cord as a child and being told that it was weird.

We turn everything into an intellectual tangle. For the first time, I can't keep up mentally with a lover. She twists and turns through conversations, mixes emotions and theory with deadly ease. Dinner parties with her friends always end up 'interrogating the discourse'. I'm the dumb jock in our relationship, without the raw confidence of the dumb jock.

I flounder. A sleeps over and leaves behind a book on knots and a length of red rope. I put them in my wardrobe where they seem like a rebuke to my lack of ability, and like they'd be useful if I was the kind of queer who liked rock climbing. I take myself, and my intellectual insecurity, to class. I don't tell A I'm going. This pursuit of knowledge seems shameful, like when I was eight and still couldn't tie my shoelaces (I pretended I liked them undone). There's a DIY element to everything A and her friends do: a hangover from their anarchist days, living in squats and dumpster-diving. A can cook a meal for twenty people with a kettle and a few packs of noodles. Dropping eight hundred dollars on a class to learn how to spank someone would be a joke, contributing to my already fussy-femme, not-quite-queer-enough rep. I'm learning that I hate not knowing. It brings on the same wild fear and humiliation of my childhood, when I was clumsy and fat and bullied, daily humiliated. In the same way I run a practice journey when travelling to a new job, I run a rehearsal for being dominant, layering technical knowledge over my uncertainty. I tell everyone I'm doing a yoga class on Thursday nights.

In class, we're eleven cis women and one cis man. We meet in a hot room above a sex-toy store in a busy suburb on the way out east. Our mistress is a New Zealander like me, her accent still strong though she's been away longer. She's been a mistress for almost a decade. She's brought along one of her slaves (the term 'slave' is problematic, something I've seen both addressed and glossed over in different scenes. I use it here because it's pretty much pervasive and was part of my introduction to BDSM. I don't use it in my own practice): a cheerful, red and bearded man in his fifties, who gets down on his leather-clad knees to serve us all water. As usual these days, I find myself in the middle of the age spectrum. Everyone else is mostly under thirty and over forty. There are a few sex workers who want to expand their services. A large number of the rest of the women are newly divorced, exploring kink and polyamory with new partners. One woman is there to add some authenticity to a novel she's writing about kink. She's in her sixties, abrupt and stern. A man sent her Louboutin heels from the US, just so he could dial in and hear her walk down a wooden hallway. Her husband is 'the reason vanilla was invented' and works interstate all week, so she can do what she wants.

That first night is mainly talking. We explain the reasons we're here. We say: exploration, freedom. We all want to escape something: our mothers, our fathers, our small towns, our old friends, our first lover or our last one, ourselves. One beautiful girl will say: 'You just have to keep re-learning yourself, over and over again,' which rides the line of new-age self-discovery bullshit and total truth for me. I'm somewhere in the middle of re-learning myself: as queer, as a domme. I'm as far from myself as I thought I could go, something that does keep happening again and again.

There's a lot of talk about the goddess Inanna, which I couldn't give a shit about, though I know I should be open. A and I will later discuss this aversion to earnestness and meaning as a barrier to truly being part of anything. We're too cool (and too afraid) for the scenes we want to be a part of, unwilling to speak the language and wear the clothes and play the part.

I'm told to think about the kind of woman I aspire to be, and I can only think of Charlotte Gainsbourg. A lot of people say Lady Gaga. The man in the class says James Bond, and that's what we'll call him for the next eight weeks. In the next class I'll tie up his cock and balls with a shoelace, getting down too low as I've been told not to, at blow-job height, where you lose all your power. It's hard to see from up high.

The mistress tells us that she's never met a woman with a real fetish, not in all her research and work. She's written a book and interviewed hundreds of mistresses. Men have fetishes. She tells us about a man she used to truss up with twine, herbs poked in the ties, a carrot up his arse, who she would then threaten to cook. Men want to be schoolboys, caned and held to musty bosoms. Men want to lick the soles of your shoes. Men want to be suctioned into latex. Men have fetishes. She appreciates the current temperament of us all being the same, but sorry, our biological differences cannot be ignored. In saying this, although everything in the class is geared towards dominating men, it can be applied to women as well. I take this, in the moment, at face value. Why couldn't it be? Over the coming weeks I'll learn that nothing fits me and A perfectly, or even near enough. So much of being a dominant woman in this context seems geared towards getting what you want, or what you should already have: your shower scrubbed, your feet rubbed, your pussy licked. I don't want these things from A. Apart from my dislike of cunt worship (when applied to myself, it's tied up to a trauma I can actually name), I don't want to add to my girlfriend's already considerable labour. I'll shamefully and incorrectly label myself as a 'service top' – something that's looked down upon by most dominants and tops as being not quite here nor there, somehow a little bit soft. Later, in another re-learning, I will recognise myself as a stone top and a dominant. I can imagine a future where I get men to do my laundry after I piss in their mouths, but between me and A, the give and the take isn't so clear.

That first class I'll dutifully write notes: 'Use any excuse for a caning.' 'Think about how you want to be spoken to.' 'You own your own want.' The advice I most want to take into my life is: 'Don't soften your language.'

At the end of the class, the mistress tells her slave he deserves a reward. He fetches a small square stool, about forty centimetres high, with a hole in the centre of it. He takes his pants down and lies down in the semi-circle of students. He places the stool across his mid-section and pulls his cock and balls through the hole. That hot, musky dick smell wafts across the room. We take turns standing on the platform, letting it take our weight as we step on his chest, or his genitals, with one foot. This is his fetish, trampling.

Over the next few weeks we'll learn the basics of impact play, cock and ball torture, bondage. I'll see the beautiful girl in my class have an orgasm in a vac-bed, ripping the latex breathing hole around the mouth with her upwards arch. We'll hear about men who work with their dommes for forty years towards the ultimate goal of castration, and mistresses who are made beneficiaries of million-dollar wills for their work, but the work takes their whole lives. Mistress tells us of couples who break each other's collarbones, who suspend each other off cliff sides for entire nights. This is work for true experts. Not for us – we're just dabbling at the edges. We know enough to be aware of how much we don't know. In the last class, I'll take off my dress and be flogged by Bond, so softly that I'll barely feel it.

There's a BDSM scene in Melbourne. We want a way in. We go to kink magazine launches and listen to bad spoken word about pussies and assholes.

We go to rope bondage classes. We go to fetish events that double as psytrance raves, where there's a few limp spankings on the edge of the dance floor. A will often clock herself as the only trans woman in the room. There's not a lot of visible queerness. Nothing happens to us at these events. If play happens, it happens after we're home and in bed. We're not shunned, but we remain our own little private couple, watching from a distance.

We're convinced there must be an underground queer scene, something we catch a whiff of from a distance but that doesn't open up to us. I stumble across a 'non-cis-male-centric' hook-up group who are planning an orgy, but we're not in the right frame of mind. The invite is sternly worded and mentions tea and biscuits will be provided.

I go to a class run by a world-renowned body modification artist. He's running a workshop on kink rituals. The class is run on a Sunday morning in a loft space in Brunswick.

There are six of us in the class. The guy running it is a top-of-the-line example of what I'll come to think of as the utilitarian military Daddy look. He's in all black, shaved head dotted with dermal fillers, tattoos right to the jawline. In place of glasses he wears what look like old-fashioned flying goggles. His calves are wrapped in riding gear, a kind of velcro-leather mix that accentuates how muscular he is. This is what it means to create a 'look', something A and I have been tossing back and forth between us. Who are we, and who do we want to look like?

He gets us to take our shoes off and sit in a circle.

He sits in front of us, and a girl in a robe kneels in front of him. He slowly strokes her face, her neck, her chest, opens her robe and slips it off her shoulders. We watch. He pulls her back against his chest, still stroking her neck, then the tops of her breasts. She's very beautiful, with short blonde hair and bright red lipstick and pale skin. He holds his hand over her nose and mouth for a few seconds and this is the only moment of the two-hour workshop that I will find even vaguely sexy.

For about fifteen minutes this stroking goes on, and all I can think is that her legs must be killing her, bent underneath her like that.

Then he pulls her robe back on and smiles at us. We smile back and nod. The girl continues to sit in between his legs, where she'll remain for the rest of the class.

For the next hour he will talk. He will tell us that when we talk in a scene we 'break something' and instead we should pull the string of fear as far as it would go. He talks about lighting incense before a scene, and playing music. I've read the same tips on setting the mood in *Woman's Day.* Eventually he goes around the circle and asks us what we think about what he's said. One woman talks about tantric sex for a really long time, another one talks about another workshop she attended, where she was encouraged to explore her masculine side. He asks me what I've been writing. I look down at my notes: 'This is excruciating', 'Men are always going to want to talk long after they've stopped having anything to say.'

The legend of male mastery lives on here, like everywhere.

We haven't found the heart of the queer kink scene in Melbourne. Not because there isn't one, but because we don't need it so much anymore. We don't have so much trouble calling ourselves things: we've stopped making air quotes when we say: 'as your "sub"' or 'I want to be a good "domme"'.

We try things on. The staple, the standard, is that she's my doll and I'm her mistress. Below this, I'm some dumb jock and she's my put-upon girlfriend, being pawed at and paraded about. It works because she's a girl who didn't get to be a girl at high school, and at high school I was the girl fucking the dumb jocks. I'm the dumb jock of my sixteen-year-old dreams.

Samantha Byres is from Whanganui. She is a graduate of the International Institute of Modern Letters in Wellington and currently lives in Melbourne. Her work has appeared in *Sport*, *Turbine | Kapohau*, *JAAM* and *Other Terrain*.

Sara Knox

In the Garden of Unearthly Delights

It's April, 1998. I'm in my room in the Buena Vista Palace Resort and Spa in Orlando, Florida, writing a letter to myself. The letter is a series of disjointed notes: things I don't want to forget, and things I don't want to think about. My printing doesn't stick to the horizontal, or to the places meant for writing on; there are words scrawled all the way round the icon for the Buena Vista Palace. Above the silver 'E' of the word PALACE is written:

37-pound white cat

I can't remember what the 37-pound white cat had to do with anything. I've never practised remembering – that was the point of the letter. To put the whole bewildering business away from myself; to defer making sense of what the fuck I'd been doing for the last forty-eight hours with a guy who was ex-CIA and ex-Army Intelligence – ex-human race, really, a psychically and emotionally ruined individual in the tip-top shape you'd expect for the tennis coach / massage therapist he'd become in the year since he'd been out of the service. The year he'd spent heading back toward the human race.

Orlando's main export then was citrus fruit and homeless people. The homeless people were sent east or north on a one-way bus ticket. I'd seen a homeless person dead in a shopping cart in San Francisco, but I don't think he was from Florida. He had a Yankees cap on, and no tan. The soles of his sneakers were bald. All that walking, looking for someone to give a shit.

Orlando purged of its homeless was a whiter city than it should have been. White, and clean, and empty but for the holidaymakers and service workers. That was the attraction for the ex-Army Intelligence / ex-CIA operative, that blond coil of sinew and suppressed intention who'd picked me out of 300 people queued for a theme-park ride at Disney World with an opening line that still staggers me.

'I wish I hadn't sold my uniform,' says he, 'You'd look great in it. And it would be about your size.'

I'm standing there in nondescripts. Jeans maybe. A T-shirt. There is no sign around my neck that says: *I'm a uniform fetishist*. He just knows. Much later, I'll think long about that, and wonder. It makes me suspect (then, now) that he was the real deal after all, not just some random fantasist.

Nowhere in that letter is the ex-Army Intelligence, ex-CIA operative named. I remember *him*, but not his name. Let's call him Charlie. Or Mike. Or Victor. 'Disney World's so clean, and orderly,' Victor says that first day, gesturing at the man-made lake and the pink flamingos standing, placid and indecisive, on their reflections. 'I come here all the time,' he says. He shades his eyes. They're very blue, those eyes, like the sky Disney has rostered on for the afternoon. 'Nothing ever happens here,' he says. 'It's safe. There's no dirt. There's no violence.' He looks toward the far shore, where the Japan pavilion has just sprouted Taiko drummers. That thousand-yard stare could poleaxe goats – was trained to do so, in point of fact (or fantasy – I will spend forty-eight hours, then the rest of my life, trying to decide which). Victor is trained in remote viewing. He can sense his way, map-less, through the tangled highways of America, seeing his destination arise in his mind's eye long before getting there, vectoring to the end of the road with some instinct the rest of us don't share. That was one of the skills he was recruited for: a preternatural grasp of space.

He tells me this as we're getting into the elevator in the Tower of Terror at Disney World's Hollywood Studios. The dark swallows us. As promised, we've come at the best time and don't have to share our descent with too many people. I can't concentrate on the sensation of my feet dropping out from under me because I'm too busy sizing up Victor. He looks like a serial killer from the West Coast. He looks like the victim of a serial killer from the West Coast. I can't decide which. I will spend the next forty-eight hours trying to decide whether he's going to take me somewhere and kill me. I'll risk it. Since I'm in the US as a *bona fide* murder expert it would be too much of a coincidence for me to be spirited off by a serial killer and murdered. Shit like that doesn't happen.

The letter I write to myself at the end of that weekend is full of shit that doesn't happen, that cannot be organised into the sensible world. It's my way of consigning to the page what I couldn't say out loud. Before I'd sat down to write it, I *had* telephoned my girlfriend back in Sydney. She wasn't happy, although whether she was unhappy *for* or *about* me I couldn't tell. 'So you had sex with him,' she concluded, before I could even admit I had. 'How come you had sex with him?' That was a good question. I didn't answer it. There was a lot I wasn't saying. For instance, about the aliens. I'd have risked ear-ringing detail about the sex long before I'd have risked the subject of those little grey corpses (I think of them as *little grey*, though he never stipulated a colour), and the larger grey corpses of their downed spaceships. Better think about this later, that thirtysomething me says to herself as she puts down the receiver. Think about it in the light of the everyday, back home in Sydney.

So I think about it later: twenty years later. Now, telling you about it.

Since it was Easter weekend there wasn't a vacant hotel room to be had in all Orlando. Victor's been kind enough to show me two theme parks, and the EPCOT Center, so I figure the least I can do is offer him a bed. I'm still thinking he might be a serial killer, but what the hell. When we're sitting in my hotel room watching television with the sound down I try to winkle some proof out of him. Something to persuade me of the world he's described, the world a GS15 security clearance makes you privy to.

'So, they wouldn't let you off the plane at Lake Papoose, even someone with your clearance, because of what was in the hangars?'

He see-saws a hand. 'I didn't see what was in the hangars, that's the point. But my father worked for McDonnell Douglas. He was an engineer. He saw things.'

'And you have a map of America in your head?'

'Not just that,' he says. '*Everything.* I've got everything in my head.'

'Show me,' I say, because anyone can say anything about anything. It doesn't make it true.

'Stop me when you get bored,' he says. He reels off the script of a Looney Tunes cartoon, verbatim, doing the character voices too. He recites *Treasure Island*.

'Give me the bit where Jim is hiding in the apple barrel,' I say. And he obliges. In the end, I stop him – not because I'm bored, but because I have a muscle cramp from all the walking.

'I can look after that for you,' he says. He spreads his fingers, and flexes them. Army Intelligence trains a person to know just where the most vulnerable spots on a human body are. Just one more of the maps in his head: a map of the fragile human body. Useful stuff for a massage therapist.

When I turn the light out he tells me about the time *his* people sat in on an interrogation as a courtesy to *their* people. Things had drifted to the point where someone hacked the suspect's arm off beneath the elbow. He'd watched the whole thing drift to that point, and beyond that point – to the screaming and the bloody rags catching under the feet of the five men crowding a windowless room. He'd watched, and not been able to do anything.

Sometime during the night, he starts shaking. He cries out in his sleep. I hold the muscled curve at the top of his arm until he calms down.

The next day we go to the Aeronautical Museum out on Cape Kennedy. On the way back to Orlando he stops at a pharmacy to buy condoms. By then, I'm pretty sure he's not a serial killer. He's left the car running, with me in it.

That night, in the bed in my room at the Buena Vista, I take the last long step off-world. The time machine that is my cunt – a time machine that seats only one – takes me back: past the 37-pound cat and the playdough grey aliens in their hangars by the airfield at Lake Papoose; past the Mossad interrogators in the room with the blood-slicked floor. I am brought back to myself with lurching finality. Or back to one of my selves: in this case, the eleven-year-old me, in the dark house just up the road; the eleven-year-old me with the carpet chafing her naked back, and buttocks.

That reality comes and claims me. Since there's no room in it for the blond-haired man who looks like a serial killer, I ask him to leave.

Dawn comes. Before the call to the girlfriend, and the writing of the letter, I call my mother in New Zealand. 'I'm lonely,' I say. 'I don't feel right.'

'Oh pet,' she says, with the breathy voice that means she's got a cigarette in the hand not holding the receiver. 'You'll be home soon. Cheer up,' she says. 'Take a long walk.'

And I do.

Sara Knox was born in Wellington, New Zealand, in the year that country got television. Having been raised in a writerly family (her father was a journalist and editor, and her older sister Elizabeth would become one of New Zealand's leading novelists), she started her writing career as a poet. Leaving New Zealand to take up a doctoral scholarship at La Trobe University, she lived happily in Melbourne for several years, then settled – with a teaching position, partner and cats – in Sydney. Her first novel, *The Orphan Gunner* (Giramondo Publishing, 2008), co-won the Asher Prize for the best novel by a woman about war, and was shortlisted for both the regional Commonwealth Writers' Prize and the *Age* Book of the Year. She is also the author of an earlier work of scholarly non-fiction titled *Murder: a Tale of Modern American Life*, and her poetry and literary essays have been published in *Sport*, *Meanjin* and *Landfall*. Currently she is an adjunct associate professor in the School of Humanities and Communication Arts at Western Sydney University.

Sarah Jane Barnett

The Geographer

Brief Historical Overview

The geographer has come to stay for a week. He is going to run the North Island Orienteering Championships. This is his first visit since the news. He opens his case: 'I'm still your Dad, just kinder,' he says.

*

It is near midnight. I tell the geographer I am going for a run. In the oily rain I sprint urgent loops of the terminal and then hold myself in the marked spaces and dull windscreens of long-term parking. The airport is dead tonight, a stretch of slaggy ash on the bay. The sea is a flash on the grey seam. At a school camp, when I was a child, we played a trust game. A girl blindfolded my face and my feet stretched away in the cotton dark. 'How does it feel?' she asked before her turn. When I arrive home I undress in the porch light. My legs have puckered into red welts, and my ungloved hands are bright and translucent.

*

Through the night, rain beats the skin of the land like genetic echoes.

In my dream a man runs into a woman
with a small papoose. When he was young my father was a runner.

My father is also a woman.

'What makes someone a runner?' my friend asks.

Theories and Figures

A relaxation exercise tells me to shimmy my neck and face like a horse. I close my eyes and try to find my inner horse. He is coal black. Outside cars sluice over the road. The horse is loose: a wheeled wooden mare melts into a rodeo chestnut. Huh-ha like an accordion. I shuck my shoulders and try to be the idea of *horse*: a mane and downy nose, but I slide back into a rider and look up the slope between two tulip ears. He takes off with a glide and push. He steps into my idea of his idea of horse.

✷

The geographer teaches human geography: the bluff of a woman's shoulder or a deposit of hair. He talks about the space between people. 'You'll want to see the competition course map,' he says. He is wearing a blonde wig and a cerise cardigan. It's a good colour. He spreads the creased paper over the coffee table and shows me where we will stake the hills with flags and punches. I study the shape as if it were an ink blot.

In the concrete gulf of the wildlife reserve we park the car. I hide slender orange flags in bushes and behind the corpses of trees. At the stream he explains conservation. 'It's not what people think,' he says as he leans on the bridge. 'Everything needs to change.'

✷

A woman is sometimes the cartographer of her body. She shaves its slow limbs. Her cavities, a great idea, split into descendant branches. A geographer measures the way a bank shapes the water, which shapes the bank's space. At the branch mouth the groin is a shore-protection structure, narrow in width but permeable (openings). His mother's name becomes his first name.

✷

His face is a closed atlas. 'I never know what to use,' I say as we drive into town. 'Use either, dear. Either he or she,' the geographer says.

'Would you two ladies like to order lunch?' asks the waitress.

Models

The geographer once told me that running soothes the tidal fluctuations of the human brain. It helps focus the body until the mind spins like a wheel in water. In the blue light of the morning the pavement is broken with mirrors. The sky is an airless shield over the streets. Outside the Supersaver a woman sucks and balloons a bag like a throat. His mother had a throat of pearls. At the funeral my Aunt Shirley ate sausage rolls and told stories. 'Your gran loved her stilettos,' Shirley said. 'She wore a fur cape while doing the hoovering.' The geographer stood pressed and grey at the coffin in his double-breasted suit.

*

The first day I met the geographer: 'Here she comes, the Queen of Sheba,' my mother said.

'It's the clothes that make the man,' I said.

Questions

A human geographer must condense the distribution of natural complexities. This requires a synoptic dance of planes and levels. My father is a dune of questions: How is a place created? Does the lateral expansion of plume block the distributary mouth? Can a bridge transform a mountain from one region to another? The river has a still surface but flows with moderate speed. We shout instructions over the bridge in echoing cascades of sand. Geography is a field of middle grounds.

*

In one photograph the geographer slides on a jacket in front of a mirror with the help of my mother. For a moment he is his own father, his arms raised. They are off to the musical adaptation of *As You Like It*.

'Are you going to change?' my mother says.

Epilogue

Late evening I cook dinner and we watch a black and white Western. The geographer wears their old dressing gown and Sellotaped reading glasses. They will leave in the morning. With a whistle the cowboy turns his horse, winks from under his hat and rides homeward. As the sun compacts in tangerine slow motion the horse's legs wheel away. For a moment they exist in the air.

Sarah Jane Barnett is a writer and editor from Wellington. Her poetry, essays and reviews have been published widely in Aotearoa. Her debut poetry collection *A Man Runs into a Woman* (Hue & Cry Press) was a finalist in the 2013 New Zealand Post Book Awards. Her second collection *Work* (Hue & Cry Press) was published in 2015. Sarah is currently writing a book on the multifaceted theme of womanhood and midlife: sarahjanebarnett.net

Sarah Laing

Faux fur pas

... who seemed to live such interesting lives.
I JUST ATTACHED THE ELECTRODES ABOVE HER BREAST AND GAVE HER A LITTLE CHARGE AND VOILÀ! BOOB LIFT! IT LASTS A FEW WEEKS – I'LL DO IT FOR YOU IF YOU LIKE.
I hoped, by association, I'd become interesting too.
WANT A TOKE?
I HAVE TO GO TO WORK.
DON'T BE SO BOOO-RING
One night, Drew heard about a party we could crash.
HOW ABOUT THIS ONE?
YEAH, GO GLAM. HEY, CAN I BORROW YOUR FUR COAT?
IT'S IN MY WARDROBE.
I'd bought the fur coat in an op-shop, rationalising that it was better to wear it than to let the poor dead fox languish, having died in vain.
WHAT DO YOU THINK?
TRÈS GLAMOUR!

The party was in a converted warehouse, the guests an alternative, activist crowd.
I didn't know anyone but I spotted a guy that I'd had my eye on for a while.
THE SMITHS
I'd met him at an animal liberation stand, where he got me to sign a petition banning sow crates.
HE'S CUTE. I DARE YOU TO GO TALK TO HIM.
I THINK HE'S COMING OVER! MAYBE HE LIKES THE LOOK OF US TOO!
I FEEL SO NERVOUS! WHAT AM I GOING TO SAY?
I HOPE HE'S STRAIGHT
MAYBE HE'S GAY. HE BLIPS.

HI, IS THAT A FUR COAT YOU'RE WEARING?
IT DIED IN THE SIXTIES!
I DON'T CARE, I'M A VEGAN AND I'M GOING TO HAVE TO ASK YOU TO LEAVE. I CAN'T STOMACH IT.
OH, IS THIS YOUR PLACE?
We were pretty shocked.
IT'S YOUR COAT.
LUCKY HE DIDN'T HAVE A BUCKET OF BLOOD.
I CAN'T BELIEVE WE'VE BEEN KICKED OUT. I'M SO NOT LEAVING.
DO YOU THINK HE WAS BALDING?
We found his room...
CHECK THIS OUT— THE SMITHS!
BINGO!
...and finished off the party there.
THIS BEAUTIFUL CREATURE MUST DIE... A DEATH FOR NO REASON & DEATH FOR NO REASON IS MURDER...

What New Zealand needs

Do you have a character? You need to create a character.
Well, I have one on my blog. But that's not what I'm doing at Metro...
You need to create a stroppy, feisty Claire Bretécher character who talks about edgy current events.
What you do is read up what's been happening in the country & write about that. That's what NZ needs! You could syndicate it!
Sell it to the Waikato Times, the Timaru Herald for $20 a pop - you could make a living.
Well, that's what I've always wanted to do anyway.
So why haven't you?
Oh, I've been too busy.
Me too.

Sarah Laing is an award-winning cartoonist, short story writer, novelist and graphic designer. *Let Me Be Frank* (Victoria University Press), a collection of personal comics, is her fifth book, and she has also illustrated children's books, made zines and co-edited *Three Words: An Anthology of Aotearoa / NZ Women's Comics* (Beatnik). Her most recent graphic memoir, *Mansfield and Me* (Victoria University Press), was longlisted in the 2017 Ockham New Zealand Book Awards, and was published in New Zealand and the UK, where it was favourably reviewed by the *Guardian* and the *Sunday Times Literary Supplement*. She lives in Wellington.

Semira Davis

Hiding

Mum,
you said it was okay
if I came home pregnant
as long as I was not a lesbian

I was thirteen

and it wasn't milking cows
that had my fingers
dripping cream

and if it were a boy
who gave me that hickey
would I still have scratched it
with split driftwood
to make it look like a wound?

Into the garden

come into the garden where your mother
and uncle lean the bamboo corpses
into triangle arches for the beans

the garden where the earth reads your palm
and the life line the love line the heart line
are dirty and mud

come into the garden and watch your mother
bleed into loose denim overalls wearing only
a bra for underwear and nothing inside

the garden full of unmade fishponds
gurgling scratch up chickens
and the smell of fresh depression

come into the garden and sit dangling
on the swing in silent thought of your lost
virginity while your uncle waters the lettuce

the garden where your mother lives
next to the pig sty where your mother lives
for she does not enter the house anymore

then come into the garden and find
the maggots and the bones among
the weeds beneath the fallen bean arches

the garden you've forgotten
because you have been forgotten
because things weren't left forgotten

and you've come into the garden
with a barrel with a lighter
with a diary and you don't want to read

Pink roses

The petal sits perfectly on the curve of her thumb. Vibrant, as if painted with lipstick. She strokes it in tiny circles against her finger. Around and around until she's forgotten her hand is moving. The petal feels like velvet. Her fingers have warmed it and it feels like the silky crinkle of lips. And she remembers the sound of another's breath. That first sinking of knuckles, and the wet pooling on each other's prints. Her fingers part to find the petal bruised, stained brown in the middle with dark lines spreading to the edges. It is damp. Like skin scratched repeatedly till there's moisture without blood. It smells acrid, when moments before it had smelled like showered skin.

Semira Davis is a writer whose poems have appeared in *Landfall, takahē, Ika, Blackmail Press, Ramona, Catalyst, Stasis, Poetry New Zealand Yearbook, Mayhem* and *The Friday Poem*. In 2019 they were a recipient of the NZSA Mentorship and runner-up in the Kathleen Grattan Poetry Award.

Simone Brighton

[Poem]

The O in no
Man

O tree
O sun-
beam

give till
& toil

way
& bramble

breast

vine & bough

world woe-fruited

break
in word
s, cold

caesura dark in dawn

gold arc & pinion

orb for
ever

in line

hundred-honeyed
suns &
bleed silver

| hoop hove

out
o'er
hour
&
pour , our use

still weightless

& unwaited

&
no
thing
stirs

brief burial
sky ;

still lip

& moon loom

an empty bell

torn, starless, shod

birdborn

circum-
flex
counter-
nance

fur furl

gold   pinion   & hoof
                                        shod bright,

                                        all seen as seam,

&
river,
arch,
door,
wave,
hill

Poem

I believe in
I believe in
I have lived one thousand deaths hauled from
through the jaws of hate
(there was a you there standing
standing wearing personhood like a cloak)

inertia is a thing
the first personal pronoun is owned by
the first personal pronoun falls through cavernous space
swing
swim
sing through
exalt for

four time decays luminescent in the slipstream of fingers
fingers luminesce
imma burn
imma burn
imma burn
burn triumphant
in excelsis

fire
space
fire

are you ready to go now?

the thousand sunshines of love
immolating terrible
toward every monadic site ever addressed as you

Simone Brighton is a non-binary, transfeminine poet currently renting substandard housing in Auckland. They (/she) fear God, and are a sometime-musician and medical patient-cum-beneficiary. Their gender is unnecessarily abstract and difficult, which may or may not be reflected in their work. They've been published a bit but that's all under their deadname so we'll ignore that for now, thanks. Their appearance here is also probably news to some people, so hi, I love you, burial-sample-from-rival-dealer-voice this is who I am. Also dubstep is cool, check out my Soundcloud.

Sinead Overbye

The River

it starts with a drip
drop down
a trickle it starts
with a tear – just one

another & then

i'm gone melting

overflowing
with

emotion
&

it's a cliché i know – i don't care – it's kind of genuine
it's kind of the most honest i've ever been
look what's become of me – i've lost my face
my hands my arms
my entire body
i'm losing my mind – maybe –
for a girl who doesn't love me

here's how it began:

we sat together in an empty flat
scrubbing the marks of our year off the walls but not speaking
it'd been too long for words to matter anymore

i put the last of my belongings in two shoeboxes
she said she didn't want to stay with me the night

she said i can't do this anymore it's not your fault
i'm thinking about our future
i'm thinking of a future you without me a me without you

&

remember that time we went to that party
you left halfway through a conversation to go buy cigarettes
that was embarrassing & remember when you started yelling at me
in our bedroom when all the flatmates could hear
that was embarrassing too & when you never forgave me
for the bad thing i did it felt like you were trying
to make me depressed

& that's how it happened
things changed – they always do –
she left with a bag of dirty cleaning cloths

& i cried in the kitchen because
that's how i cope
i have watery eyes always waiting for
something to overflow about

when i was a child i cried about everything –
loud noises from the neighbours' backyard or losing my scarf
in the supermarket or the muppet movie
set in outer space – i was too young to be unafraid but still
too old to be crying at puppets –

& when nan died i cried for days
the sky cried too there was mist rising
from the grass –

& i need to harden up i know i have tried

but already
my body's
dribbled down
i seem to have melted into myself
to have liquefied i'm being set free

i'm becoming liquid flow

&
the flow won't stop i can't help it i cry

& watch my body melt & then keep crying

i started as a puddle – a little pool of a thing –
in the house on the hill on the kitchen tiles
which we'd just finished cleaning

i was nothing too substantial at first
now i'm growing – flowing – into a kind of stream
rushing down the driveway onto the street
you could place your hand in me feel the water on your palms
hear me speak
– here i am – at last – the water is me –

did you even notice
can you even hear me
above the sound of your loud music

i see you cross at the traffic lights
with headphones in
i want to know if you miss me now i'm gone
please
please
look at me

i'm changing fast
watch how
i trickle
down
drop
drip
drip drop
drop

drip

& it's kind of fun
to be undone
to become no body

no thing

pouring through streets
where people go for coffee

& you no longer recognise me
i try to wave
but my waters aren't
big enough yet
for waving

oh & it's been such a long journey

i've grown too big
for this countryside
rippling
carving grooves into the earth

i deepen widen
the land ushers me out
towards the sea –

only now am i grateful for the tears

the grass bows down as i pass

the trees tower beside me
the sand sinks

the ocean is calling me home to her

i release you

&

become the river i was always meant to be

Sinead Overbye (Te Aitanga-a-Māhaki, Ngāti Porou) completed her MA in fiction in 2018, and has since been published in *Turbine | Kapohau*, RNZ, *Starling*, *Oscen*, *Sport* 47, *Tupuranga Journal* and other places. She was a co-founder of *Stasis*, which operated during lockdown in 2020. She currently works as a staff writer for *The Pantograph Punch*.

Siobhan Harvey

In Transition

when she comes out

her parents reject her
as if she's an uncomfortable thing;

a scratch upon a chalkboard or jag
in a cauterised limb. The heart wrenches

in uncaring ways. The mind spurns
those it refuses to love. To imagine,

parents who cast a daughter – *out,*
out brief candle! * – as the villain

in the story of their lives. How could they
rid themselves of this? Close the door

on unwanted visitors. Silence
the phone. Delete the junk mail.

So in transition, the child finds shelter
in a halfway house, where she dreams

of her parents, unresolved and reduced
to eviction and living rough;

while she searches for a different home.

* Quote from *Macbeth* by Shakespeare (Act V, Scene V).

The Past

We belong to the past. Like spirits
belong to the scream, like music

to the instrument and air. *Daylight almost gone*
It seems there's something I should know . . .

The body the child doesn't want. Another
name for her memories: *freak!* Cry of bullies;

weeping herself to sleep; coming out,
as if absolution, to strangers. Here lives

a past the child aches to ghost. Not alone;
we all possess remnants we want erased. Life,

reduced to the present, seems simpler; so
where's the harm? Sometimes, we disappear

'search' histories or 'Facebook' friends.
Sometimes, we are the disappeared. In fault-

system and erosion, the land sets free its past.
Earthquake, hurricane and eruption: delete.

Cardiac arrest, disappearance and suicide: delete.
Yet in open vein, absence and arrhythmia, memory

survives. In magma, storm and rupture, memory
survives. Even the infirm body, weak of heart,

buried and decomposed, endures. Even in Lazarus-
taxon, tuatara and horseshoe crab, even the fossil

remains. Silent yet perpetual as a god, the past – our
troubled companion – never abandons us. Accept it

and hold fast, as a child does their identity. Silence it
and concede, it will haunt you forever from within.

* Lyrics from 'Ghosts' by Japan, 1981.

Why I Don't Own a Closet

There's never been a closet that I've been in
— Harvey Bashion

Because it's always self-assembly.

Because it's always one size fits all.

Because it comes with hidden instructions.

Because it's made of walls and darkness.

Because its doors are always closed.

Because its catches and hinges break
down words like love and acceptance.

Because it's like undressing in public
or writing a poem, a personal thing.

Because one day I woke and deconstructed it.

Siobhan Harvey is the author of eight books, including *Ghosts* (Otago University Press, 2021) and 2013 Kathleen Grattan Poetry Award-winning *Cloudboy* (OUP, 2014). She received the 2020 NZSA Peter & Dianne Beatson Fellowship, and won the 2020 Robert Burns Poetry Award and the 2019 Kathleen Grattan Award for a Sequence of Poems. Her work appears in recent anthologies: *Arcadian Rustbelt: Poets Emerging 1980–1995* (University of Liverpool Press, 2021), *Feminist Divine: Voices of Power and Invisibility* (Cyren, 2020) and, translated into Italian, in *HerKind: Anthology of Contemporary New Zealand Poets* (Editione Ensemble, 2021).

Sophie van Waardenberg

do not blame me for loving the 2003 film love, actually

because it should snow
all the dogs should wear stupid shoes
noses are beautiful
at christmas when you are in love
even when you are a grown man
a body double in a porn film
airports are beautiful
if you don't cry –
the beach boys at heathrow
and people in love immediately again
– you are not worthy to criticise
even the planes hold hands
between their gates
though this does not happen and the flowers
wilt from changing arms I know I am wrong
colin firth and bill nighy and emma thompson
should make better art
snow does not look like that
body doubles probably do not fall in love
you cannot blame me it is maths
to like the 2003 film love,
actually
an idiot in a cold street
unfairly criticised pie
a lobster in a nativity
every possible demonstration of easy emotion
nipples censored by christmas hats
sometimes
we like bad films just like sometimes
we choose bad poems
to read at christenings
and the funerals of loyal pets
and later we are embarrassed
they belong in cross-stitch
in hospital waiting rooms

instead pin them to our child hearts
that love whatever they feel
sometimes the things that hurt shouldn't hurt too much
love like snow shouldn't care
if you can't speak its language
should fall you into it anyway

unfortunately pam beesly I fell in love with you briefly

by which I mean
your season one hair is the easy life I long for.
it is clear to me for one second that I love you,

by which I mean
you are a driverless van full of flowers.
it is always, isn't it, the boy with the stupid hair
with the nose like a good and hopeful christmas ornament
who looks at you nicely and points you
in just the right direction

by which I mean
if I do not love something I do not remember it.

by which I mean
if I love something I do not watch it only once,
but over again, looking to the corner of the room,
the reception desk, you in the chair, tinselbright,
waiting for love to fit itself over you
like a jumper.

by which I mean
five episodes are enough to know I am enough in love
to reverse out of the warehouse and down the street
and into anyone's wedding, destroying the ceremony,
the whole cake. pam beesly, I'm bored of you

by which I mean
it's not your fault but mine
for wanting too little, wanting to choose
an uncomplicated and unstoried love: never
a statement and only a light, one light of many lights
like in the christmas episode you never film
with the tree that is real and decorated perfectly.

schön

my girl watered her cacti until they drowned
my girl filled my house with flowers until the house coughed and fell down

my girl ties yellow ribbons to my hair with her cold hands
and calls me beautiful in swooping german and my girl laughs

when my girl laughs she cuts my life in two and two again
where she kisses me there is love fizzing from my cheeks to the car windows

and we walk into the supermarket at midnight when the lilies have gone quiet
and hold hands past the eggs and milk and cut-price easter bunnies

when my girl wakes up she looks at me close and still smiles
my girl nearest to me in the world plucks her eyebrows and frowns and proves her face

my girl and I, here we are, refusing to decide what to feed each other
in the crumbed kitchen with the lights off

my girl and I spill our egg yolks on wednesday's astrology
forget that we are paper boats pushed out to sea by wistful hands

my girl forgets with me the drycleaning ticket
my girl forgets with me the breakfast cost

my girl becomes a calendar and I curl up inside her
my girl becomes a tongue twister and I curl up inside her

my girl lets the spring in through her hands
she puts her hands over my ears and I remember how it feels

it is nice and nice and nice

Sophie van Waardenberg was born in London, grew up in New Zealand, and is now studying towards her MFA in Creative Writing (Poetry) at Syracuse University in upstate New York. She holds a BA (Hons) in English and history from the University of Auckland, and her first chapbook-length collection, *does a potato have a heart?*, was published in *AUP New Poets 5* (2019). Her work can be found in *Starling*, *Sweet Mammalian*, *Mimicry* and elsewhere.

Stacey Teague

Beat

/\
when
you're
homesick
you wear your
greenstone around
your neck let it beat
against your sternum
as you walk wear it on
days when you can't feel
your power sometimes it
just goes it reminds you of
something vast and enterable
like the ocean that pushes your
edges are you abandoning your-
self your place of birth being
drawn backwards into these nation-
alities at home you walk on the
same ground as your ancestors
you belong on this scrap of earth
you can put your hands into the
heart-shaped leaves of the
flowers with a darker throat
feel the shape and form of
treasures there are things
that good to feel what
you need is beating
against the bone
that protects
your heart
between
the
pul-
ses
\/

Ipu Whenua

we bury the placenta
in its vessel
pressed deep inside the dirt
not only of the land but as the land

*

the woman grows things
inside her / outside her
they float to the surface
creating islands

*

before the birth we etched out spirals
into wood like skin
made shells for eyes
binding the person to place

*

before they came to tame us
she lay on her back
letting her legs fall either side
hips open on the flax tīenga

*

she becomes like all things
that are lost / things
that bleed when
you cut them up

*

he wāhine he oneone
e ngaro ai te tāngata

Angelhood

after Lesbia Harford – 1891–1927

a lady has a thousand ways

across the sea and all day long

beauty does not walk through lovely days

he looks in my heart

I am no mystic

I can't feel the sunshine

I dreamt last night

I had a lover who betrayed me

I hate the people I love

I know a room that's dark in daytime hours

I have golden shoes

I know more about flowers

I lie in the dark

I must be dreaming through days

somebody brought in lilac

sometimes I am too tired

there are tall trees along the road

the love I look for

this morning I got up before the sun

this evening I'm alone

a lady has a thousand knives

across the body and all the way down

beauty does not travel

he looks into space

I am no mother

I can't feel the fire I started

I dreamt a terrible plague

I had a lover who mourned me

I hate the contradiction

I know a room where we can go

I have bad news

I know more about breath

I lie in the water

I must be awake in the night

somebody broke the vase

sometimes I lose

there are lilies in the garden

the love I conjure

this morning I went swimming

this evening I'm anchored

when the day is over
you want other loves
you who spring to life

when the day is ruined
you want a bone to gnaw on
you who are dead

Stacey Teague (Ngāti Maniapoto / Ngāpuhi) is a writer from Tāmaki Makaurau currently living in Te Whanganui-a-Tara. She is the poetry editor for *Scum Mag* and *Awa Wahine*, has her masters in creative writing from the International Institute of Modern Letters, and has published one book, *Takahē* (Scrambler Books, 2015), and two chapbooks, *not a casual solitude* (Ghost City Press, 2017) and *hoki mai* (If A Leaf Falls Press, 2020).

Stevan Eldred-Grigg

from Shanghai Boy

Feeling hungry, I pop out in shorts and bare feet to the nearby shop and buy some yoghurt for my breakfast. Pines Beach has been baked dry and dusty. A hot northerly gale scorches through the treetops. Trees are bending, springing. The world feels very alive. Getting back inside my cottage with its creaky cane settees and white salty windows, I find a message waiting on my answerphone.

'Me here, just ringing with an update about Dad,' booms the mighty mezzo. 'Gastroenterology called to say he's bleeding at his new stoma. We don't really know what it means.'

I press *Delete*. Carmen's words, in a trice, are wiped away.

I don't want to think about my dreary dying old doddery dad right now. I want to go for a walk along the beach. Who wouldn't rather go for a walk along the beach? Above all somebody like me, back home at my cottage, escaped from the cold crowds of China. Carmen and I flew home for a break two weeks ago. Over there, where it's deep winter, those bundled-up crowds are bringing in the New Year. Here, it's high summer. I scarf down yoghurt with oats and apples while listening to Schumann and reading André Schwarz-Bart. Afterwards, I slip on trainers and set off.

The hot wind whistling across the sky.

I toil in the heat over the soft passive weight of the dunes. I come out onto the open seashore. I feel sad, though I don't know why. Nothing to do with Dad. Somehow it's something to do with Pines Beach. Pines Beach seems a bit of a comedown after my having longed for it so strongly while in Shanghai. Sea hisses rhythmically and repetitively – monotonously – onto the sand. Somehow it seems not quite what it once was, before I went away. Now that I've been away it seems – well, a beach.

Only a beach.

A long, grey and windswept beach.

As always, I set off at a smart pace southwards. Seashells are everywhere on the sand. As a little boy and as a grown man I've never wanted to know that all these riches, these thousands upon thousands of shells sown so wonderfully, mark nothing more than a vast graveyard. Always the knowledge has been shoved down, stowed in one of the deepest drawers of my grey matter, while drawers for storing the riotous, the hopeful, have dealt with the shells as shape, texture, colour, symbol, dream. A limey wrack has been made to seem not so much an ossuary for bleak bones – bleached skeletons – but as something that formed geologically, like stones.

Stopping at a wet spot, stooping to tie my laces more tightly, I glance at some little damp volcanoes.

Well, that's the way I thought about them when I was a boy. Tiny wet mounds spouting water. Tiny wet cones. I loved the thought, when I was a boy, that unlike a death-dealing volcano these cones spout life. Now my quick thought is that even a volcano, once its ash has settled, its lava cooled, its pumice eroded, will be found to have fed the land, to have breathed life in spite of its killing white heat. Which makes me think next of breasts, tits, paps of the women of our species, squirting not white heat but white milk – and briefly I feel wistful for the days when I was a lover of women, not boys, and could gnaw and suck away at those silky smooth mounds. Maybe my longing to drink white cum from a hard, yet teasingly soft cock is the same longing.

Anyway, as a little lad I knew about the tiny wet mounds, knew that beneath those small spouts were the living shellfish, but I wasn't quite able to get my head around it since for us who walk on top of the sand, with our skulls in the sky, the world beneath is where we dig holes for our dead. The world of the shellfish grows the other way. The world below the sand is rich and nourishing, a world where you can live and feed and thrive – and then, in the fullness of shellfish years, die, upon which your white skeleton will be lifted by time and tide, or perhaps by the beak of a marauding bird will be strewn on the surface of the sand, that place which for mammals is a place to be alive but for a shellfish is grim, bald, bare, untoward.

I walk for hours.

Dad may well have bled to death by now.

After coming to a crowd of swimmers and sunbathers, strutting, strung with scraps of bright lycra, I spin on my heels and head back north.

The wet sand gleams blindingly in the sunshine. I watch a few gulls wheeling over the waves. Next, lowering my eyes, I pick out a pair of pied oystercatchers. Oystercatchers are often to be found in pairs. Walking northwards, squinting into the sun, I follow their firm, tight bodies. The two winged ones land on the sand, stalk on their sharp red feet, strike downwards with the sharp red skewer of their beaks. They're plunging those blood-red bills into the sand, seeking shellfish.

They catch sight of me coming. They take fright.

Pee-peep.

Beating their wings, they swoop forward into the wind.

I'm peckish when I get back to the cottage, so I sling together some sandwiches and brew myself some powerful coffee. Gnawing and slurping, I go online to open my latest emails. A lot from China. Greetings from students, mostly, wishing me happy New Year. I send the same message back to them.

I wonder about Dad.

I surf a few websites looking for world news.

Has he indeed bled to death?

I feel empty, despite my mouthfuls of chewed and swallowed cheese and wholemeal, my cups of strong coffee. I feel lonely. Why not check out a chatroom? My mouse clicks, a room opens, and in a couple of ticks I find myself linked with Chatwoman.

'Cheers, Big Ears!' she says.

'What do you reckon about Dad?'

'Well, frankly, am feeling wracked with guilt.'

'Wracked?'

'If that's a word.'

'Racked with guilt. Wrack = stuff washed up onto a beach. Just been looking at same. Also just been feeling guilty myself. I take it you mean guilt about Dad?'

'Yeah. Ooh but I didn't know about wrack. We could turn it into a verb cause it kinda describes the feeling. Trash not wanted. Crap on sand.'

'Where's the old guy exactly? Hospital or Palm Grove?'

'He was at the hospital for an hour or two, where they gave him the once-over in Gastroenterology. He's now gone back to the farm for old farts.'

'Okay, maybe I'd better go to town and check him out. Did you take a look at him in Gastroenterology?'

'Ocular contact with Goatman? Ewwww! Don't think there's any need to go that far! Did however take pains to get oral reports from Gastroenterology. How do you feel about this latest blip in his terminal decline?'

I wonder, briefly.

'As always,' I type. 'Nothing.'

'I've been thinking all morning about the things he did for me when I was a kid,' says Carmen. 'Trying to work out if I owe him anything.'

'And what are your preliminary conclusions?'

'To keep thinking about it in lieu of doing anything real,' she types quickly.

'Sounds good to me!'

'Well, it's a tried and true method in our family. How much longer are we going to have to waste our perfectly good brains fretting over this sort of stuff? What's that old codger waiting for? Why hasn't he shuffled off this mortal proverbial, kicked the proverbial, snuffed the proverbial, exited, left, passed over, pushed up daisies, gone to a better place – in his case not that hard – etc? Damn him!'

*

Clicking off the computer, I look out one of the windows of my sun gallery. Too hot in here in summer. A window slightly warped, faintly blanched with its crust of windblown salt. I look at my washing. Shirts, jeans, have been pegged out on a line and now whip back and forth in the northerly. I listen to the whistle of the wind and the sounds of bushes and trees. Pines are sighing, cypresses threshing, willows flailing. Also I listen for the sounds of birds. I hear heron, stilt, crake.

Okay, get going. Out the door. Jump into my rental car.

Let's go to Palm Grove.

*

Palm Grove Senior Care Centre is a solar system of sunny bungalows in orbit around a central hospital, which itself looks like a very big bungalow. Always, all his life, my dad has lived in sunny bungalows. Palm Grove is brand-spanking new. Windows are wide and shiny. Walls are buff brick. Outer bungalows are for old folk who can look after themselves with no need for nursing, while the inner hospital, according to a posted map of the complex, is a *central facility* for those *needing care*. Dad lives in the central facility.

No right turn says a painted sign.

Apartments open by way of glass doors onto wide carparks whose glossy blacktop has been scored by parallel lines and dashes, sharply painted in white and yellow. Staked shrubs, pruned cherry trees, flank the black tarmac. My car and I crawl forward with safe slowness. Glass glistens listlessly. Lawns have been newly scalped. Roses have been ruthlessly deadheaded. My hands steer my wheels to a stop. I jump from the car gingerly. I slip into my dad's room by way of an unlocked glass door opening from his little courtyard with its picnic table. Always he's disliked locking doors. The old bloke proves to be fast asleep.

Knackered, no doubt, by the flap earlier today.

Poor fellow.

I sit. I look at him. His veiny worn arms, whose worms of weary blood still slowly wind over chalky bones, lie limp on stiff white linen. Two rows of teeth are grinning inside a cup. The teeth are blindingly white. Nothing else on or about my dad seems to be a clean colour. Everything else is pinkish blotchy brown or greyish scurfy pink or brownish grimy red or – only those teeth, not his, not him.

Loathsome old man.

Die, bastard!

Dad has been fitted with a *peg tube* for feeding and drinking and for getting his doses of drug. Peg is an acronym for *percutaneous endoscopic gastrostomy.* A hose of flexible plastic – like a slender garden hose for watering roses, which will then want deadheading – it burrows into his stomach by way of a hole stabbed through the skin and tendon of the abdominal wall. Doctors stuck it into him two weeks ago. How do doctors do it? Well, a general surgeon and gastroenterologist working together will drive a long thin needle from outside the body into the stomach. A wire is passed into the needle from the outside, and then is drawn through the stomach and out the mouth. The tapered tip of a peg tube is attached to the wire. The surgeon drags the wire back down the throat and through the stomach, and as that happens the peg tube is pulled down too. A soft round plug stops it in the stomach. One day then needs to be spent in recovery. Afterwards, liquids can be injected several times a day by syringe.

The job of getting grub or drugs down that tube isn't easy. I know because I've watched my dad do it. One day he won't be able to do it himself any longer, and the nurses will have to start squirting the stuff into him. One day, a bit further down the track, they'll plug him into a morphine drip. They'll do that for him when he asks.

'Beware the morphine drip,' was what Carmen said to me the other day. 'The morphine drip will be the beginning of the end.'

'How d'you mean?'

'The morphine drip kills the patient.'

'So why should we beware? That's what we want, isn't it? Dad dead?'

'Oops, course we do! Sorry, slip of tongue, force of habit. Hippocratic oath and all that.'

I sit stranded inside the small white room with the old, withered, sightless, wordless semi-corpse. Dad doesn't wake, let alone look – or speak. After an hour or so I clear out.

*

At the cottage once more, kicking off my trainers, I grab a bottle of mineral water and go online to open more emails. Yippee! Today's letter has turned up. A letter from Jay. My boy sends me emails daily.

What does he say, my Shanghai boy?

'I always think of our relationship and our future. Will I lose u eventually? Read all of your email many times and very sad. Miss U and all of ur body. Wanna touch ur body and hold u on the bed. Write soon! Wanna get ur email hurrily! U know I still remember that the last time we make love, I lie down and u look at my eyes, and kiss my nipples and my chest. I like ur face, so handsome, and ur hair, so soft. U know at that moment I fall in love with u again and again. I wait for u here in cold China. No snowing today, but the wind is very cold! But ur love makes me warm!!!!!! I am honor to know u and get ur passionate love. Are u my lover? Are u my heart?? I love u forever, forever.'

Now, looking away from the screen, I think for a bit about two guys.

One, the old gaffer I've just seen lying lifeless on white linen on what will likely prove to be his deathbed. A man known to me all my life, yet a stranger. A man I don't love, have never loved and will never love.

Two, a young boy waiting for me, with golden skin, with brown eyes full of life, on the other side of the world. A boy who – *the* boy—

Frightening thought.

A trilling. The phone. Carmen.

'I'm sitting at some traffic lights. Hear that mewing sound?'

'Can't hear anything but cars. Why would I hear a mewing sound, anyway?'

'Oops, lights changed! Hang on. Okay, scorching along expressway one-handed now. Let's start at the very beginning, a very good place to start. An hour ago I hooked up with a guy. We first found each other a couple nights ago courtesy of cyberdating. Online the guy billed himself as tall and an air traffic controller. Always been keen on submitting to control, at least when in the mood, so seemed like a plan. We met on Oxford Terrace. Now, as you might expect, the first question I asked at our rendezvous was *How are you?* And he – oops! Am being tailgated. Hang on again. Gonna put both hands on the wheel for a bit and slam my hoof down on the accelerator to beat that speeding bitch behind me – her in her bloody Audi!'

'Carmen, don't talk to me while you're behind the wheel, okay? Call me when you're home safely.'

My words float away feebly while my earpiece fills with a revving roar.

'Hah! Shook off the silly sow. Now – where was I?'

'Call me when you're back home safely.'

'Oh, yep – so we met, and my opening ploy was the deeply lame yet blameless *How are you?* Phatic communion, right? The guy then proceeded to start droning on in an unending monologue about his recent disastrous relationship and how he was depressed and suicidal, etcetera. So he was losing points fast! Not to mention having already lost a lot more when I saw at first glance that he was way shorter than me, and chubby. Chubby, by contrast with me, who am of course voluptuous. Also it turned out that he's no longer working as an air traffic controller. He's not working, full stop. Consequently, I told him the truth. Which is, that I don't want to spend my time listening to the troubles of someone I don't even know. So, after a civil referral to the services offered by his nearest mental health facility, I hoofed it off to a coffee house with the thought that it would be good to drown my sorrows with a double mochaccino and maybe throw in a cake – well, admit it, a couple of cakes – without aforementioned loser. However, a pet shop caught my eye. I walked straight in and bought myself a cat.'

'A cat? Well, that'll be nice and cuddly.'

'Very. Why won't he die?'

'I know.'

'Why doesn't he just fucking *die* and get it over?'

*

One hour later, flicking on the tele while fixing myself a bite of cold tucker, I look at the news. The president of the Council of Trade Unions is talking about Chinese breaches of intellectual property rights. Our factories are having to close down or shift their operations to China because competitors over there keep stealing our patented products. Cut to a local manufacturer of saw blades saying that one Chinese manufacturer not only stole his company's designs down to the finest detail but even copied a batch number onto every blade rather than sequentially numbering the batches. Cut back to the trade union leader saying that another worry is that our government isn't lobbying the Chinese government enough about labour rights for factory workers in China.

Killing him would be easy, wouldn't it?

'Failure to enforce China's own minimum labour code has kept down the price of Chinese labour,' he says. 'If you buy goods made in Chinese factories you're exploiting Chinese workers—'

So tired of waiting for his death.

Bolting down my food, swilling down a beer, I watch the rest of the news. Jumping up, I dump the dishes. I slip on my trainers. I head out for another lonely walk along the beach in the warm screaming wind.

*

Noon next day, having got myself home from a third long walk – this time through a forest for a change – I find another message from my sis waiting on the answerphone.

'Bucket kicked. Call me.'

*

'How did it happen?' I squawk into the plastic handset after keying in her number quick smart.

'Drowning, basically. Water inhaled into his lungs. Some sort of glitch with the peg tube in the middle of the night. He must've tried to get a drink while he wasn't thoroughly awake. No sign that he was thrashing about or anything. So maybe he carked peacefully.'

'You've had a look at his body?'

'Not yet. Still can't bring myself to go that far. We can do it together, holding hands, okay?'

'Course.'

'Overwhelmed with grief as I am, I'm having a latte and a tiramisu. Next I thought I'd nip out to grieve a bit with you over another latte at the Lido. A latte and maybe some of their yummy boysenberry cheesecake. After fortifying ourselves in our sorrow, we can then go back to town together and check out the cadaver at Palm Grove.'

'Sounds like a plan.'

'You're not very chatty. Are you okay? Are you in shock?'

'I'm okay. Maybe it's shock at our good luck.'

'Mm, well, as for me, dunno how I feel, really. Goatman going so much sooner than we'd expected is a definite boon. I'm scared, though.'

'Scared of what?'

'Scared that now I'm really going to have to feel something about the old bastard, and that won't be good.'

One hour later we're walking together in the northerly on our way to the Lido. The wind blows even more strongly today than yesterday. Pines Beach seems restless, distraught – agitated by the hot gale. The boughs of trees are tossing frantically. Hedges are surging and swaying, alive yet rooted helplessly, bound to live and die forever in one spot. We skirt the river, whose silted waters grow while running high between the stopbanks. We pass the lagoon. Kids are screaming, splashing, running in and out of its warm shallows while their mums sweat under the sun. Willows on the stopbanks welter in the wind, heave, send streaks of themselves into the sky, raw branch and dying green leaf, launched by the wind, ripped away by the fiercer gusts. The sky seems almost yellow, yet with low, livid clouds. Black pods on the broom bushes crack open to shoot black glittery little seeds, sending it flying wildly.

'When we look at his body what'll work best for me will be to sit with it for a bit to try and find out what I feel,' says Carmen ten minutes later, chewing cheesecake.

'Me too, I think.'

Yep, that sounds right. Yep, sit yourself down inside the white walls of his room and stare at his corpse. Allow yourself to emote. All sorts of feelings must be lurking inside your skull, waiting to burst out, wanting to be felt, needing to be known. You've got to get yourself in the right mood. You've got to feel all your feelings, finally. All your feelings for that remote and unseeing and unheeding stranger whose name is entered on your birth certificate as your father but who for the whole of your life has seldom seemed more than an ersatz interloper.

After leaving the café we take a slow walk around the domain. Carmen's still a blonde, but it's no longer the colour of straw. She's more what you'd call ash blonde, with lowlights of honey.

'I had a complicated dream about our family last night,' she says. 'Dad sexually abused me.'

Dad *what*? Dad – of course! Fuck. The dirty prick. Shit. My little sis. All of a sudden everything makes sense to me. Somehow I must have known already. Somehow I must have known subliminally. A blink of an eye and it makes sense why we both feel so bad about the old bugger.

'Carmen, you poor kid. You poor baby.'

'No – no, it's okay.'

'It's not okay.'

'No, I mean he didn't. He didn't do it. He didn't do anything like that in real life. That's what I mean by okay. A strictly relative okay.'

'Oh, I see. Got ya.'

Now, once more, it seems not quite to make sense that we should feel so bad. Why do we hate our dad? You could understand our feeling this way if we were the victims of some gross violation, couldn't you? Sexual abuse has a good, solid, sordid sort of certainty to it.

'Look at that gull beating into the wind,' says my sis pensively.

'Mind you,' I try, 'maybe it would've been better to have been groped by him than ignored altogether.'

'Doubt it.'

'Maybe not better, but something we could get a grip on. Something we could get our teeth into. Something other than the truth, which is just nothing. Nothing is all there ever was. Not even the proverbial big fat nothing, just a small scrawny nothing. Something's better than nothing, isn't it?'

'Nothing's the card we were dealt,' comes the crisp reply. 'Anyway, while he was doing it to me in the dream you were standing in the sea watching, holding some banknotes, and when I got angry with you and threw your money into the water you were anxious cause you needed the notes to buy off bullies at school, which in turn straight away made me feel bad.'

We sit in the shade, not saying much more. A slithering tangle of some shiny fine ribbon, caught in the branches of a lemonwood bush, is glittering in the sun while whipping back and forth in the wind. Plastic? Nylon? One of those audiocassette tapes, unravelled, which were a common sight in the seventies of last century and aren't so common now. My mind flips back to those days. Audiocassettes were the latest technology. You binned your big old outmoded plastic disks, disks you'd been spinning on your stereo turntable. You swapped the lot for dinky little audiocassettes, which you'd poke into a plastic slot and then play. Yet not a lot later the audiocassettes were old technology, fit only to be binned. You swapped them for the newest technology, iridescent little compact disks. A lot of tossed tapes went astray. Tossed, they unravelled, like this tangle on the lemonwood. Open spaces those days were often gay with unravelled tapes, glossy and flimsy – like tinsel on a tree at Christmas.

'Hey,' says my sis, 'I forgot to tell you that last night I got a phone call from Godfrey.'

'Godfrey? Who's that?'

'Our brother.'

'Blah, *that* Godfrey. Wanting news about Dad?'

'Ostensibly, but I think what he really wanted was to talk about his new boyfriend.'

'Get any dirt? What's the boyfriend like?'

'Well, the most salient fact is that he's no *boy*friend. He's seventy years old.'

'Fuck!'

Godfrey, you'll recall, is only one year older than me.

'Our prat brother offered a bit of self-psychoanalysis on the topic. He reckons that his preference for an older man stems from the fact that when he was a kid he didn't really have a father.'

'Hmm, so on the one hand we have me attributing my near-paedophilia to lack of a dad, while he comes out with an entirely opposite diagnosis.'

'You're both just bloody sick, is what I say.'

'Did he ask you about you?'

'Only one question: *Do you own your own home yet?* And when I said no he asked why. Apparently he now owns a townhouse and a house in the country and he's about to buy a rental property. I said I prefer to blow my money on life, not bricks and mortar. Hoping like fuck he wouldn't ask me for a definition of life. Luckily he didn't. Anyway, he plans on retiring to live off his investments after another year or two. Wonder how he'll fill his days. Join a bowling club?'

'Look for a boyfriend who's eighty. I think I'm ready to call Palm Grove.'

'Okay.'

I pick up my cellphone. A nurse answers. I ask whether my father is still in his private room.

'Oh – no,' says the nurse somewhat emotionally. 'He's been taken away.'

'Away?' I say. 'Has he been moved to another room?'

'No, he's been taken away by the undertakers. We're very sad. He was a delight, your late father. So patient and cheerful and friendly, and always ready with a bright word for everyone.'

Everyone except his own children, I think, though I say nothing. 'Oh, I see – um—'

'He left instructions with the undertakers. He asked them to take him straight away. He didn't want to trouble the family.'

Family meaning two unloved daughters and two unloved sons, by no means a full rollcall of the seven embryos he and his wife with their lack of contraceptive skill foisted upon an already burdened planet. Four embryos allowed to survive the abortionist to grow into, among other things, depressives, near-suicides and then, in the fullness of time, men who needed to be fucked by men old enough to be their dads, or by boys young enough to be their sons.

'Thank you,' I say.

'A lovely man,' she says, crying slightly. 'We'll all miss him so much. Our thoughts are with you.'

Which of the two of us knew the real man? I wonder, putting down the phone.

Both of us, maybe.

Next, a call to the undertaker. The undertaker, like the nurse, turns out not to have custody of my dead dad. She, also, has been given clear orders by the oracle. An oracle she calls, like her counterpart who tends to the breathing rather than the unbreathing end of the death trade, *your late father*. Not only were the orders clear, they allowed no compromise, and have been acted upon in the same spirit.

'He's been cremated,' she says.

'Cremated!' I yelp. 'You mean you've had him burnt already?'

Carmen, having till now lolled on a bed of dry pine needles like an opulent fakir, jerks upright.

'Your late father was cremated early this afternoon,' says the undertaker edgily, annoyed I think by my use of the very unprofessional word burnt. 'He didn't wish to trouble the family.'

'The family was troubled already!' I snap back. 'Not an uncommon circumstance, I would've thought – one which in your work you'd encounter not infrequently, I also would've thought!'

'What? Well – we—'

Climbing onto my high horse won't turn our done dad from a pile of ash into a whole corpse, however, so after a few more waspish words I give up. After all, what could fit better with the feeling that you never really had a father than for that putative pop not only to vanish like a genie or a ghost in a puff of smoke but to do it without your say-so, without your okay, without even your knowledge?

*

Now it's already more than a week since the old stranger kicked the bucket and I still have no idea how I feel about it. How can you come to grips with the truth about this bloke? When I think about my mum she's there, real, a big slack woman, a whirl of feelings, smells, words, songs. Always she was very much somebody, in her body – a body with boobs drooping, eyes watchful, lips thin yet moist. Shut my eyes and she's there – her shiny red arms as she swings a shiny black steel tray of shiny hot scones out of the electric oven, her armpits damp, the kitchen swooning with the scent of her sweat blended with the scents of baked butter and baked sugar and baked soda, the aroma of those hot crumbly yummy toothsome scones we'll soon eat, piping hot, scooped out of a swaddling teatowel, slashed with lashings of yellow butter and bolted greedily, scalding the tongue in their hurry to the belly.

Dad? No words, no warmth – no body.

A quick flurry of little printed lies.

MORSE, Malcolm Cyril. Dearly loved father and grandfather to Lenore, Daniel and Louise. At peace at last.

'Hah!' says Carmen. 'Who's at peace exactly? Dad? Or Lenore?'

Yet we don't care enough about our brother and sister to bother following up this line of inquiry. We sit looking at each other across our lattes, feeling stumped. So he's dead. Yet somehow I seem to lack *emotional closure*, as we say these days, speaking our psychobabble. How could I hope for closure, anyway, when the old coot never once during his lifetime even gave me an opening? You can't close something never opened!

'My new cat turns out to have some sort of scarring on her neck.'

'Oh.'

I'm not so very far away from my own death these days. Certainly much closer to my death than my birth. And as I sit thinking about my lack of grief for the old coot now that his cankered corpse has been slid into the white flames of the crematorium, I also think with a kind of grim comfort about the day to come when the same white flames will sting my own corpse. Comfort, because I know that my corpse will be mourned by real mourners. Tears will fall. Wails will rend the air. Carmen will be there, sorrowful. My daughters will be there – and maybe Jay. Will my lovely lad be there too? Comfort doesn't last long, mind you. After I've thought for a bit about the day they'll see off my body my next thought is – but they'll die too! My witnesses. Carmen first, most likely. My daughters a lot later, and Jay. We'll all switch off our cellphones. No witness of my dad's life, of my life, or my sister's life, of my daughters' lives, of my lover's life, will stay too long. Afterwards, after we've all gone – no knowledge, everything lost, everything forgotten. Gobsmacking, isn't it? We scoot around, living our lives, yet always knowing that it ends with a blank. All the lessons we learn will get lost. And then in the end the sun itself will flare up, red, and afterwards will hunker down, white, whiter than the throat of any volcano, any crematorium, and our small ball of dirt and water will scorch away like a drop of sweat or snot on a nuclear reactor.

'I took the scabby tabby to the vet,' says my sis. 'She's now on a course of antibiotics, but the vet says she's in good nick otherwise.'

'Cool.'

'Want a chocolate?'

'Yep, okay – wouldn't say no.'

'Good. Buy some for me when you buy yours, would you?'

'Ha de ha.'

'You think I'm not serious, don't you?'

Stevan Eldred-Grigg is an award-winning novelist and historian. He grew up in the South Island, graduating with a history doctorate from the Australian National University. He has lived in Blackball, Christchurch, Canberra, Whangārei, Wellington, Hamilton, Berlin, Mexico City, Singapore, Shanghai and Beijing and now lives once more in Blackball. His latest novel is *Pru Goes Troppo* (Piwaiwaka Press, 2020), a comedy about the ups and downs of two rich privileged parasites living on a Canterbury country estate who go on holiday in Samoa. His most recent history book is *Phoney Wars: New Zealand Society in the Second World War* (Otago University Press, 2017).

Sue Fitchett

1981

the gals in ponsonby
doing their bit

& we all sang
the topp twins chorus

graffiti raiders
graffiti writers

my ears still play
the same trick

I like it better
& this grainy
black & white photo
women's bodies
& motorcycle helmets
leaning into each other
easy arm across a shoulder
thighs planing thighs
a line more solid than a jumbo bin
I know
I'd *cross that road* again
islingtono'neilpompalier
orargyle
eyeball the red squad
AMANDLA with you

wheeling above the gluepot
on a toppie yodel

* Lyrics quoted are from 'Graffiti Raiders' and 'Paradise'. Quoted with permission of Jools and Lynda Topp.

playing leather

she puts on a growl
a second skin
takes hold of her

she ventures out
butch butch
people gaze shout

'a cute butch'
purrs a woman
at a party

she grows new toes
feet binding the earth
no longer a pushover

she likes her feral smell
her sharper teeth
biting at the boundaries

a small nibble
just enough spice
to jog her pulse &

torch her music
take pleasure in her
own hard arms coming

home in twilight easing
off her great coat
bedding it with a wet kiss

in a public place people are watching

heat swirls round her body sliding
under her clothes until her skin weeps into the air
everybody's skin must be weeping into the air she thinks
& what about their heart beats

the two women on the screen
are kissing each other's breasts they are naked

she is back in the park with her
lover they walk & hold hands a man in a navy raincoat is
watching them his eyes keep pace running over their
bodies a man in a navy raincoat is watching us she tells
her lover her lover does not look you're paranoid he's
feeding the pigeons she takes her mental editing knife &
swish swish her lover is walking backwards she is
walking backwards their hands swing back a man in a navy
raincoat is watching us she tells her lover her lover
turns on her heel aims a bone at the man the navy
raincoat catches fire

the women on the screen are
sucking each other

she sinks further down in her seat
& forgets to breathe she tries to remember the foyer a
big crowd milling she pushes herself up to the ceiling
floating scanning each row each seat a man in a navy
raincoat is snaking out an exit she's faster flames shoot
from her fingers

Sue Fitchett is a conservationist and Waiheke Islander. She is the co-author or editor of several poetry books and anthologies. She authored *Palaver Lava Queen* (Auckland University Press, 2004) and *On the Wing* (Steele Roberts, 2014). Her work has appeared in various publications in New Zealand, the United States and Australia, and in art shows. She was the recipient of the Louis Johnson Bursary in 2001.

Uther Dean

from Massive Crushes

Bodies

(*Elliot, prim and proper to a fault, talks to the audience.*)

ELLIOT Other. People's. Bodies.
(*Beat.*)
There is *nothing* more revolting than other people's bodies.
(*Beat.*)
I'm not saying my body is perfect. Far from it. But I try my best. You won't find me perspiring in public. You won't find me confessing to ablution. You won't find me eating. (*Shudder.*) Eating.
(*Beat.*)
I recently found myself – due to circumstances beyond my control – at a food court.
A Food Court. Such a perfect name for such an imperfect place.
It is a court, yes.
(*Pause.*)
It is a court and I am *judging* you.
You wild creatures tearing at flesh with your juicy sound gaps, like rabid beasts. And then . . .
(*Gob-smacked.*) You *talk*. You talk like we all don't know what precisely you've just been doing with those very same mouths! We know what you just did to that mouth! We all saw you masticate! Filthy!
People have no shame.
Sometimes I am overcome by the urge to tackle these masticators to the ground, get them in a headlock, stitch their mouth closed and explain to them that a mouth is a privilege not a right.
(*They take a moment, positively harrowed.*)
Lollipops are a particular irritant and it only shows just how far gone society is that I am the one who has been ejected from more than one town fête simply for logically and calmly explaining to children that no one wants to see their sick fat pink mouth worms snail lazily across egregiously over-sized sugar discs.

(*They reflect for a moment.*)

Parents really are letting their kids down these days.
Teachers too. Don't get me started on teachers. Ooooh do not get me started. Do not get me going on teachers because I will go off! Don't get me started. Don't. Don't tempt me to talk about teachers! You don't want to hear it so don't ask me about it.
You wouldn't like it so don't tempt me. Don't ask me what the problem with teachers is! I know you want me to talk about it but I flatly refuse. There is no way I am going to talk about—See the problem is that teachers are 'teaching' – and I am using quotes deliberately there – children, children who are young enough to *drive*, about intercourse.
Sexual intercourse!
It gets worse! They don't just 'teach' children to have mechanical passionless sex through an ajar door so that a child may be conceived and nothing else, no. They are 'teaching' children to (*Scoffing.*) prevent conception. As if there can be any pleasure derived from intercoursing!
Let me tell you this: I speak from experience. Oh yes, don't be shocked. I've lived. I've been near sex both pre-, post- and once, I suspect but cannot confirm, during.
So believe me when I say: There is no pleasure in intercourse.
There never has been and there never will be. Have you heard the noises people make during intercourse? They sound like they are being attacked! Have you ever seen people post-intercourse?
They look positively harrowed. Like the very essence of their being has been pumped out of them by the Scratchman's Samba.
It's horrific.
The French call an orgasm or intercoursial gesture a tiny death for a reason.
(*Beat.*)
Oh yes. I have heard of orgasms. And, if you ask me, they seem incredibly stressful. If people could just put down all these modern distractions and gadgets like recorded music, and photographs of landscapes, they'd come to the same conclusion as I: that intercoursing is abject and everyone is making a fool of themselves by doing it.
Let's break it down. First: kissing.
Kissing is little more than a short-form physical theatre piece about the most efficient way to share and spread bacteria. I suspect but am not yet able to conclusively prove that kissing was invented by peppermint companies, the same way marriage was

invented by diamond miners and fiction was invented by Big Ink.
Then there's what occurs next: frottage.
Frottage is an act that really only exists so that teenagers have something to do during movies. And what are they doing watching movies? They should be doing what all good children do: drinking room temperature water while crying.
And why would you want to touch another person's skin? That's where sweat comes out, people!
Next comes nudity.
People willingly expose their saggy flesh prisons to each other. As if to say 'Look at this decaying wrinkled flabby beige lump. Look at my meat prison, gaze upon this map of abuse and disrespect.' And what do they expect the other person to do? Say 'Oh, yes, I like how your body is riddled with the disrespect of age! It really gets me off how it's a massive pile of sputumic sickness barely held together by a moist charcuterie of skin. Let me touch it!'? Ha.
In conclusion: No one ever actually wants to see another naked body.
People just think they do because of the media and their minds. Both of which are provably wrong.
Nudity! Disgusting! Next!
Fellatio, cunnilingus and-slash-or anilingus, all I should note, perfectly charming names for a baby ruined, as all things are, by the insertion of genitals.
I could speak for days on why oral intercourse isn't fun so I'll leave it at this: Oral intercourse seems like someone looked at eating and decided that it needed to be much worse.
Then (*Shudder.*) penetration.
Have you ever really thought about penetration? Have you ever really rolled penetration around in your mind? Have you ever really unpacked penetration as a thought? Have you ever penetrated penetration?

(*Meaningful TED talk pause.*)

Imagine if you will: A couple at home of an evening. One turns to the other and says . . .
'Dear, what would you like to do tonight?'
'I would like to eat a single slice of untoasted bread, my love, and then take a walk along an industrial road, staring right ahead, thinking very hard about my life, as I do every night.'
'Ah yes, I do like to do that too but could I suggest that I,

a rational human being of standing in my community, adored by my friends and the heart of my family, repeatedly insert my blood-hardened urine evacuator into an aperture perilously close to both your urinal and fecal sphincters?'
'Yes, I, a woman of learning and achievement, a leader in my field and beloved by my peers, think that is not only an acceptable offer *but a tempting one*. I do hope I experience something akin to death!'

(*They pause to let that sink in.*)

And, yes, I know there are other possible pairings of other possible genders that partake in intercourse and, honestly I've not put enough thought into such 'alternative lifestyles' so I don't want to speak out of turn except to say they are definitely morally in the wrong and should be illegal. So what is there to be done? I assume you all agree with me by now. My arguments are so rigorous and well delivered that it would only be the most clod-headed simpleton that would dare to pick holes in the dense weave of my tapestry of facts.
And yes, they are facts. How do I know they are facts? Because I think so much that if I think something it must be a fact.
And that's a fact.
It's hard for me.
Heavy is the head that thinks the facts.
Do I wish I thought less so I could maybe find a little company with another disgusting person to waste away my life pretending to experience the empirically fictional feeling of love?

(*Long thoughtful pause.*)

No. Because someone out there has to be right and I fully intend for that person to be me.

Uther Dean is a writer and director. As a part of My Accomplice, the theatre company he co-founded and co-runs, he's written and directed work in all of Aotearoa's major centres. An award-winning critic, he reviews culture weekly in his email newsletter The Dean's List (bit.ly/utherlives). He has two podcasts: Shite and Sound (shiteandsound.com), a film review podcast, and The Witching Hours (thewitchinghours.com), a radio drama anthology. He's also written for *McSweeney's Internet Tendency*, *Shortland Street*, the *Listener*, *Sport*, *The Pantograph Punch*, RNZ National and *Power Rangers*. He's a bit of an acquired taste.

Vanessa Mei Crofskey

two-piece bathing suits

i.

I was never the girl brave enough to undress in public changing rooms.

Some girls, like Annabel, would get straight to it, whipping their tops off like they were born naked or something. They shimmied their limbs into sparkly two-piece bikinis while still managing to convey with hushed delivery how Harry had confessed to Emma after school yesterday up the tree at Ben Burn park. *But what did she say?* We whispered through the changing room turned auditorium.

When I was a gangly, nine-year-old amphibian, I loved to be in the water. I had weekly lessons and regularly ran from our car door all the way to the waves. Swimming pools only became terrifying once I noticed the public audience to my limbs, that the boys in your class could see you for what you were: naked and ashamed under chlorinated spandex.

Plastic bands wrung our hair out like flannels as we wobbled a wet line between child and adult, wisps of adolescence jutting out of nylon underwear.

ii.

Before one of our regular swimming lessons, Annabel turned to me and Cathy as we were juggling between togs undies togs undies togs public decency and whispered:

Did you know I heard from Sarah who saw Cathy getting dressed by accident that Cathy has hair down there?

By *there*, she meant pubic region, the scariest neighbourhood a girl could live. Annabel was waiting for me to react so I gasped half-heartedly, because she scared the shit out of me and I didn't want to be the weird kid.

Cathy was the weird kid. Her family had wacko problems like mine and everyone thought she was secretly a lesbian. Fearing the worst, I mumbled *real strange* and backed into a private changing room, Annabel's eyes piercing though the wood. I hunched into a plain black bathing suit that hid as much of myself as possible and made sure not to look at anyone's bodies while I exited.

iii.

The first time I remember feeling the divide between what I looked like and what I might grow into was sharing the shower with my mum. She had river lines across her stomach. I was soft toddler limbs and pink puppy fat. God did not answer my pleas to stop growing, so I turned pliant under hormonal tweezers. My limbs swelled in response to B cups fondled under the pretence of watching movies. My thighs thickened to trunks. I filled out and grew higher, bigger, similar still. I took my baths fully clothed, my body a wrong no amount of soap could erase. And then I swam naked.

iv.

We were born into buoyancy. Our births were the first great waterpark features. We were born into cellulite publicity, each wrinkle practised a thousand times over. Before I move, I practise how I might be seen, scrutinise the pores of my laughter. Goggles are my only defence each time I try and swim through public space.

v.

Sunday evenings are my routine swim days. I walk to Tepid Baths as the sun casts its showcase and leave by day's ovation. The way I reclaim muscle memory is to swim faster than attention, up and down the lanes. When I am in the water, I am nothing but a concerted effort to keep moving. I wade through the swim caps and bobbing lanes, heavy enough to sink, and save myself from drowning.

Peanuts Pickled in Aged Vinegar

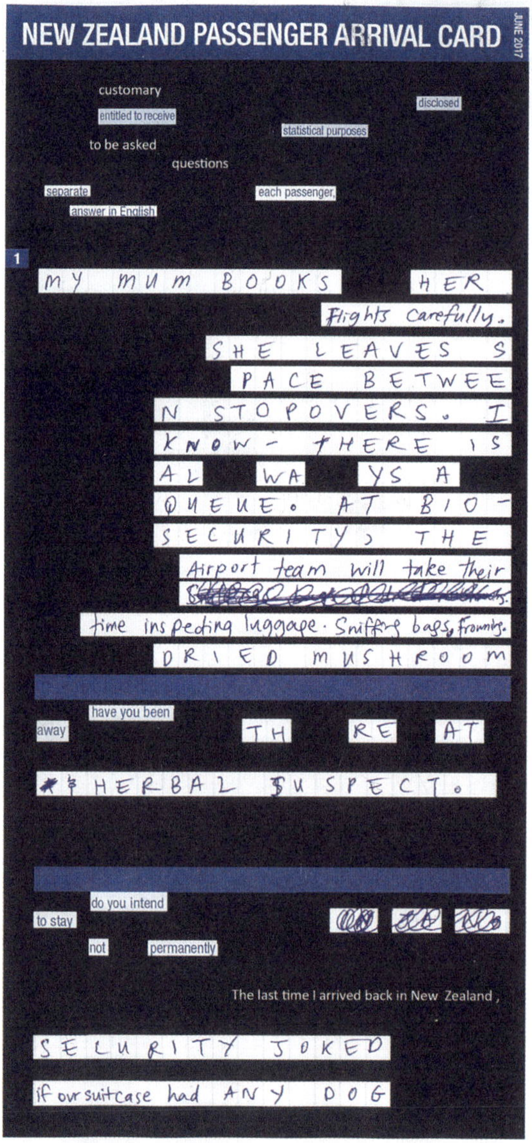

NEW ZEALAND PASSENGER ARRIVAL CARD
JUNE 2017

customary
disclosed
entitled to receive
statistical purposes
to be asked
questions
separate
each passenger,
answer in English

1

MY MUM BOOKS HER
Flights carefully.
SHE LEAVES S
PACE BETWEE
N STOPOVERS. I
KNOW – THERE IS
AL WA YS A
QUEUE. AT BIO-
SECURITY, THE
Airport team will take their
time inspecting luggage. Sniffing bags, frowning.
DRIED MUSHROOM

have you been
away TH RE AT

HERBAL SUSPECT.

do you intend
to stay
not permanently

The last time I arrived back in New Zealand ,

SECURITY JOKED
if our suitcase had ANY DOG

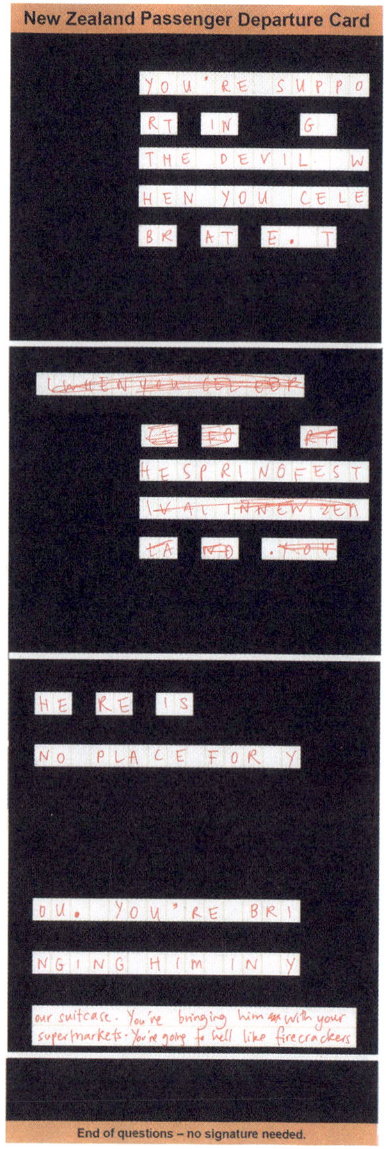

New Zealand Passenger Departure Card

YOU'RE SUPPO
RT IN G
THE DEVIL W
HEN YOU CELE
BR AT E. T

~~WHEN YOU CELEBR~~

HE SPRING FEST
~~IVAL IN NEW ZEA~~
~~LA ND .YOU~~

HE RE IS
NO PLACE FOR Y
OU. YOU'RE BRI
NGING HIM IN Y
our suitcase. You're bringing him with your supermarkets. You're going to smell like firecrackers

End of questions – no signature needed.

I love mooncake & lantern fest

AliExpress & Nikes

I love Lim Chour, Gong Cha

New Flavour & Spicy

I love anime, your crescent face,

smooth features & body

But they are right that there are

too many Asians in Auckland

GUIDE NOTES 5

Tear
each step

your own handwriting
a disability a language difficulty, someone else can

relate to We can only
miss
contact there may be a delay

scanning

BLACK
box
mistakes use correction fluid

the name you want to appear

commonly known as
your last
given

space
a diacritic contact

this

married
want

process
in centimetres
your own
hazel

entitlement

indicate your

birth
the first time

you were outside and
obtained
descent

colour
6 months and
paperclip the
damage

We strongly recommend that you

avoid the most common problem

the front cover of

an

oval

a clear gap around the
head

gloss coated

heavy-backed

red-eye

not white

a neutral expression
frowning

clearly showing
no reflection

obscure your eyes.

for
medical reasons.

Actual photo size

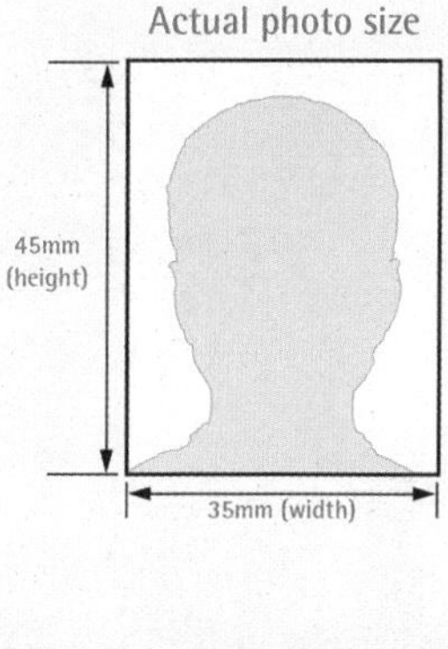

Actual head size
(including hair)

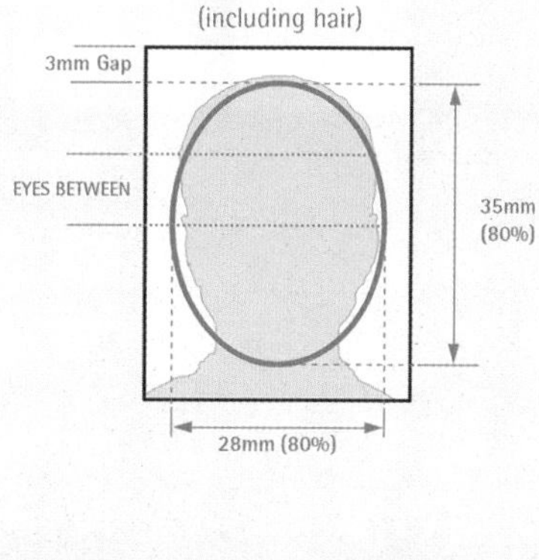

i just hate all
new migrants
over here

be proactive
have

better
values

expecting
a welcome

why are you
here

those wealthy
who come
and can't speak
english

they should

learn/ed
the language

吗

what
are you

☒☒☒

even

doing

一

It's the
New Zealand born
who are the first to
turn away from their
lotus root
cousins

二

They were taught
how to chew
with their mouths closed,
to spit when looking
at the mirror

三

Learned
an anthem
of glottal repetition
what was said
about their
family members

五

It felt so empowering
standing on a field of red carpet
talking our stories
in the light of sinophobia

We had a sold out show
we had a standing ovation
we had misplaced shoes
overwhelming compassion

Outside of the theatre,
I forgot where I left my feet

Dragged through the mud
the whispered ching chings of a man
on the corner of a milestone

Saw a drunk guy look in our direction
then scream to his friends about
overpopulation

Vulnerability in numbers

Once he saw
clouds of wiry black hair
pass together,
proudly-shaped eyes
or
no human in isolation

Vanessa Mei Crofskey is an artist and writer based in Te Whanganui-a-Tara. Through her writing she examines how trauma intersects with race, queerness, love and pop music. Over the years her poetry has been included in a wide range of New Zealand literary journals, including *Turbine | Kapohau*, *Sport*, *Starling* and *Hainamana*, with a collection published in *AUP New Poets 6*. Previously, she was a staff writer at *The Pantograph Punch*, after graduating from Auckland University of Technology with a degree in visual arts. Currently she acts as the director of Enjoy Contemporary Art Space and is chipping away at her first full-length book.

Victor Rodger

Donny's Dialogue

Donny had a muli[1] on him that looked like a couple of bowls of just-set jelly, a muli that rippled when Robert smacked it, a muli that felt like dough as Robert pushed Donny's buttocks apart before plunging his tongue into Donny's asshole.

Donny moaned softly with pleasure in the darkness of their London hotel room.

They had met online just before Christmas when Robert had made his first hunting expedition on Grindr after landing in London from Auckland to begin a writer's residency. He had been pleasantly surprised to recognise another Polynesian face and soon discovered that Donny was in London on holiday from Oxford University where he had won a prestigious scholarship to complete a PhD in something that Robert did not entirely understand. After meeting later that day in Robert's hotel room, they had slept together and subsequently met up whenever their respective schedules allowed.

Earlier that afternoon, Robert had met Donny outside King's Cross Station when he arrived from Oxford. It was Valentine's Day and they were surrounded by couples, straight, gay or otherwise, who held flowers, chocolates, each other's hands.

Donny was still closeted – Mormon – so instead of showing any outward affection they had walked side by side towards the hotel in an anticipatory silence. Robert supposed that to passers-by they may have looked like cousins: two hulkingly tall, broad Samoan men – one dark skinned and one lighter – but both with thighs and mulis that stretched the fabric of their 4XL ASOS jeans to their very limit.

Donny had caught Robert eyeing up his muli as they walked towards the hotel.

'Sole, *'aua*.'

But Robert wouldn't stop. Couldn't wait to get Donny naked, which he did even before their hotel room door closed behind them.

As Robert's tongue went deeper and deeper into Donny and Donny continued to moan, Robert hoped that this time might be different. That this time Donny would simply keep moaning.

1 Muli means 'ass' in Samoan.

But instead Donny was soon talking to Robert the way he eventually always did whenever they had sex, which was to say that Donny was talking to Robert as if they were in a clip on Pornhub.

'Oh yeah. You got your tongue in my hole? You got your tongue in my hole, daddy?'

Robert withdrew his tongue and looked up at Donny over Donny's wide muli, which lay in front of his face like an enormous smooth mountain made of Whittaker's Creamy Milk chocolate.

'Sole: Daddy? Really?'

In fact, Donny's employment of the term 'daddy' wasn't the actual problem – Robert was self-aware enough to know that he had left his ingénue days well behind him on a dance-floor somewhere, sometime during the last century. But Robert didn't feel like he could be honest with Donny – not completely – without hurting his feelings. He was, relatively speaking, just a boy: twenty-five to Robert's fifty. And in their brief time together Robert had already seen how sensitive Donny was underneath his seemingly laid-back exterior, how something that Robert considered a gentle mock could wound him.

Donny craned his neck to look back at Robert over his own mountainous muli.

'Uce; what'd you stop for? You don't like it when I say "daddy"?'

If there was one thing that the writer inside Robert could not abide it was bad dialogue.

'Look . . . if I'm being completely honest,' said Robert, '. . . it's just . . . I'm not into running commentaries while I'm rimming you I guess.'

Donny frowned.

'What do you mean?'

The bad-dialogue-spouting porn star side of Donny had surprised Robert: not because he was Mormon – but because Donny was smart. Smarter than his 'fuck me daddy' dialogue would suggest. In between sex they often talked about race and class and gender and their terrible fathers; they discussed everyone from Frantz Fanon to Donny's Mormon namesake, Donny Osmond.

What made Donny so porny? Robert sometimes wondered.

Donny rolled over onto his back, his knees bent and legs wide open so that Robert was now directly facing his thick erect penis and his ball sack with its light coating of hair.

Donny repeated his question, this time more firmly:

'What do you mean? Just say it, uce.'

Robert knew he was entering new and dangerous territory with his smart, young lover, so approached his response with care.

'Sex with you – it's great.'

'Awwww gee shucks.'

'No I mean it. It's hot. It's really hot. You know that.'

'But . . . ?'

Robert hesitated for a moment:

'. . . but when you start talking like a bad porn star it really turns me off.'

Donny's penis immediately began to go limp.

'Like a what?'

Robert was worried that he'd gone too far but knew there was no going back now.

'So, for example when you say: "You got your tongue in my hole, daddy?"'

'Yeah?'

'I mean, you gotta admit that's kinda porn star-ish, right?'

'So?'

Robert wasn't quite sure what to say to this. Donny straightened his legs and closed his eyes.

'Dead.'

(Donny's generation's shorthand for 'you're killing me,' as Robert had recently learned.)

Donny lay still, looking indeed as if he were dead. For a moment there was no sound in the room except for the soft whir of the air con and the vague sound of traffic below them.

Donny suddenly opened his eyes.

'So you just want me to be quiet when we fuck? Is that what you're saying?'

'Well . . . I mean . . . I don't want to squash your self-expression but, uh, yeah, that would . . . that would work for me.'

Donny shrugged.

'Sweet as.'

Robert felt relief.

'So I'm not cancelled?'

More youthspeak that Robert had cribbed from Donny.

Donny smiled as he rolled back over onto his stomach.

'Sole: I cancelled you a long time ago.'

Robert wasn't entirely sure if Donny was joking or not but before he could investigate further, Donny lifted his beautiful muli into the air.

'Take two . . . and action.'

Robert chuckled, squeezed two large handfuls of Donny's buttocks and then started to work Donny's muli again with his tongue.

Donny moaned softly.

'Mmmmmmmmm.'

And again.

'Mmmmmmmmmm, yeah.'

Robert, pleased with the restraint that Donny was showing, kept going faster and deeper, spurred on by Donny's moans.

'Ooooh fuck yeah, daddy.'

Annoyed, Robert slapped Donny hard on his muli.

'Sorry.'

Donny returned to simply moaning with pleasure.

But then, just as Robert was really finding his rhythm, Donny said:

'Oh yeah, daddy, you got your tongue all up in my ass. You like that, don't you, daddy?'

Robert immediately withdrew from Donny.

'Shit. Sorry. It just came out,' said Donny.

Donny reached behind himself to try and force Robert's head back towards his ass but Robert batted his hand away. Instead he knelt back onto the bed and looked down at Donny. Even in the darkened room his smooth caramel skin was in stark contrast to the crisp white bedspread.

'You watch a lotta porn? I mean when you're not hard at work on your PhD?'

Donny scoffed then shrugged.

'Yeah. Sure.'

'Who's your favourite actor?'

Donny laughed.

'I don't know any of their names. Why? Do you?'

'François Sagat. I used to like him back in the day.'

'Who?'

'French. Muscly. Tattooed hairline?'

Donny looked blankly.

'What about Colby Jansen? You know him?'

'Show me.'

And so together they watched a clip of Colby Jansen on Robert's iPad with another actor by the name of Rocco Steele. Colby Jansen was saying things like 'It's so fucking big' (which it was) and 'Use that fuckhole' (which the other actor most certainly did).

Donny frowned.

'So why can this guy say all that shit and you don't say anything but when I say it, you don't like it? I don't get it.'

'Maybe because it sounds scripted when you say it.'

Donny looked at Robert with derision.

'Cancelled. Definitely cancelled.'

Donny rolled over onto his side, his back to Robert.

This was not the Valentine's Day Robert had envisaged when he had first arranged to meet Donny in London. Robert looked over at Donny's back, idly ran his index finger up and down his spine.

'Sole? Sole?'

When Donny didn't respond, Robert grabbed the remote control and turned on the hotel television. He was taken aback to see some familiar New Zealand faces in a murder mystery that looked like a lot of other British murder mysteries. As far as he could tell, this particular mystery was something to do with a lady duck hunter who had come a cropper. He was certain the murderer would turn out to be the vaguely unhinged palagi woman with the severe bowl cut.

Eventually Donny turned back towards Robert and laid his head on Robert's shoulder.

Robert felt relieved to feel the warmth of Donny's skin against his again and was taken aback to realise how unsettled the tension between them had made him feel.

Robert began to stroke Donny's coarse black hair, which was already generously peppered with grey and together they watched the show.

'They're duck hunters?' said Donny.

'Uh huh,' said Robert.

It soon became clear that the woman with the severe bowl cut had indeed shot the other lady duck hunter because the lady duck hunter had been having an affair with the chicken farmer who the lady with the severe bowl cut had had a crush on.

'Palagis,' said Donny as the lady with the bowl cut was handcuffed and placed into a police car.

'Uh huh,' said Robert.

Donny raised his head from Robert's shoulder and looked at him.

'Would you change any of their dialogue?'

'Absolutely.'

Donny seemed to consider this for a moment.

'Has anyone ever accused you of being really critical?'

'Once or twice.'

Donny wriggled further up Robert's shoulder.

'No shit.'

Donny grabbed Robert's hand and began to move it up and down Donny's hair again.

'This is nice,' Donny said sometime later.

'Yeah. It is,' said Robert.

After a while, Donny said: 'Sometimes I want to rewrite your dialogue too, you know.'

Robert stopped stroking Donny's hair.

'Like when?'

'Don't worry about it.'

Donny grabbed Robert's hand, placed it back again and began to move it up and down Donny's hair.

'When?'

But Donny stayed silent.

They lay side by side in silence for some time until finally Robert spoke into the night:

'Interior. London Hotel. Night.

'Robert strokes Donny's head on Valentine's Day.

'Looks at him fondly.

'Neither of them speak.'

Donny remained still but hugged Robert tighter.

In the morning they were surprised to wake up in the same position, still entwined.

After they showered and dressed, Robert and Donny walked down to King's Cross Station with their bags. Robert was catching a train from St Pancras to Manchester but Donny had to get the tube back to Liverpool St and then connect with a train to Oxford.

Robert felt an uncommon surge of affection for this young man who he knew he'd hurt and wanted nothing more than to enfold him in the kind of hug he only gave Donny behind closed doors, but he remembered only too well the time in his own life when he himself had been scared of showing such affection to another man in public.

'I wish I could kiss you,' said Robert into Donny's ear as he pulled Donny in for a shoulder-to-shoulder bro hug. Robert began to pull away but Donny held him close as he whispered into Robert's ear:

'Exterior. King's Cross Station. Morning.

'Sometime in the not too distant future.

'Donny looks at Robert.

'Kisses him on the lips.

'For a long time.

'A long long long time.

'People watch.

'And Donny doesn't care.'

Donny released Robert's hand, winked at Robert.

'Fa, daddy.'

Robert smiled.

'Ia, fa.'

Donny turned and began his descent into King's Cross and Robert watched him until he disappeared from sight. Then, breathing in the crisp February air, he headed towards St Pancras, still smiling and warmed.

Victor Rodger is a critically acclaimed playwright of Samoan and Scottish descent. His work often deals with issues of sexuality, race and identity, and has been praised for its boldness, candour and freshness. Since his first award-winning play, *Sons*, was produced in 1995, he has written eight plays, including *Black Faggot*, *My Name is Gary Cooper* and *Club Paradiso*. A collection of his work was published by Victoria University Press in 2017, while his personal essay 'Voyage Round My Father' was published in *The Best of E-Tangata* the same year. Victor has also written extensively for television, as well as children's stories for RNZ National.

Witi Ihimaera

from The Uncle's Story

The photograph fell out of Uncle Sam's diary:

SAM WITH CLIFF HARPER, VIETNAM, 1969.

In it, Uncle Sam and Cliff Harper look as if they've just come up from the beach after a swim. It must have been taken when they were on leave in Vũng Tàu, some time after Operation Bucephalus.

Harper is sitting on the sand. Uncle Sam, in the middle of the photo, is resting in the harbour of his arms. Uncle Sam's upper body is strongly developed. Around his neck is a greenstone hei tiki. His right arm is up in protest, as if he doesn't want the photograph to be taken. He is laughing and his lips are curved in a resisting, 'No.' But the one who really draws the attention is Harper, who looks directly into the camera. With his boyish grin and half smile he traps you in his gaze. He seems to absorb the light. Wherever there are shadows – on his shoulders, in the definition of his back muscles as he encloses Uncle Sam in his arms – they serve only to highlight his skin's extraordinary translucence.

Some men are lookers, but Cliff Harper is something else. His looks transcend time. Blond, clean cut and devastatingly handsome, he is breathtaking – yet, in his unswerving gaze is a mixture of innocence and knowing. He seems to come wrapped in a shyness and modesty that makes him the boy next door or the brother you wish you had. Or the boyfriend you dream about.

'Michael? I know you're there.' My sister Amiria's voice. 'Pick up the phone, pick it up right *now*.'

I put Uncle Sam's diary, and the photograph, aside.

'Hello, Amiria. How was the honeymoon?'

'I knew you were there, I'm your twin, you can't hide from me. The honeymoon was great but—' Amiria wailed, 'I'm pregnant.'

'Already? Nobody gets pregnant on their honeymoon.'

'You know what they say about the Mahana family.' Amiria didn't sound too happy about it. 'The women are always so fertile. A man only has to look at one of us and she gets pregnant – though I guess a woman wouldn't have to worry in your case! But that's not the reason why I'm ringing. Tyrone and I are leaving from Auckland by United Airlines for Texas this weekend. His dad wants him to start work at the casino immediately, and I'm starting to get cold feet. I may be leaving New Zealand for good.'

Amiria was sounding tearful. At the moment I felt the same sadness. My twin was going to the other side of the world.

'Will you come up and say goodbye to me?'

'I don't know whether that's wise. Mum and Dad will be there. I don't want to start World War Three.'

'Please, Michael. We might never see each other again.'

I caught the afternoon flight from Wellington to Auckland where the international terminal was crowded with Cook Islanders returning to Rarotonga. Bedecked with flowers, they looked so festive and relaxed. Across the sea of flowers I saw Mum and Dad with Auntie Pat. For a moment I considered backing away. Perhaps I could pretend I hadn't come, ring Amiria in Texas and give some excuse about work or fully booked flights. But Auntie Pat saw me and pulled me towards Mum and Dad.

'Now, Monty,' Auntie Pat said to Dad, 'we're all adults—'

Dad's face went red with anger and Auntie Pat had to intercede again.

'You've already spoilt Amiria's wedding. Let's try not to spoil her going away, shall we?'

Dad glared and said nothing. Mum looked awkward, as if she wanted to hug me but was being restrained by her loyalty to Dad. For a while we just stood there, a silent knot in that singing crowd. What can you say to a father who has made it quite clear that you don't belong in his life any longer?

Amiria and Tyrone joined us. They had been doing some last-minute duty-free shopping. As soon as she saw me, Amiria began to cry. When we had been small children we were always trying to push each other out of the pram. As teenagers, there had been times when we wanted to throttle each other. The gap in her teeth was bigger than mine. How would we get on at opposite ends of the world?

Auntie Pat started the conversation.

'I suppose your sister's told you that she's pregnant?'

Amiria sniffled and glared at Tyrone.

'I told you to keep on using your condoms.'

Mum gave a nervous laugh, and Dad tried a different track. 'Better start thinking about buying that double pram for the twins,' he said.

Tyrone blanched, Amiria started to wail, and you could count on Mum to make things worse.

'What did you two get married for? To have children of course!'

Another family argument began. Dad apologised to Amiria that he had only been joking. Mum folded her arms and said she didn't know what the fuss was all about. Tyrone tried to hug Amiria and reassure her that he didn't mind that she was pregnant.

In the middle of all of it, Auntie Pat pulled me away. 'They won't miss us,' she said.

But I saw the look Dad gave her, as if she was doing something he disapproved of. Despite the fact that she was older than Dad, he was the head of the family. Auntie Pat had always been somebody who said yes to him, a sister he had sometimes gently ridiculed because of her submissive nature and her spinsterhood.

'Am I causing trouble for you, Auntie Pat?'

She stared at Dad and turned to me – and I sensed that the relationship between her and my father was changing.

'Yes,' she answered. 'Your father doesn't like me taking your side. He's used to me being the kind of girl I was when Dad had us under his thumb, and the kind of sister I've been – up until now. He doesn't like it when I argue with him or speak against him. He's not used to it.'

We went to find some of the stuff that passes for coffee at an airport. Auntie Pat was tense – but for another reason. I guessed it was the diary.

'I've begun reading Sam's story,' I said.

She sighed and took both my hands in hers and held them tight. I was surprised at the intensity of the gesture and the force she put into it. Any further pressure and her grip would have hurt.

'I never realised how much of a relief it would be to share his story with someone else. To share it with you—'

I knew what she meant. Once, I had simply been her nephew and she had been my aunt. My coming out had led to a particular act of trust – the giving to me of the diary. And like Auntie Pat's relationship with Dad, hers and mine was changing. I liked this new Auntie Pat, this spirited woman whom I was becoming close friends with. Our alliance was shifting the shapes of both our lives.

Then Auntie Pat said something strange, as if speaking to herself. 'And now that the lid is off Pandora's Box, I guess whatever is in there, for good or ill, will come flying out—'

She closed her eyes and sighed.

'When you get back to Wellington I want you to go out and talk to George.'

For a moment I didn't know who she was talking about. Then it clicked: 'George? So he didn't die in Vietnam?'

'No. What makes you think that! I haven't seen him in many years but I rang Emma—'

'Turei's sister?'

'You know about her? She gave me George's number in Porirua, just outside Wellington. I told him you might want to talk to him about Sam. He's expecting you at the Porirua Tavern eight o'clock Friday night, next weekend.'

'Can he tell me about Cliff Harper too?'

A look of fear crossed Auntie Pat's face. 'How much do you need to know about Cliff Harper?' she asked. Her expression was angry, almost bitter.

We rejoined Mum and Dad just as Amiria and Tyrone's final boarding call was made.

It was obvious that Mum would cry. But none of us was prepared for Dad's sudden grief.

'Amiria,' he burst out. Tears were rushing down his cheeks like a river.

At the sight of Dad's sorrow, tears sprang to my eyes too. Part of it was because of the emotion of the moment. Another part of it was because here was my father, weeping for Amiria who was only going to America; and here I was, his son whom he had thrown out of the family. Had there been any tears for me? No. None. Even so, I tried to close the gap between us.

When Amiria and Tyrone went through Customs, Dad was still weeping. I went to offer support. He looked at me, dabbing at his tears with a handkerchief, and turned his back on me.

'Your mother and I have decided,' he said. 'Don't come home for Christmas.'

Auntie Pat began to argue with him: 'Now, Monty, that's a stupid thing to say.' But he was already walking away with Mum through that roistering Polynesian crowd.

My anger made me walk after him and force him to turn and look me in the eyes.

'Dad, why do you think I stayed away from home? Why do you think I live in Wellington? It makes no difference to me.'

Did I mean it? Yes. No. Yes—

'Then don't come back at all,' Dad said. 'Ever.'

It was raining when I returned to Wellington. I was depressed and angry with myself for having pushed Dad too far, for mishandling the situation. But there was no use crying over spilt milk.

What's done was done. The gloves were back on.

The taxi queue was chaos, with men in business suits jumping the queue and grabbing taxis without apology. A guy carrying a large, bulky canvas bag over his shoulder bumped into me, and for a minute I was on the defensive. Bloody idiot. Why didn't he look . . .

But I was drained by the altercation with Dad and by Amiria's departure. So I let the moment go – until he bumped into me again.

'Remember me?' the culprit said, laughing.

Shaven head. Taller than I had expected. Lasers had limned his profile with green fire. 'Carlos.'

'Good boy! You've passed Go and been given a hotel on Mayfair. Why didn't you tell me that the person you were with at the club was your auntie! I met your girlfriend, and she told me. I thought you were with another guy. Are you available?'

His boldness took my breath away.

'I'm in a relationship right now, but it's rocky. I'm not right for anybody. I don't want to get involved.'

'Damn,' Carlos answered, making a teasing gesture. 'Here I was hoping we'd do the wild thing! Look, I'd give you a lift but I've got to get this gear back—' Apart from his canvas bag, he had a pile of aqualung equipment on a trolley. 'I've been doing some diving up around the Hen and Chickens.' He took out a piece of paper, and scribbled his telephone number on it. With another grin he pretended to throw dice.

'If you don't call me soon you lose your hotels on Mayfair and go straight to jail, you hear?'

Back at the flat, I dumped my bags and opened a can of beer. Life was changing all around me and it was happening so fast. In less than a month I had come out to my parents, my boyfriend had walked out, and my sister was now on her way to live in America. My parents no longer talked to me, and my aunt had given me the diary of an uncle who I had never known existed. A history that once I had been part of and belonged to was disappearing as surely as if somebody had pressed the *Delete* button on a document named Michael Mahana. Correction. *I*, Michael, had pressed the button and consigned the file to the Recycle Bin. By my own act I had rendered myself a man without a history. And now a guy named Carlos had given me a hotel on Mayfair.

Later that night, however, my thoughts turned to Jason.

'The thing is that I do think I love you,' he'd said. 'If I do come back to you it would be nice to know that you will be waiting.'

I truly believed Jason. I wanted to believe him. Love was always the problem. Before you knew it you could only think of one person to the exclusion of any others. I had to admit to myself that I loved Jason. Although I was now writing myself a new history, I wanted to include him in it. I wanted a partner to walk with me into that brave new world. Too much time had passed already. There was a shapeshifter at work in my life, shifting the shapes according to forces I had myself set in motion. The shapes were out of control now, and I was afraid if too much time went past they would move Jason and me further apart. And I needed him. Physically as well as emotionally.

The next morning I telephoned Jason at work. I was so confident. I felt that all I had to do was talk to him and he would melt. That all I had to do was to say 'I miss you', and he would come running back.

But Jason wasn't in. 'Sorry, Michael, nobody knows when he'll be back. Do you want to leave a message? All right, I'll tell Jason you called.'

I put the receiver down. I was frustrated. I replayed the conversation I'd just had back in my head. You know what it's like. You start becoming suspicious. You begin to imagine a hidden, unspoken text:

Sorry, Michael, Jason isn't in, *not to you*. No, nobody knows when he'll be back, *but even if he was he wouldn't talk to you anyway*. Do you want to leave a message? *You can if you like, but it'll end up in the trash can*. All right, I'll tell Jason you called, *but quite frankly, Michael, can't you take a hint and take a hike*?

I was really spinning out of control. I needed somebody to talk my anxieties out with. Who better than Margo, Jason's analyst? I decided to telephone her.

'I'll see if Margo can talk to you,' her secretary said. 'Yes, she's just finished with a client. I'll put you through.'

The phone clicked and buzzed, and Margo's voice came down the line. 'Hello, Michael, how lovely to hear from you.' She sounded warm, reassuring, like a soft couch you could sink into.

'Margo, I need your help. Jason's left me and I haven't heard from him since. Do you know where he is?'

'You don't know where he is?'

'No, and I'm going out of my mind with worry. When he first started to go to you I thought it was for simple issues. Like why is he unhappy? Or what he wanted out of life.'

'You thought those were simple issues?'

'I never anticipated that they would escalate like this. Three months down the track and he's questioning everything and everybody. What's happening to him, Margo? How can I help him?'

'You don't know what's happening to him? You want to help him?'

I began to feel my temperature rising. Sometimes, talking to Margo was like listening to an echo or having a talking parrot in the room.

'Michael, there are two issues here. One of them is what Jason wants and the other is what *you* want. Are you sure you're ringing because of your concern for Jason – or is it because you're really concerned about yourself? Have you considered that the reason Jason hasn't let you know his address is because he doesn't want to be found? He needs time to think these things out. He's given himself permission to explore who he is, what he wants and where he wants to be—'

I listened as Margo put it all on the line for me. She was right: I *was* concerned for myself. Secretly I had hoped to hear her say that Jason had spoken about me, that he had told her he loved me and that he wanted us to be back together. Instead:

'I have had to guide him through some very serious matters. While this might mean that some of us might not be happy with the outcome, what is more important is that Jason defines the outcome for himself. So if he chooses not to be in touch with anyone, we have to respect that choice.'

It all sounded so reasonable. And, obviously, if Margo knew where he was staying, she wasn't telling. I tried another tack:

'In that case, Margo, can you give me Graham's telephone number?'

A pause. 'You know about Graham?'

'Yes.' Her intonation had risen a few decibels. Why?

'Well, I suppose it will be all right.'

A few moments later, I was talking to Graham, the buddy who had become Jason's closest friend.

'You've got a nerve ringing me,' he said. 'But if you want to know, Jason's moved in with me.'

Moved in?

Graham went for the jugular.

'Why don't you leave him alone, Michael. Why don't you admit that all he ever was to you was another scalp you could hang on your belt.'

Later that day Roimata asked me to meet her for lunch to talk about the submission I had written for Toi Māori – her Board was delighted with it. As usual she had chosen a restaurant where we would stand out: the only brown people in the room. She liked to make visual her political position – that Māori were a minority but, dammit, we could still walk through the front door and play with the family silver.

'So things look really bad for you and Jason, right?'

'You don't have to sound so pleased.'

'Well, you know how I feel about Jason. We've never liked each other.'

'Can you blame him?' I reminded her. 'Who was that certain Māori maiden who tried to break us up by introducing me to an alternative candidate!'

'He wasn't only an alternative,' Roimata said. 'Don was Māori, he had mana and, from what I've heard, he wasn't called Long Dong Silver for nothing. He was totally suitable but what did you do? You rejected him and became a – a potato queen.'

'Look,' I answered. 'I like white boys. When I put my brown hands on them it makes me feel so dirty.'

Roimata knew I was joking. Even so, she couldn't resist pushing home her point.

'I only wish, Michael, dear, that you would see that you've been colonised twice over. First, by the Pākehā. Second by the *gay* Pākehā. Even in the gay world the White majority holds the power, the money, the decision-making power – and it is their images that tell you what is desirable, what you should be like and what you shouldn't be like.'

Roimata always had a particular strength, a particular vision. It came from her university training in Māori studies, women's studies and art history – a potent combination that had turned her into an outspoken Māori activist. Add to this her lesbian identity and world, watch out.

'Take, for instance, the Pākehā gay attitude to family,' Roimata continued, warming to her subject and talking academic-speak. 'The Western model de-privileges any notions that gay men or women might have children. Therefore, the White gay species is the only one that doesn't replicate itself. But our Māori model is a tribal one. It should therefore include the possibility of growing a tribe. Of having children.'

Roimata's passion was overwhelming, pouring out of her, and her eyes were glowing and luminous.

'Don't you understand, Michael? The issues of identity and space – of sovereignty, of tino rangatiratanga – that our people have been fighting for within Pākehā society are the same issues for gay Māori within Pākehā gay society! That gay tribe that your Auntie Pat asked about won't just happen – it will have to be created, God dammit—'

Sometimes Roimata's words weren't expressive enough for her and, before you knew it, you became the target of her spontaneous passions. This time, she reached over the table, grasped my head in both hands and kissed me. Roimata was always helping herself to my body, leaving lipstick all over my face, so I wasn't surprised. However, this wasn't just a kiss. It was strong. Deep. Long.

'Why did you do that?' I asked. I had the feeling another shape was shifting in my life.

Roimata tried to hide her emotions with flippancy.

'Well it works in films and in television ads,' she said.

She looked at me, as if trying to decide whether to push her point or not. Then decided that the meter had gone too far into the danger zone, so backed off – for now.

'But that isn't why I asked you for coffee. Are you able to come to Canada? Next month?'

'Canada?'

'There's a big indigenous arts conference being held in Ottawa. The First Nations people of Canada are hosting it and they've invited indigenous representatives from all around the world – Black Africa, the Caribbean, Asia, Europe and, of course, Polynesia. The conference will consider the models available for indigenous cultures in terms of setting up our own network. I've already been asked to go but last week, you lucky boy, I emailed them a copy of the submission you wrote for me. They want you to come with me. They're paying all travel and expenses. Will you?'

'If the dates work out, yes.'

'Great.'

'Now,' I said gently, 'that kiss—'

Roimata was silent for a moment. She hated being cornered. She nodded to herself and there was both sadness and acceptance in her eyes.

'I know you're gay,' she began, 'and you know I'm lesbian. But I love you, Michael, and I wanted you to know it.'

I took Roimata's hand and kissed it. I was surprised to see tears welling in her eyes. Our relationship had always been unspoken. Amiria was my twin but Roimata and I shared something else. Amiria was part of the old world; with Roimata there was a promise of the new.

The moment grew dangerous. Then:

'What a pity you're not a woman,' Roimata smiled.

'What a pity you're not a man,' I answered.

In every other respect we knew we were made for each other.

At that moment the waiter arrived. 'More coffee?' he asked.

'Yes,' Roimata said. Her voice was strong and thrilling. 'He'll have a tall basketball player—'

'A long black.'

'And I'll have—'

'A flat white?' I laughed.

'Yes,' she nodded. 'A dead Pākehā.'

Witi Ihimaera is a hard-working New Zealand writer committed to supporting takatāpui and LGBTQIA+ politics in Aotearoa New Zealand. His most visible expression has been through his novels *Nights in the Gardens of Spain* (Secker & Warburg, 1995) and *The Uncle's Story* (Penguin, 2000) as well as his published short fiction, introductions and essays supporting the work of other writers and personalities in our community. He was the chairman of Auckland's first group to represent Māori and Pacific gay men during the AIDS crisis in New Zealand. His most recent works are the memoirs *Māori Boy* (Penguin, 2014) and *Native Son* (Penguin, 2019), and the historical fiction *Navigating the Stars* (Penguin, 2020), all of which reference our takatāpui history. He lives in Auckland.

Zoë Higgins

Leaving Hospital

The paper curtains round the bed are blue.
I sit, leg cocked, and sip the glass of water
you told the nurse was yours. Asleep your arms
are heavy sand, still curled to hold
the shape of where I was. I face
away; set glass down. You'll be fine.

At 3am a stranger says 'She's fine
to go.' We practise walking round the ward. The blue-
clad nurse on desk ignores us, face
made pale by her screen. Outside, dirty water
flattens papers to the road. You hold
me loose, uncertain what your arms

are for. Something inside me arms
itself. A low hum, strong, fine
and long-sustained, the way you hold
a note. You speak in repetitions, like a blues
singer with a voice as slow as water
rolling through the same progressions, face

tilted and smooth. 'It wears my face;
it isn't me.' I know. Step over water
crawling down the pavement, arms
loose and flapping and stagger through fine
drizzle for the night bus driver with blue
caves under his eyes to take us home. I hold

you upright on the seat. My skin feels rigid, like the hold
of ships that bear through storms. I face
rain through the window, see your sleepy blue-
sky smile. Like a ship's captain, arm
myself. Have fathomed how fine
weather slips and storms come boiling over water.

You want a bath. You lie flat underwater,
one foot up for me to count how long you hold
your breath. 'No drowning!' (Still I'm anxious – fine
intestine-probing fingers til your face
breaks surface, laughing.) You raise exhausted arms
in glee. The sky, for now, is blue.

We are in a paper boat above deep water. Face
me now; hold me in your arms; be held. We are
fine. This season is stormy; the sky may stay blue.

A Freudian Theory of Orthography

Of course there are two kinds of letters: the male principle and the female. Related to the male principle are the upright, active and dominant letters. The 'l', 't', 'h' and especially capital 'I' fall within this category. The female principle relates to encompassing, open, receptive and passive letters. The 'u', 'n', 'c' and especially 'o' fall within this category. The combination of these principles gives language its expressive social force. This explains why words like 'loo', 'hut', and 'oi!' are among the most erotic in the English language.

The Beach

We drove over folds of land
to reach this place – a tanned arm
of sand flung out across the coast.
It smells of ghosts, which smell
like dry seedheads of grass.
The beds are not made up. We loll
sideways on a sunset blanket
laid on a double mattress.
I go to boil the jug.
When I come back you are beneath
the blanket, which falls in folds
like hills around your knees,
and I see again the distances in you,
a sleeping giant stretched for miles from the sea.

Zoë Higgins is a Pākehā poet of Swiss and British descent and also a massive lesbian. She grew up on Horomaka Banks Peninsula, and now lives in Te Whanganui-a-Tara. Her work has been published in *Sport, Starling, Mayhem, Landfall* and *Aotearotica,* and featured in the Wellington Pride edition of Naked Girls Reading. She is currently working on her first clown show.

Works previously published

Alison Glenny:

'The Propeller Club' first published by Hue & Cry Press as part of the online serial *Farlight* (2013–14).

Annamarie Jagose:

In Translation, Victoria University Press, Wellington, 1994.

Aorewa McLeod:

Who Was That Woman, Anyway?: Snapshots of a Lesbian Life, Victoria University Press, Wellington, 2013.

Ash Davida Jane:

all poems previously published in *How to Live With Mammals*, Victoria University Press, Wellington, 2021. 'Good People' was first published in the zine *Fuck You Everyone!, Food Court / Sweet Mammalian*, Wellington, 2018.

Cadence Chung:

'Girls just wanna have fun' first published in *The Spinoff* (2020); '女 (Woman)' first published in *Awa Wahine* (2020); 'The End' first published in *Stasis* (2020).

Carolyn DeCarlo:

'Winter Swimmers' first published in *The Spinoff* (2019); 'The Year I Let My Heart Go Asunder' first published in *Sweet Mammalian* 3 (2015); 'Equilibrium of a Rigid Body' previously published in *AUP New Poets* 5, Auckland University Press, Auckland, 2019.

Courtney Sina Meredith:

'Jam Sandwich on the Lawn' previously published in *Brown Girls in Bright Red Lipstick*, Beatnik Publishing, Auckland, 2012; 'The Coconut King' previously published in *Tail of the Taniwha*, Beatnik Publishing, Auckland, 2016.

Eliana Gray:

'Sometimes I wonder if my salt water mouth should be allowed to speak at all' first published in *Mimicry* 5 (2019); 'Summer's hot and so is everybody else' first published in *Sweet Mammalian* 7 (2020); 'Dirt.' first published in *Eager to Break*, Girls on Key Press, NSW, Australia, 2019.

Gem Wilder:

'Te Awakairangi' was written to accompany the drone film *The Rising Gale* by artist Murray Hewitt, and was originally presented as a live performance for the Hutt Valley Public Arts Festival Common Ground (2017), curated by Letting Space. Thank you to Murray Hewitt, Mark Amery and Faith Wilson for their role in the creation of this work.

Gina Cole:

'Melt' previously published in *Black Ice Matter*, Huia, Wellington, 2016.

Hannah Mettner:

all poems previously published in *Fully Clothed and So Forgetful*, Victoria University Press, Wellington, 2017.

harold coutts:

'poems about boys' first published in *Starling* 7 (2019); 'farewell to a gender I never loved' and 'my gender' first published in essa may ranapiri (ed.), *this gender is a million things that we are more than: poetry from takatāpui/genderqueer/trans writers from across Aotearoa* (2019).

Heather McPherson:

all poems previously published in *This Joyous, Chaotic Place: Garden Poems*, Spiral, Wellington, 2018.

Hera Lindsay Bird:

'UNTITLED 404' and 'I AM SO IN LOVE WITH YOU I WANT TO LIE DOWN IN THE MIDDLE OF A MAJOR PUBLIC INTERSECTION AND CRY' previously published in *Pamper Me To Hell & Back*, Smith | Doorstop Books, Sheffield, 2018; 'LOVE COMES BACK' previously published in *Hera Lindsay Bird*, Victoria University Press, Wellington, 2016.

Hinemoana Baker:

'born again māori' and 'last born' previously published in *kōiwi kōiwi | bone bone*, Victoria University Press, Wellington, 2010; 'rope' and 'follicle' previously published in *waha | mouth*, Victoria University Press, Wellington, 2014.

Isabelle McNeur:

'Dancers' first published in *Scum Mag* (2020).

Jackson Nieuwland:

'I am a version of you from the future' previously published in *I Am A Human Being*, Compound Press, Auckland, 2020.

Janis Freegard:

'Exhibition' was first published in *JAAM* and subsequently published in *The Glass Rooster*, Auckland University Press, Auckland, 2015; 'Trinity' was first published in Raving Beauties (eds), *Hallelujah for 50 ft Women: poems about women's relationship to their bodies*, Bloodaxe Books, Hexham, UK, 2015, and subsequently published in *The Glass Rooster*; 'Mikey' was first published online on The Open Book website (2019).

Josiah Morgan:

'BODY' previously published in *Inside the Castle*, Amphetamine Sulphate, Austin, TX, USA, 2019.

Joy Holley:

'Why Girls Always Go to the Bathroom Together' previously published in *Mayhem Literary Journal* 6 (2018).

Lily Holloway:

'i think i can feel reverberations of something further downstream' and 'the thing' first published in *Milly Magazine* (2020); 'commuting with angela' first published on the Given Words website (2019).

Lorae Parry:

Eugenia, Victoria University Press, Wellington, 1996.

Natasha Dennerstein:

'O, Positive, 1993.' first published in *Bloom* 10 (2015); 'Much Too Fast.' and 'E S T R O G E N' first published in *Seahorse*, Nomadic Press, Brooklyn, NY, USA, 2017.

Ngahuia te Awekotuku:

'Auntie Marleen' and 'Remembering Them' previously published in *Tahuri: A Limited Edition 2017*, PangoCatPress, Hamilton, 2017.

Oscar Upperton:

New Transgender Blockbusters, Victoria University Press, Wellington, 2020.

Paula Boock:

Dare Truth or Promise, Longacre Press, Dunedin, 1997.

Pelenakeke Brown:

'A Travelling Practice' first published in *Movement Research Performance Journal* 52/53 *Sovereign Movements: Native Dance and Performance* (2019).

Peter Wells:

'Sweet Nothing' was previously published in *Dangerous Desires*, Reed Books, Auckland, 1991.

Pip Adam:

I'm Working on a Building, Victoria University Press, Wellington, 2013.

Rachel O'Neill:

'Your dead language' first published in *Mimicry* 4 (2018).

Ray Shipley:

'The Catholic-Mobile' first published in David Stavanger and Anne-Marie Te Whiu (eds), *Solid Air: Australian and New Zealand Spoken Word*, University of Queensland Press, St Lucia, Queensland, 2019.

Rebecca Hawkes:

'Fairy floss' first published in the zine *Food Court* (2019); 'Quad bike farm tour' first published in *Starling* 8 (2019); 'Dairy queen' first published in *Scum Magazine* (2018) and subsequently in *AUP New Poets* 5, Auckland University Press, Auckland, 2019.

Renée:

The Skeleton Woman, Huia, Wellington, 2002.

Rhian Gallagher:

'Between' and 'The Gospel According to Longing' previously published in *Shift*, Auckland University Press, Auckland, 2011; 'Embrace' previously published in *Salt Water Creek*, Enitharmon Press, London, 2003.

Robyn Maree Pickens:

'Moving in' first published in *Brotherton Poetry Prize Anthology*, Carcanet Press, Manchester, UK, 2020; 'Malaysian love story' first published in essa may ranapiri (ed.), *this gender is a million things that we are more than: poetry from takatāpui/genderqueer/trans writers from across Aotearoa* (2019).

Rose Lu:

'Notes from Mandarin Class' first published on the Britomart website as part of the 'Notes from Self-Isolation' series (April, 2020).

Ruby Porter:

'A list of dreams' first published on The Open Book website (2018); 'eel' previously published as a poster by Phantom Billstickers (2020).

Sam Brooks:

Riding in Cars with (Mostly Straight) Boys previously published in *Here/Now: 8 Plays By Award-Winning NZ Playwrights*, Playmarket, Wellington, 2015.

Sam Duckor-Jones:

'On Intimacy' and 'On Isolation' previously published in *People From the Pit Stand Up*, Victoria University Press, Wellington, 2018.

Sara Knox:

'In the Garden of Unearthly Delights' first performed at Queerstories in Sydney on 6 July 2018.

Sarah Jane Barnett:

'The Geographer' first appeared in *Sport* 39 (2011) and was subsequently published in *A Man Runs into a Woman*, Hue & Cry Press, Auckland, 2012.

Sarah Laing:

'What New Zealand Needs' and 'Faux fur pas' first appeared on Sarah's website and were subsequently published in *Let Me Be Frank*, Victoria University Press, Wellington, 2019.

Semira Davis:

'Hiding' first published in *Poetry New Zealand Yearbook 2018*, Massey University Press, Auckland, 2018; 'Into the garden' first published in *The Spinoff* (2019).

Simone Brighton:

both poems first published in *arkeia | archive 2010–2020*, Placeholder Press, Norwich, UK, 2020.

Sinead Overbye:

'The River' first published in *Starling* 8 (2019).

Sophie van Waardenberg:

'do not blame me for loving the 2003 film love, actually' first published in *The Three Lamps* (2017); 'schön' first published in *Mimicry* 4 (2018); 'unfortunately pam beesly I fell in love with you briefly' previously published in *AUP New Poets 5*, Auckland University Press, Auckland, 2019.

Stacey Teague:

'Beat' first published in *Turbine | Kapohau* (2019); 'ipu whenua' and 'angelhood' first published in *hoki mai*, If A Leaf Falls Press & Glyph Press, Edinburgh, UK, 2020.

Stevan Eldred-Grigg:

Shanghai Boy, Random House, Auckland, 2006.

Sue Fitchett:

all poems first published in Sue Fitchett, Marewa Glover, Cary McDermott and Rhona Vickoce (eds), *Eat These Sweet Words: The New Zealand Anthology of Lesbian and Gay Poetry*, Giant Publishing Press, Christchurch, 1999.

Vanessa Mei Crofskey:

'two-piece bathing suits' first published in *Turbine | Kapohau* (2018) and subsequently published in *AUP New Poets 6*, Auckland University Press, Auckland, 2020; 'Peanuts Pickled in Aged Vinegar' first published on *Hainamana* (2017) and subsequently published as 'New Zealand Passenger Arrival Card' and 'Guide Notes' in *AUP New Poets 6*.

Victor Rodger:

'Donny's Dialogue' first published on the Verb website (2020).

Witi Ihimaera:

The Uncle's Story, Penguin Books, Auckland, 2003.

Zoë Higgins:

'A Freudian Theory of Orthography' first published in *Mayhem Literary Journal* 6 (2018); 'The Beach' first published in *Starling* 6 (2018); 'Leaving Hospital' first published in *Starling* 3 (2017).

Acknowledgements

We could not have completed this anthology without the contributions of many others. We are immeasurably grateful for their help, encouragement and support as we forged our way through the challenging and, at times, overwhelming task at hand.

Creative New Zealand awarded us an Arts Continuity Grant that enabled us to complete the editorial work for the anthology and to pay our contributors.

The team at Auckland University Press have been a dream to work with at all stages of this process. Thank you to Sam Elworthy, Katharina Bauer, Sophia Broom and Lauren Donald.

Hugest of thanks to our copy editor Caren Wilton and designer Kalee Jackson for their part in turning a stubborn track-changes-riddled Word document into a beautiful real-life book, and to Madison Hamill for proofreading. Thank you to Jack Trolove for letting us use his gorgeous art for the cover.

Thank you to Eboni Waitere at HUIA; Frances Faulkner at Penguin Random House; Murray Lynch at Playmarket; and Craig Gamble at Victoria University Press.

Thank you to Sam Orchard and the team at Same Same But Different; Chris Brickell; Elizabeth Kerekere; Jan Logie; Michael Farrell; and Chris Yee.

Thank you to all the writers who submitted writing to us or agreed to be included in this anthology, for trusting us with their work.

Thank you to our families, whānau, friends and writing communities. This anthology is infused with the love you have shown us.

Thank you to Simon Carryer. Thank you to Michael Gibson.

About the editors

Chris Tse was born and raised in Lower Hutt. He studied film and English literature at Victoria University of Wellington, where he also completed an MA in creative writing at the International Institute of Modern Letters. He is the author of two poetry collections published by Auckland University Press: *How to be Dead in a Year of Snakes* (2014) and *HE'S SO MASC* (2018). *How to be Dead in a Year of Snakes* was a finalist at the 2016 Ockham New Zealand Book Awards and received the Jessie Mackay Best First Book Award for Poetry. His poetry, prose and reviews have been widely published in Aotearoa and overseas. He lives and works in Wellington.

Emma Barnes (Ngāti Pākehā, they / them) studied at the University of Canterbury and lives in Aro Valley, Wellington. Their poetry has been widely published for more than a decade in journals, including *Landfall*, *Turbine | Kapohau*, *Cordite* and *Best New Zealand Poems*. Alongside Pip Adam, Emma started Cats and Spaghetti Press where they published Sugar Magnolia Wilson's *Pen Pal*, *Rejectamenta* (previously rejected work alongside its real or fictional rejection letters), and a series of poster poems where poets worked alongside artists. In 2018, they developed a performance piece for three voices for Wellington performance art show *Obscene*. Their first book, *I Am in Bed with You*, was published by Auckland University Press in 2021.